Making American Industry
Safe for Democracy

Making American Industry
Safe for Democracy

*Comparative Perspectives on
the State and Employee Representation
in the Era of World War I*

JEFFREY HAYDU

UNIVERSITY OF ILLINOIS PRESS
Urbana and Chicago

© 1997 by the Board of Trustees of the University of Illinois

Manufactured in the United States of America

1 2 3 4 5 C P 5 4 3 2 1

This book is printed on acid-free paper.

Library of Congress Cataloging-in-Publication Data
Haydu, Jeffrey.
Making American industry safe for democracy :
comparative perspectives on the state and employee representation
in the era of World War I / Jeffrey Haydu
p. cm.
Includes bibliographical references and index.
ISBN 0-252-02289-0 (acid-free paper). —
ISBN 0-252-06628-6 (pbk. : acid-free paper)
1. Trade unions—United States—History—20th century. 2. Strikes and lockouts—
United States—History—20th century. 3. Industrial relations—United States—
History—20th century. 4. Labor policy—United States—History—20th century.
5. Industrial policy—United States—History—20th century. 6. World War, 1914–
1918—United States. 7. Reconstruction (1914–1939)—United States. 8. United
States—Social conditions—1918–1932. I. Title.
HD6508.H36 1997
331.88'0973'09041—dc21
96-45881
CIP

To my parents

Contents

Acknowledgments

Writing books has much in common with rearing children. You become blind to their faults; you may experience rejection; it can be a very lonely endeavor; and it is hard to let go. I'm grateful to all who lent a hand raising this book.

Support for field trips and writing time came from Syracuse University, the American Council of Learned Societies, the Office of the Vice Chancellor at the University of California–San Diego, and UCSD's Academic Senate. Peter Erickson provided research assistance and good humor. Visits to archives would have been less fruitful were it not for knowledgeable staff members at the National Archives, Cornell's Labor-Management Documentation Center, the Labor Union Collection and Bancroft Library at the University of California–Berkeley, the Ohio Historical Society, the Western Reserve Historical Society, and the Institute for Great Lakes Research. I owe special thanks to Bill Creech at the National Archives, Richard Strassberg and Martha Hodges of the Labor-Management Documentation Center, and the Institute for Great Lakes Research's Robert Graham and Jay Winter.

Michael Burawoy, Sanford Jacoby, Richard Price, and Kim Voss gave helpful suggestions on the project in its early stages; close readings by Melvyn Dubofsky and Howard Kimeldorf of the penultimate draft guided one more round of revisions. Over the long haul in between, I benefited from the comments and camaraderie of Steve Cornell, Dave Edelstein, Howard Kimeldorf, Martha Lampland, Tim McDaniel, Akos Rona-Tas, Gershon Shafir, and Ken Teitelbaum. I also appreciate the support of Dick Martin and the careful editing of Bruce Bethell at the University of Illinois Press; and thanks to Trisha Stewart for last-minute help with the index. I would like to attribute any remaining flaws in the book to the mischievous influence of my son, Colin, but they are in fact my responsibility. Colin generously shared his own perspectives on representation and authority.

Kathy Mooney has an uncanny ability to detect the imprecise idea and the infelicitous phrase, and she refused to lower her standards for her husband's writing. There is little in the book—or its author—that she has not improved. My thanks, finally, to the authors Bill and Mary Haydu for always standing by their work. The dedication is to them.

Introduction: How Many American Exceptionalisms?

"While we are fighting for freedom," President Wilson counseled American Federation of Labor convention delegates late in 1917, "we must see, among other things, that labor is free."[1] American labor made greater use of its freedom than Wilson intended. Empowered by the war economy and inspired by democratic ideals, workers joined a wave of insurgency that by 1919 was easily (and often) mistaken for mass insurrection. Labor mobilization in the United States had much in common with upheavals in Europe. Union membership boomed. Strikes broke out in unprecedented numbers and broke down previous obstacles to class solidarity. And workers sought to apply democratic principles in new areas, demanding a larger voice in managing their workplaces, their unions, and their industries. As it did in Europe, labor's challenge in the United States involved new forms of organization in the shops and local communities: shop committees and labor councils provided vehicles for militancy and promised to serve as building blocks for a more democratic industrial order.

All along the arc of labor militancy, governments were key actors. Wilson's address to the American Federation of Labor (AFL) is symptomatic. His very presence—the first by an American president—marked a closer relationship between the state and organized labor, and his message demonstrated a new commitment to labor reform. The state's more activist role echoed Europe's "war socialism," and as in Europe, it politicized and destabilized traditional industrial relations. Yet wartime intervention also fostered new mechanisms of industrial stability that would become visible once the dust of 1919 had settled. Among these mechanisms were new forms of employee representation,[2] institutional arrangements and procedures for giving labor some voice and certain rights at work. While the government waged war for democracy abroad, it also had to make industry safe for democracy at home—it had both to accommodate and to limit labor demands for participation in industrial governance.

This book explores how the American state, in coping with the wartime labor crisis, helped to restabilize industrial relations through the reform of employee representation. One theme is that new approaches to employee representation made important and lasting contributions to industrial and political stability; another is that wartime government interventions deserve more credit for these enduring reforms. The book turns on a series of comparisons deployed to explain state policies and labor relations reforms. Part 1 juxtaposes the U.S. experience with two very different cases, those of Germany and Britain. Playing off the United States against Germany, with its socialist labor organizations, autocratic state, and revolutionary possibilities, connects changes in employee representation to familiar features of American "exceptionalism." Shifting the comparative focus to Britain's militant trade unionism, conciliatory employers, and democratic stability points to a less familiar—but perhaps no less "exceptional"—causal dynamic, rooting government policies in long-standing characteristics of work and industrial relations. Part 2 compares industries *within* the United States, adding more detailed studies of railroad shops and shipyards to the better-known case of munitions plants. These interindustry comparisons confirm the causal importance of prior labor relations for wartime employee representation reforms. They also offer two broader lessons. First, sociologists are ill-served by models of government policy that give theoretical pride of place to state institutions, working-class power, or business influence. Policy outcomes over 1917–22 prove to have been highly contingent both on changes in state responsiveness over time and on the balance of class forces in particular settings. Second, these case studies remind us that arguments for American exceptionalism do more than homogenize the European experience. They also generalize too glibly across regions, industries, and epochs within the United States.

WARTIME RADICALISM, EMPLOYEE REPRESENTATION, AND RESTABILIZATION

These were the Red Years, when heightened class consciousness, worker militancy, and revolutionary movements threatened old regimes throughout Europe.[3] Labor insurgency never seriously jeopardized political order or private property in the United States. Even here, however, the war fueled support for industrial unionism, independent labor politics, and workers' control.[4] And although rank-and-file ambitions rarely matched the goals of radical ideologues, the sheer scale of insurgency convinced anxious American elites of a Red menace that only government repression could defeat.[5]

The labor rebellion of these years had many roots in the United States and Europe, including changes in urban working-class community life, the large-scale entry into the labor movement of workers unaccustomed to union discipline, and the most basic material hardships. One contributing factor of particular importance for this book was the state's wartime role in supervising work relations. Government efforts to maximize output by diluting craft skills, regulating labor mobility, and restricting strikes antagonized workers and turned shop floor grievances against the state. To win support for the war effort, moreover, governments enlisted union leaders in labor administration; those leaders were expected in return to hold their constituents in line. In his address to the AFL, for example, President Wilson noted how often he conferred with "your president, Mr. Gompers," and emphasized the quid pro quo in a homely metaphor: "I like to lay my mind alongside of a mind that knows how to pull in harness. The horses that kick over the traces will have to be put in corral."[6] Cooperation between union and government officials bred rebellion in the ranks, however: members increasingly repudiated their leaders' concessions, and they developed local and shop floor organizations to defend their interests in the absence of union support. These bodies posed formidable challenges to union authority and to government efforts to keep the peace. Where local organization enabled craftsmen[7] to enforce customary work rules in defiance of union compromises, they also created serious obstacles to management control and vital war production. Such defensive action was commonplace, and wartime insurgency often reflected not radical commitments but the narrow self-interest of privileged work groups. Yet even in these cases, shop steward systems, works councils, and citywide workers' committees created an organizational base for more inclusive alliances and more militant leadership, above all by industrial unionists, syndicalists, and left-wing socialists unfettered by union obligations.

Wartime rhetoric joined organizational opportunities in politicizing insurgency. Wilson was not unique in highlighting the AFL's new political role and using democratic ideals to legitimate popular sacrifices; moves of this sort were common fare in Europe as well. Such appeals fortified workers with visions of an industrial order more representative of labor and more democratic in governance. *Democracy*, of course, covered a multitude of virtues. The substance of democratic aspirations varied both across groups within each country and between nations. Perhaps the most common democratic ambition among American workers was to be free of arbitrary and unilateral management authority—the freedom alluded to by Wilson. During the war U.S. workers assailed unchecked employer power as "Prussianism," and they warned that "we who comprise Uncle Sam's industrial army can not stand idly by and see the 'Kaisers' of American industry continue their un-American practices in the workshop."[8] The alternative to employers' "autocratic control" was "effective trade unionism,"[9] the right to union representation in dealing with management and setting working conditions. For most British war workers, the rights to organize and negotiate through union representatives were no longer contested issues. Wartime insurgency commonly involved a strong commitment to democracy *within* the labor movement, however, with calls to expand rank-and-file control over both unions and collective bargaining. Finally, German workers shared with their American counterparts the goal of abolishing management autocracy. Under the influence of a mass socialist movement, however, these workers often linked the goal of democratizing work to workers' control of industry as a whole. And, unlike the situation in the other two countries, in Germany democratic ideals applied directly to the state itself; indeed, revolutionary workers were probably committed more to political reform than to a socialist economy. These different visions of a more democratic order each gave a privileged role to institutions of employee representation. Germany's left socialists assigned to workers' councils responsibility for both political rule and economic management. Leaders of Britain's Shop Stewards' Movement saw in workers' committees an alternative to craft unionism and an instrument of workers' control. Finally, local militants in the United States sought to enforce craft standards and achieve collective bargaining rights by building on wartime union shop committees.[10]

These were not only ideological differences, and they did more than motivate protest. They also expressed the key contradictions—distinctive to each regime—between the old order and the demands of total war. Wartime economic mobilization empowered workers and led government officials to cooperate with union leaders in all three countries. In Germany, however, neither traditional management nor constitutional autocracy could accommodate the labor movement's new power and legitimacy. In Britain, by contrast, industrial relations stability had long relied on centralized collective bargaining and the internal authority of craft unions. Wartime labor conditions stimulated a rank-and-file movement that undermined both these pillars of order. Employers in major American industries, finally, denounced unions as incompatible with management control and organized their labor relations accordingly. Trade unions' indispensable contributions to the war effort, however, and their new role in wartime labor administration could be fully recognized only at the expense of open shops.

In all three cases, then, the practical necessities of speeding production and coping with unrest were bound up with larger problems of industrial and political restabilization. Whether handling day-to-day disputes in munitions plants or looking ahead to the "reconstruction" that should accompany peace, elites had to decide how best to incorporate labor into the war effort and, ultimately, into postwar society. And whether in Europe or the United States, they faced some common choices. In the sphere of industrial relations, what was the proper role for unions in representing employees? What were the minimum rights and standards for workers—including the right to a voice in management—and what responsibility did the state have to guarantee those rights? Which institutions for handling conflict were most likely to avoid strikes and "harmonize" the interests of labor and capital?[11]

The answers differed sharply among the three countries, but they all involved a restructuring of prewar class relations and—of particular significance in the following account—a reconstruction of employee representation. The changes were most dramatic in Germany. Even before the revolution, political realignments enhanced the legitimacy and influence of the Social Democratic Party (Sozialdemokratische Partei Deutschlands, or SPD) and brought union leaders together with government and business elites in a common commitment to industrial control. This alliance would handily defeat the revolutionary challenges of 1919, but not by force alone. Weimar labor laws also consolidated war corporatism, guaranteeing unions' right to collective bargaining and giving the SPD and unions—pariahs before the war—new political responsibilities. The system was anchored in state-mandated works councils through which unions exercised control over employee representation. No such revolutionary changes occurred in Britain. In comparison to that of Germany, the British case is striking for the rapid dismantling of "war socialism" and an apparent return to the prewar status quo in labor relations. Labor's role in wartime governance, however, helped to establish the Labour Party as the dominant (and legitimate) political opposition after 1918. It also expanded the scope of union representation and collective bargaining. Here too, unions disciplined employee representation, but Britain's government eschewed direct control. Instead it encouraged organized employers and unions to bring workplace labor relations under joint regulation through industrywide agreements rather than legal mandate. In both countries these changes benefited organized labor at the expense of rivals to the Left. They also put industrial relations on a more stable footing and made industrial conflict less of a threat to the political order during the 1920s.[12]

This sketch of German and British outcomes is a familiar one. Scholarly treatments of these two cases routinely emphasize the links between war-time experiences and the postwar order and between industrial and political restabilization. For the United States, by contrast, these links are rarely visible. Studies that do connect wartime government policy with the post-war political economy focus on business rather than labor,[13] and issues of collective bargaining and company unionism in the 1920s are most often treated in terms of industrial relations, not political history.[14] There are some good reasons for these omissions. In contrast to German outcomes, wartime state intervention here ended abruptly after the armistice. And compared to experiences in Britain or Germany, the war brought American labor no lasting gains in union strength, collective bargaining rights, or political voice. What was new in the 1920s was a remarkable combination of rapid economic growth and labor quiescence, based in part on reforms in the "handling of men" undertaken internally by large corporations.[15]

These reforms included measures to put employee representation under unilateral employer control. Other parties advanced rival ideals, and historians have examined how competing ideologies of labor representation and industrial democracy gained or lost support by the early 1920s.[16] My own concern is more with institutional outcomes and their roots in concrete U.S. government policies. Shop committee plans fostered in the United States by key wartime labor agencies organized employee representation on an open shop basis. Particularly by improving workplace communication and the "rule of law" without union involvement, these plans became influential models for postwar management. Here a comparative perspective proves to be useful. Reformed open shops, like the very different reconstructions of British and German industrial relations, were a response to the wartime labor crisis. They also had political consequences, making industry safer for democracy by preserving labor peace during a period of rapid economic growth. In the United States as in the other cases, moreover, they had political origins: the federal government served as both architect and general contractor in building the new industrial relations regime.

Part 1 elaborates these distinctions among employee representation under state tutelage, under union-management control, and under employer auspices; relates patterns of workplace representation to postwar restabilization; and explains why states undertook such different reforms. The causal account developed through comparisons of the United States with Germany and Britain emphasizes, first, the contradictions between prewar class relations and the demands of war. These shaped the nature of the labor crisis—particularly the extent to which insurgency developed autonomous organization and political claims—and thus framed the problems confronting wartime governments. Political alignments, together with industrial class relations embodied in the labor process and industrial relations, also defined what options were open and feasible in government efforts to restore order. They did so in part through the dispositions of employers. Like government officials, employers were more or less likely to embrace particular industrial relations reforms in the light of their past experiences, present problems, and perceived opportunities. The logic of this argument makes Germany and Britain especially useful comparative reference points for the United States, because they offer striking contrasts in labor's challenges, employers' dispositions, and political alignments.

The importance of prewar labor relations in shaping employee representation reforms stands out sharply in part 2, where the focus shifts from comparing nations to comparing industries within the United States. This combination of cross-national and internal contrasts, rarely used by historical sociologists, is particularly fruitful for exploring government policy and employee representation. Whereas chapter 2 focuses on munitions as a "typical" American case, chapters 3 through 5 turn to the "deviant" cases of railroad shops and shipyards. Shipbuilding, railroad repair work, and munitions production involved many of the same occupations and unions, they were all of strategic importance to the war effort, and all were sites for serious labor unrest.[17] They differed, however, in prewar union power, production practices, and industrial relations. Making a "natural experiment" possible, each fell under the jurisdiction of a distinct government agency (the National War Labor Board was most important for munitions production, the Railroad Administration regulated shop crafts, and shipyards answered to the Shipbuilding Labor Adjustment Board [SLAB]). The three cases are thus well suited for showing the independent influence of labor relations on government policies. The comparison of two regional centers of the shipbuilding industry (the San Francisco Bay area and the Cleveland vicinity) in chapters 4 and 5 serves a similar purpose. Here too, one finds the same occupations and unions on the job but subject to surprisingly autonomous local SLAB administrators. These two centers also present contrasts in production practices, union organization, and labor-management relations similar to those between railroad shops and munitions factories.

Although my selection of cases implies the logic of a controlled experiment, my conclusions conform more to historical sensibilities. We can profit from asking of the United States questions usually posed only for Europe. Similar questions, however, may prove to be useful even if (or especially when) they yield different answers. I seek to identify important differences between the United States and other cases rather than causal uniformities among them,[18] and Britain and Germany make good benchmarks precisely because they differed so sharply from the United States in their industrial relations, politics, and patterns of restabilization. Part 2 may appear to offer a more "scientific" comparison. By zeroing in on the United States, it controls for political influences and isolates the impact of differences in industrial relations on wartime unrest and government policy. But the conclusions drawn from these case studies do not aspire to universal applicability. Rather, the sectoral comparisons are deployed to better understand the causal configurations behind particular outcomes, and the interpretation of these cases is unlikely to travel far. For any given industry or country, I attach too much weight to particular historical legacies (notably from prewar labor relations) and to the idiosyncrasies of timing and sequence (the fact that labor mobilization *preceded* government intervention in the United States, for example, had important consequences) to expect that the account will fit other cases.

Acknowledging the limits of explanation may violate certain canons of social science, but it echoes recent methodological discussions among historical sociologists. These routinely emphasize that the causal efficacy of one variable or another may depend on *when* it occurs, that causality may be multilinear and path-dependent, and even—most subversive of all—that unique events may be indispensable components of an adequate explanation.[19] In short, history counts. To these familiar cautions about explanatory generalizations I add one more. The logic of the comparison—moving from nations to industries to geographic districts in order to assess the impact of industrial relations on policy—itself makes sense only for a fleeting historical moment. Political alignments during the war briefly opened a window for variations in U.S. government policy. That window, with its opportunities for interindustry causal comparisons, closed by the early 1920s. As the progressive alliance (and impulse) collapsed amid labor militancy and Red Scare, federal intervention in the three industries became more uniformly unfavorable to organized labor. The opportunity for more supportive government policies would not reappear until the New Deal.

EMPLOYEE REPRESENTATION AND
AMERICAN EXCEPTIONALISM

This study shines a narrow beam on the federal government's role in reconstructing employee representation. Looming in the shadows are larger issues of American exceptionalism. The debate over exceptionalism has used misleading vocabulary to ask legitimate questions about working-class formation in the United States. Skeptics have rightfully asked what there is to explain. Sombart's well-focused question, "Why is there no socialism in

America?" has long since been expanded to include such issues as the character of working-class political culture, the marginal role of working-class parties in the American electoral system, and the political dispositions of labor unions. For any such marker of class formation, labor studies have marshaled evidence that the United States is no solitary exception to some general rule of capitalist development. If American working-class politics is not uniquely different, however, it is at least an outlier. The best work on exceptionalism accordingly renounces both the single exception and the general rule, turning instead to the business of explaining how and why working-class formation has been different in the United States.[20] Debates have been lively and often fruitful, as scholars have defended competing accounts of American exceptionalism (no feudalism, early suffrage, racial cleavages, social mobility). For most of this venerable controversy, however, a common concern with class formation and American politics has been evident.

More recently the debate over exceptionalism has colonized the field of industrial relations. Characteristics of American unions, employers, and industrial relations have been rethought in comparative terms and recast as further symptoms of the country's exceptionalism among advanced industrial nations. These features of American industrial relations appear both as problems to explain and as clues to more familiar national puzzles. Studies of American workers' presumed aversion to union organization and their employers' hostility to collective bargaining, for example, line up the same historical suspects that are held accountable for political exceptionalism, including an individualistic culture and the nature of working-class incorporation into the state.[21] To complete the circle, some scholars have attributed America's exceptional working-class politics to features of the nation's industrial relations history.[22]

Industrial relations rather than working-class formation and politics occupy center stage in my study, but the latter forms of exceptionalism are never far in the background. A major concern is to connect industrial relations outcomes to wartime political alignments and state policy; a minor one is to trace links between employee representation reforms and the character of the labor movement in the 1920s. The first theme departs both from historical interpretations of federal intervention during the war and from state-centered theories of comparative industrial relations and policy making. The second theme, *sotto voce*, holds that state-sponsored industrial relations reforms reinforced organizational obstacles to cohesive and sustained working-class protest. This link between employee representation and labor protest has broader relevance for theories of American class formation and political stability in international perspective. One other general lesson for

American exceptionalism deserves introduction. The explanatory narrative of prewar labor relations, wartime struggles and reforms, and postwar restabilization reminds us that American exceptionalism is neither a fixed characteristic nor a uniform property of American industrial relations. As conditions have varied across sectors and changed over time, exceptionalism has been reconstructed in different ways.

Employee representation in the 1920s provided new support for America's distinctive open shop order, and I assign to the wartime state much of the credit for this achievement. The claim that the state "counts" is a familiar one. Much recent work on the history of labor and industrial relations has rediscovered institutional influences, the state and organized employers above all.[23] On specific points of historical interpretation, I contest other views of war labor policy. Prevailing historiography depicts a marked discontinuity between wartime intervention and postwar labor relations. In the area of industrial relations, the Wilson administration's approach is seen as anticipating (and serving as a model for) the New Deal system, not the retrograde 1920s.[24] My interpretation stresses instead certain continuities between wartime reforms and "up-to-date" postwar open shops. State intervention during World War I is often regarded as giving workers both the protection and the inspiration to build a mass labor movement.[25] I instead highlight some government contributions to employer hegemony after the war. Unionists certainly had good reason to feel that they had friends in Washington (although a booming labor market ensured that unionization and successful strikes were well underway before federal officials got involved), but the government's wartime responses to insurgency helped to lay the organizational foundations for open shop stability and a fragmented labor movement *after* the war. These disagreements aside, I share with other students of American industrial relations and labor movements a healthy respect for the influence of the state.

It is in explaining the character and direction of that influence that I part ways with state-centered accounts of industrial relations and government policy itself. The prime mover in my analysis of employee representation reforms is not an autonomous state or characteristically "American" political alignments but the balance of class forces embedded in prewar production practices and labor-management relations. My study accordingly offers no support for the view that states and employers, rather than the struggles of ordinary workers, are the keys to understanding work relations and labor organization.[26] State strategies during the war were themselves shaped by and varied with the character of popular insurgency. Nor should comparative work on postwar industrial relations put America's political alignments at center stage to the neglect of its industrial class relations. David

Montgomery, for example, briefly compares the accommodation between German labor and capital in 1918 with the insistence on open shops in America. In his view the revolutionary threat faced by German employers explains the difference. Sanford Jacoby combines Germany and Britain in a single contrast with the United States and Japan to reach a similar conclusion. In these European nations but not in the United States or Japan, he maintains, labor's threat to political stability motivated employers to accept unions and collective bargaining as the price for political peace.[27] Holding Britain and Germany apart in a triangular comparison with the United States suggests a different view. In Germany employers abandoned their customary anti-unionism in response to revolutionary threats, and the postwar political power of the SPD sustained the deal. In Britain, however, employers faced no comparable political challenge, and the Labour Party had no comparable clout.[28] The solutions to wartime crises promoted by the government and accepted by employers must be explained not in terms of politics but by way of class relations in industry, for the latter both structured wartime upheavals and rendered certain reform strategies viable.

The "exceptional" character of American history and institutions also informs theoretical debates over the origins of public policy. Neo-Marxist accounts have generally been "class centered," rooting state policies in class interests (however indirectly represented) or the imperatives of containing class struggle and reproducing capitalism. Exceptional class relations beget exceptional policies. The peculiar ideological affinities and electoral behavior of U.S. workers, for example, are invoked to explain the late arrival, limited scope, and grudging character of America's welfare state.[29] For "state-centered" theorists, by contrast, characteristics of political institutions determine policy. Classes count, but the very identities and weight of political actors are in part the creation of state institutions. Exceptional institutions generate distinctive policies. America's minimalist welfare state, for example, is traced to the early development of patronage-based mass parties, the weakness of centralized administration, and the power of the courts.[30]

In explaining policies governing employee representation, the state-centered model offers little leverage. Familiar characteristics of the American polity, particularly its "exceptional" electoral alignments and its underdeveloped administrative apparatus, are certainly part of my story. They did not determine the substance of state intervention, however, instead, they made an unusually wide range of policies politically feasible. Wilson's electoral debts to the AFL, for example, were repaid with federal staffing and programs more sympathetic to organized labor than was anything seen before 1912 or during the 1920s. Furthermore, administrative fragmentation permitted officials responsible for different industries to maintain separate fiefdoms and pursue distinct policies. But these features of the state cannot explain what those policies were; the character of wartime insurgency and prior industrial relations determined which options would prevail. My account thus falls in the "class-centered" camp, but with a twist. These interpretations typically show how social factions (corporate liberals in one version and politically mobilized workers in another) act on or from within the state.[31] In the case at hand, class exerted its influence indirectly, as a relatively neutral state entered the field of industrial relations, with its various forms of congealed class power. Wartime government officials had powerful and autonomous interests in maximizing munitions output and maintaining industrial peace, and they often overrode the objections of organized labor and business. Where class "counts" here is in the nature of the threat to government objectives and in the solutions that seemed to be viable. Class relations embodied in prewar production practices, union power, and employer strategies created distinctive labor problems and policy opportunities for government administrators and in this way led to specific employee representation reforms.[32] Comparisons among U.S. industries showcase the causal importance of prewar labor relations, for here one sees distinct traditions generating contrasting patterns of upheaval and restabilization.

Most of this study invokes the causal sequence of prewar industrial relations, wartime crises, and state intervention to explain distinctive government policies and employee representation reforms. Those same policies and reforms influenced the postwar labor movement, however, reinforcing American exceptionalism in its more familiar guise. Sociologists usually trace the influence of states on social movements through political opportunities—the costs and benefits of pursuing particular tactics or goals.[33] I emphasize instead how the state influenced the organizational vehicles for mobilization. Employee representation institutions favored by the wartime state and widely imitated after 1918 raised new barriers to broadly based organization and mobilization by labor. Such limits to working-class solidarity hardly confirm American exceptionalism, because they are neither wholly characteristic of the United States nor entirely different from what is found in other countries. Historical and even contemporary case studies uncover striking expressions of class solidarity among U.S. workers in particular moments and settings, even amid cleavages of skill, gender, and race.[34] On the other side, recent labor historiography finds that working-class unity and socialist class consciousness are more the exceptions than the rule in Europe as well as in the United States. Historians more often make the opposite assumption, viewing race, religion, family ties, or place of employment as more typical bases for allegiance. As expectations change, so do the key questions. The explanatory problem is now less likely to be why class consciousness or solidarity did not prevail; it is more likely to be how, if at all, class interests and solidarities ever emerge. The fashionable answer is that class identities are constructed through language and, Rick Fantasia adds, in the heat of conflict.[35]

One polemical target of these arguments is the economic determinism that lurks within many labor histories. Recent historiography goes well beyond the Weberian point that class standing is merely one among several potential bases for group formation.[36] The more ambitious claims are that class identities and solidarities are ideological strategies more or less unrelated to economic position or that those economic positions are themselves cultural fabrications.[37] This reorientation of social history parallels new theories of social movements that also stress the open-ended and constructed character of collective identities in postindustrial societies.[38] These rethinkings of class formation usefully remind students of labor that collective identities and actors are contingent outcomes. It does not follow, however, that class alliances and goals are wholly constructed through cultural practices; we can repudiate determinism without disowning institutional analysis. One recurrent theme in this book is that workers' solidarities are also constructed by the organizations through which they act. Organizational forms, lifeless though they may seem to be, are important for at least three reasons. First, they affect coalitions, institutionalizing solidarity or divisions along occupational, ethnic, geographic, or other lines.[39] Second, organizations shape leadership, consolidating conservative control or opening opportunities for influence by radicals.[40] Third, organizational forms and boundaries determine the probability that specific grievances or goals will become the focus of collective action.[41] To this unfashionable emphasis on organization rather than culture I add the claim that alliances and goals cannot be reduced to or predicted from the underlying dispositions of participants. We will see that snobbish and conservative craftsmen often had good pragmatic reasons for joining solidary organizations under radical leadership. Those organizations, in turn, could mount serious challenges to government, business, and union elites without ever converting craftsmen to radical doctrines. For all these reasons, my interpretation endorses social scientists' appeals for renewed attention to formal institutions in the study of workers' collective action and politics.[42]

The fleeting and constructed nature of class formation throughout the West rules out a strong exceptionalist thesis that America is uniquely deficient in class-based solidarity. This does not save us the trouble of comparative analysis, but it does reframe the question of exceptionalism. We should not ask why American workers are immune to class identities and action. We should ask instead why occasional cultures of solidarity or explosions of class militancy are so rarely linked to other workplaces or sustained over time, whereas similarly small-scale and episodic labor mobilizations abroad have more often escalated into broadly based, coordinated movements.[43] Part of the answer must again highlight organizations and in so doing link the fields of industrial relations and social movements. The institutions of labor relations are some of the crucial organizational forms through which workers mobilize collective action and consolidate solidarities of one kind or another. Unions are familiar actors in sociological studies of labor movements. Workplace institutions for employee representation have received much less attention in this context, yet they may be just as important in shaping coalitions and mobilization, joining workers (or severing their ties) to coordinating institutions and fellow workers outside the factory gates. In the 1920s employee representation plans pioneered by the wartime government were particularly inhospitable to such coordination and linkage.

Reformed open shops in the United States renewed American exceptionalism by denying even conservative unions, much less radicals, an institutional footing for popular leadership. The Left fared little better in Britain or Germany, and here too reconstructed employee representation helped to circumscribe labor protest. In the latter cases, however, "responsible" union leaders acquired greater authority to discipline rebellious workers. If union fortunes differed dramatically between Britain and the United States, however, the terms of restabilization in these two countries ultimately made industry a good deal safer for democracy than did the reconstruction of employee representation in Germany. By mandating union control of workplace representation, the Weimar state uprooted the council movement's challenge to bourgeois society. This response to revolutionary crisis suited employers for the few years in which the political alternatives appeared worse and the economic costs seemed manageable; the SPD's continued ability to act as political guardian for union power sustained the system for the rest of the 1920s. By the end of the decade none of these supporting pillars remained standing. Because the system of employee representation tied the fate of union control to that of the Weimar state, industrial conflict inevitably escalated into political crisis and put democracy itself at risk.[44] Employee representation reforms in the United States and Britain, by contrast, allowed their governments to disengage from industrial relations, insulating the political order from labor conflict. America's reformed open shops, like German works councils, would break down under the strains of economic depression. In the U.S. case, however, this collapse in the industrial relations order posed little threat to political democracy.[45] The separation into independent variables of political and industrial class relations, urged in this book for scholarly purposes, was also a historical achievement of considerable value to the stability of liberal democracies.

Exploring the origins and consequences of employee representation reform forces us to rethink but not renounce American exceptionalism. Open shops as a managerial strategy for controlling work and workers set U.S. industrial relations sharply apart from conditions in Britain and Germany. Compared to its counterparts in these latter cases, moreover, the U.S. labor movement was distinguished by insular organization and fragmented action. But the roots of employer practices and labor politics were neither constant over time nor consistent across regions and industries. Employee representation in the 1920s provided new reinforcements for an open shop order undermined by war; reformed open shops, in turn, would collapse in the Great Depression, and America's exceptional industrial relations and labor movement would be reconstructed once more.[46] Workers, employers, and state actors contributed to each crisis and contested the terms of each restabilization, so that the outcomes varied not only by time period but from one sector to another.[47] In the World War I era, government labor administrators fostered different institutions and procedures for employee representation in different settings, doing so in deference to the balance of class power in politics and in particular industries. Aristide Zolberg reminds us that there are as many exceptionalisms as there are cases.[48] There are also many American exceptionalisms, each with a history of its own.

PART 1

Corporatism, Collective Bargaining, and Company Unionism: The United States in Cross-National Perspective

Introduction:
Industrial Democracies

On December 7, 1918, leading representatives of business, labor, and the federal government gathered at New York's Hotel Astor to celebrate the Allied military victory and the industrial triumphs that had made it possible. All looked back in pride at their contributions to the war effort, and each drew lessons for the future. Bethlehem Steel's Charles Schwab "learned from this war . . . that this is the age of democracy" and called on labor and capital to deal with one another "collectively and honestly." Connecticut Mills Company president R. Caldwell drew a similar conclusion from the recent war for democracy: "In industry we have hitherto had an oligarchy as complete as formerly was the case in Russia. We must change that and have industrial democracy." Schwab, among several other businessmen, went on to praise Samuel Gompers for his "stand against Socialism and Bolshevism." The American Federation of Labor (AFL) leader graciously accepted Schwab's tribute, advising all present that even after the war they should avoid any "rocking of the boat." National War Labor Board chairman William Taft concurred, denouncing "extremists on both sides" of industry. Felix Frankfurter, another active participant in the government's wartime labor administration, added his weight to the dinner guests' endorsement of industrial democracy and moderation. Applauding the growing evidence of employers' liberal spirit, he reminded his audience that "there is but one answer to Bolshevism, and that is to see to it that capitalism does not spell exploitation. . . . Industrial relations prior to the war for thirty years had been oscillating between the tyranny of autocracy and the anarchy of strikes. We shall not have stability in this relation unless there comes into industry a larger share of control by the workers."[1]

In their advocacy of cooperation and workers' participation as the keys to productivity, the defeat of "bolshevism," and industrial relations stability, these Hotel Astor diners were not alone—either within the United States or in other nations fighting World War I. Among all the belligerents, war had sharpened workers' grievances and produced a sense that their own sacrifices far exceeded those offered up by the rich—a sense of injustice that everywhere crystallized against "profiteers." In each case, too, one finds a similar dynamic of insurgency. To promote production and maintain peace on the home front, governments gave union leaders new roles in wartime labor policy in exchange for their aid in curbing strikes and speeding output. Such arrangements, however, led many war workers to lose confidence in their union leadership and to pursue their interests through other means. And as governments became more closely involved in war production, they became the focus of efforts to redress grievances and the targets for blame if those efforts failed. With unions and governments increasingly discredited, and amid a mounting wave of insurgency during the final years of the war, union, business, and government leaders each had good reasons to advocate closer cooperation among themselves and more conciliatory approaches to industrial management.

This vision did not survive the brief postwar euphoria. Some Hotel Astor dinner guests already hinted at trouble. Frank Vanderlip of National City Bank urged a "return to our former individualism" in the interests of competitiveness even while Gompers warned that labor would "never go back to the old conditions." Gompers was right and Vanderlip wrong, but not as Gompers hoped or Vanderlip feared. What emerged was a third possibility, to which Taft alluded in his suggestion that employers' contributions to industrial harmony, while a break with prewar "autocracy," might bypass unions altogether: "If you would overcome the unreasonable rules of the unions, beat the unions to it in concessions and fair dealing." Another dinner guest's corporation had taken steps in this direction even before the armistice. While Charles Schwab was serving the government as head of its Emergency Fleet Corporation, his Bethlehem Steel distinguished itself by its uncompromising insistence on a nonunion employee representation plan and in its defiance of government efforts to give employees a more independent voice in industrial management. Within a few months of the Hotel Astor dinner, the call for an end to government interference and for more enlightened—but nonunion—labor relations would prevail over the hopes of union leaders such as Gompers or Progressives such as Frankfurter.

In Germany and Britain, too, postwar industrial relations outcomes did not match the radical hopes, progressive dreams, or conservative fears aroused by World War I. Like their American counterparts, European met-alworkers[2] seized center stage in wartime industrial conflict. As did similar efforts in the United States, their insurgency raised the stakes. The labor Left gained new support; employers and politicians mobilized to fight (or con-jure up) a Bolshevik threat; and progressive intellectuals promoted social reforms to resolve labor conflict and rekindle economic growth. Neither syndicalist visions of rank-and-file control nor statist programs for recon-struction survived 1919 in Britain, however; revolutionary socialist schemes for workers' councils and technocratic ideals of corporatist rationalization fared no better in Germany. One way in which German and British outcomes diverged from America's was in the role assigned to unions in restabiliza-tion. Schwab's praise of Gompers as an antidote to bolshevism was both fleeting and rare for U.S. employers. More often business leaders lumped the AFL and socialists together and fought both with equal vigilance. The Red Years in Britain and Germany, by contrast, led employers and the state to support unions as a bulwark against the Left. They did so in very different ways. British government officials and employers relied on voluntary trade agreements to preserve industrial order and regulate employee representa-tion; union-controlled collective bargaining and works councils in Germa-ny were mandated by the state. In both cases, however, unions acquired a responsibility for workplace labor relations that would be denied to most of their American counterparts until the New Deal.

Chapters 1 and 2 assess these different outcomes. The focus is on employ-ee representation (both as a central, contended issue in the crises and as a crucial component of restabilization) and on the role of the state in its reform. The central questions are why three different approaches to regulating em-ployee representation—corporatism, collective bargaining, and company unionism—emerged from the wartime crisis and why government labor policies during and after the war pushed in these directions. Although the picture inevitably opens up from this narrow focus, much that is interest-ing and important about these Red Years in other respects is deliberately neglected. The comparison is also uneven. I make use of Germany and Brit-ain less for their own sake than for highlighting some distinctive features of the U.S. experience. Chapter 1's discussions of Germany and Britain, accord-ingly, are relatively short selective summaries rather than new interpreta-tions. The chapter on American munitions production, by contrast, offers both more detail and more systematic comparative argument.

The explanatory account of national differences emphasizes a general causal trajectory in which prewar conditions molded postwar outcomes, both by shaping the nature of the wartime crisis and by narrowing the available means for restoring order. This trajectory can be traced along political and industrial tracks, and both are important for a full understanding of restabilization. Comparing Germany and the United States highlights the political determinants of labor relations outcomes; juxtaposing Britain and the United States accentuates industrial forces shaping new patterns of employee representation. That latter contrast sets the stage for part 2 of the book, which holds political factors constant and compares two "deviant" U.S. war industries to the more typical case of munitions production.

CHAPTER 1

Political Stability and Industrial Relations Reform in Germany and Britain

GERMANY

The 1919 Weimar constitution proclaimed a standard for industrial democracy that no speaker at the Hotel Astor would have endorsed, even amid the warm glow of national victory and a good meal. "Manual workers," declared Article 165, "are called to participate, in community with entrepreneurs and with equal rights, in the regulation of wages and conditions of employment as well as in the overall economic development of the productive forces." The state lent its authority as well as gave its blessing to industrial democracy. "Organizations of the two sides and their agreements shall be recognised," and workers "shall obtain statutory representation in factory workers' councils as well as in district workers' councils . . . and in a Reich Workers' Council."[1] This more ambitious agenda for industrial democracy clearly built on the political revolution of 1918; the republican achievements of the revolution, in turn, rested in part on a reconstruction of German labor relations. Supporting one another in the early 1920s, Weimar democracy and industrial relations would collapse together by the early 1930s. Postwar reconstruction of German politics and employee representation had a common origin, as well as a joint destiny. Both were precipitated by the dilemmas of wartime mobilization—some generic to all belligerents and some reflecting a clash between the demands of total war and the peculiarities of German history.

Autocracy at War

Germany entered World War I with a formidable reputation for economic and military power but socially and politically ill-equipped for modern war. To meet demands for labor and munitions, the government—like its counterparts in Britain and the United States—made enormous demands on German workers, whether on the front or in the factories. Industrial workers still lacked full citizenship, however: both the federal parliament's (Reichstag) constitutional weakness relative to the Imperial government and Prussia's three-tiered voting system sharply discounted the value of universal suffrage. Political and military authorities, moreover, had long treated the workers' major union federation (the Allgemeiner Deutscher Gewerkschaftsbund [ADGB], an umbrella organization for Germany's socialist trade unions) and political party (the Social Democratic Party [Sozialdemokratische Partei Deutschlands, or SPD]) as enemies of the state. Employers took much the same view of unions. In part because the ADGB retained a programmatic commitment to socialism, heavy industry continued its traditional opposition (in practice and principle) to independent worker organization or collective bargaining.[2] German workers thus entered the war enjoying fewer political or industrial rights than did their counterparts abroad; the Imperial government then imposed material deprivations (including lower real wages, longer working hours, and limited supplies and variety of food) exceeding those experienced in Britain or the United States.[3]

Against all reasonable expectations, the first two years of the war saw relatively little unrest. Following the SPD's infamous vote for war credits, SPD and ADGB leaders renounced political opposition and strikes in exchange for recognition as legitimate representatives of German workers—the 1914 "Burgfrieden," or public peace.[4] The Burgfrieden reflected the military command's understanding that war production could not be increased by coercion alone. Union support was needed to curtail wage movements, manage disputes, and keep workers on the job. Winning that support required concessions, such as exempting unions from liability as "political associations" (1915) and granting them the right to consultation in wartime labor policy. Many of these government concessions had to be imposed on employers (particularly in heavy industry) who had lost none of their prewar hostility to unions.[5]

The state's new treatment of organized labor is clearly demonstrated in the Auxiliary Service Law. By the middle of 1916 war industries faced acute labor shortages even as the army called for more men and munitions. The solution advocated by heavy industry and endorsed by the army's Supreme Command called for compulsory civilian mobilization to increase the pool of labor and to keep workers from leaving war industries or shifting jobs. To this end key industrialists and army leaders pushed through a new Reich War Office with responsibility for labor and raw materials, and they demanded authority to impose military discipline on civilian workers. Army officers more directly involved in labor administration, however (particularly the new War Office head, General Wilhelm Groener), argued that vital manpower policies could not succeed without union support and some democratic legitimacy. Rather than enact new laws by fiat, the government submitted its proposals to the Reichstag for ratification and, unavoidably, amendment.

As initially proposed, the Auxiliary Service Law would have severely restricted labor mobility and empowered the military to adjudicate the competing claims of army, business, and labor. But the bill precipitated a realignment within the Reichstag, joining Center and liberal parties with the SPD in a historic compromise: liberals would support many union demands for changes in the bill, and the SPD would support legislation to promote "bourgeois" democratic reforms.[6] Over the opposition of leading industrialists, this emergent Weimar coalition altered the bill in favor of union rights. Labor gained equal representation with employers on committees responsible for allocating war workers and resolving disputes over job mobility. The revised bill also guaranteed the right to unionize, and it mandated workers' committees to handle grievances with management in every plant with more than fifty employees. The War Office agreed to follow union recommendations in appointing labor representatives to joint committees, and it abetted union efforts to exclude company ("yellow") union members from works committees.[7]

The Auxiliary Service Law reflected the intense pressures on military, political, and economic elites to accommodate unions; it also marked a major advance in German labor's political standing. Yet the law heightened tensions between labor leaders and German workers. Between March 1914 and September 1916 the average daily real wage of war workers (the most privileged sector of the labor force) dropped 21 percent, and keeping earnings up required working longer hours. Along with tighter budgets and harder work came bread rationing, food and coal shortages, and the spectacle of the rich satisfying their lavish needs at black market prices while workers did without. The Burgfrieden restricted the unions and the SPD, however: fearing reprisals and pursuing respectability, labor leaders honored the pledge to abandon strikes and support the war. The Auxiliary Service Law further aggravated discontented workers by limiting their right to switch jobs in search of higher wages. And by incorporating union leaders more closely into the state's labor administration, the law widened the rift between industrial workers and their industrial and political representatives.[8]

The Council Movement and Political Authority

By the summer of 1917 little remained of Germany's Burgfrieden. Union leaders and the SPD, to be sure, retained their commitment to the war effort. Many of their members did not, however, and over the last two years of the war they sought other means to press their demands. Workers' "radicalism" consisted not in a flood of new converts to socialism but instead in the insurgent character, changing leadership, and subversive implications of protest. Tight labor markets and a relatively supportive War Office enabled munitions workers to press demands that employers recognize and bargain with union representatives (as in strikes by Silesian miners and Cologne metalworkers during the summer of 1917).[9] Such demands implied a sharp break with the prewar industrial order: many German employers saw no difference between recognizing unions and accepting socialism. In pursuit of these demands, moreover, German workers engaged in unauthorized strikes and relied on leaders willing to defy union officials and the government. Localists who had long been hostile to centralized union authority (and who typically leaned toward the socialist left wing) seized the opportunity.[10] While the head of the Metalworkers Union (Deutscher Metallarbeiterverband, or DMV), Alexander Schlicke, worked with the War Office to implement the Auxiliary Service Law, Frankfurt DMV official Robert Dissman promoted local wage movements and denounced Schlicke for selling out the workers. Citywide networks of factory delegates—the "Revolutionary Shop Stewards"—played comparable roles among Berlin and Leipzig metalworkers.[11]

A similar process of radicalization driven by practical concerns occurred on the political front. No revolutionary ideology was required to turn worker protest against the state. As they did in other countries, grievances over food, pay, or military service naturally targeted the institution that rationed bread, set wages, and continued the war. In contrast to the governments in Britain or the United States, however, the government that German workers held responsible for turnip diets and coal shortages treated them as second-class citizens. Major strikes in Leipzig and Berlin in April 1917 began in response to food shortages but quickly escalated (under Revolutionary Shop Steward leadership) into demands for peace without annexations and constitutional reform.[12] The army command and heavy industry, increasingly impatient with Groener's coddling of the labor movement, met these and other strikes with military force. Government repression in turn heightened the appeal of the Independent Social Democratic Party (Unabhängige Sozialdemokratische Partei Deutschslands, or USPD)—the only political faction that embraced workers' yearnings for prompt reform and an immediate peace.[13] Nor was the sense that the burdens of war fell most heavily on a disfranchised class confined to workers on the home front. By August 1918 warweary soldiers derided reinforcements as strikebreakers.[14]

Many of these developments came together in the formation of workers' councils over the final two years of the war. The councils typically brought together delegates elected in the larger factories throughout a city; these in turn might co-opt local socialist and union leaders sympathetic to the movement. Despite their family resemblance to the recently victorious Russian soviets, these councils represented neither radical goals nor revolutionary constituencies. They enjoyed support because they were uncompromised by ties to the government and thus more responsive to workers' immediate interests than existing unions could be. Workers' council leaders, by contrast, came disproportionately from among Revolutionary Shop Stewards, radical locals of the DMV, and the antiwar USPD.[15] Left leadership and organizational independence combined to give workers' councils their aura of— and potential for—mobilizing radical popular action. They did so most impressively early in 1918. On January 28, acting against the better judgment of union and SPD leaders, 400,000 Berlin workers struck on behalf of peace without annexations, worker representation at peace negotiations, improved food supplies, an end to military discipline in the factories, and democratic reforms. Workers throughout the city's factories elected delegates to a body they named the Great Berlin Workers' Council. These delegates selected the eleven-man "Action Committee" chaired by Richard Mueller, which recruited USPD and SPD representation in the interests of political unity.[16] The stoppage spread rapidly to other munitions centers. Although met with prompt and effective military repression, these strikes demonstrated the challenge facing the government and employers even before the revolution. They explicitly linked industrial and political demands for change in labor relations, war policy, and the state itself; they were conducted under the leadership of Revolutionary Shop Stewards and the socialist left; and they were organized largely through workers' councils acting independently of the ADGB and SPD—the twin pillars of the government's wartime efforts to base manpower policy on the consent of labor.

On November 5, 1918, German sailors at the Wilhelmshaven naval base mutinied, organized a sailors' council, and claimed control of the base. Their example was widely imitated throughout the north over the next two days, as soldiers' and workers' councils sprang up and seized control of garrisons and city governments. When Berlin councils met on November 9, they acted together with the SPD Executive in proclaiming Germany a "People's

Republic." A mass meeting the next day established a provisional government headed by the six-man Council of People's Commissars, equally balanced between the SPD and USPD. The mass meeting went on to assign
overarching but ill-defined authority to the Executive Committee of the Berlin Workers' and Soldiers' Councils, with delegates from the SPD, USPD, and
Revolutionary Shop Stewards.[17]

For all its drama, the November revolution involved no sharp break in
the character of labor unrest. Spokesmen for workers and soldiers emphasized the same demands they had made earlier: peace and constitutional
reform, not socialism. A wide range of war-weary Germans rallied behind
these goals. They found their voices through workers' and soldiers' councils,[18] which served as the key institutional vehicles for unifying revolutionary action. As they had in 1917 and early 1918, councils still appealed to
workers not because the groups constituted soviet cells for proletarian rule
but because the SPD and most unions proved to be unresponsive. In retrospect Arthur Rosenberg's summary judgment seems valid: this was "a middle class revolution won by Labour fighting against Feudalism."[19] At the
time, however, the social-democratic future was a good deal less certain.
From November through the spring of 1919, a dynamic of radicalization
already apparent during the war accelerated.

Despite initial hopes, ending the war did not eliminate wartime hardships. Nor did the SPD or ADGB suddenly champion popular claims once
the old regime fell. The SPD emerged as the dominant force in the provisional
government and became the leading party after National Assembly elections
in January. The party thus reaped much of the blame for the government's
failure to improve living conditions, and it further alienated workers by its
use of military force to quell demonstrations and strikes.[20] For its part, the
ADGB was no longer bound by the Burgfrieden or tied down by government
responsibilities. But it was committed to its November 12 pact with leading
industrialists, the Stinnes-Legien agreement, under which disputes would
be handled by orderly collective bargaining. Leftists denounced the agreement for abandoning class struggle and compromising with capitalism;
whether or not they agreed with this indictment, many workers resented
their unions' renewed restraint.[21]

Radicalization after November, then, involved the alienation of growing
numbers of workers from moderate institutions and leadership. Where labor insurgency went beyond wartime developments was in the appearance
of demands for more far-reaching political and industrial change. The November revolution enacted constitutional reforms demanded during the war;
continued disenchantment with the SPD and its army allies fostered calls for
council power as an alternative basis for government. Already in Novem-

ber and December, the Executive Committee of the Berlin Workers' and Soldiers' Councils regularly sought (but failed) to assert its sovereignty over the People's Commissars and government ministries. A minority of the delegates to December's congress of workers' and soldiers' councils fought against National Assembly elections in the name of council control—a position increasingly identified with Sparticists and the left wing of the USPD. And after January's military crackdown on antigovernment demonstrations in Berlin, radical councils deposed municipal authorities in major cities throughout Germany.[22] On the industrial front, recognizably socialist demands gained credible support by the spring of 1919, appearing in wildcats and in large-scale strikes among miners and metalworkers. In some factories workers simply deposed management (decried as "wild socialization" by moderate socialists), much as workers' councils ousted city administrators. In the Ruhr the Essen Workers' and Soldiers' Council proclaimed the socialization of mines in January; elected pit councils, area councils, and an industrywide council were to take the place of private ownership, traditional management, and existing unions.[23]

Workers' councils, left leadership, and radical protest did not line up with sociological precision. In the unsettled period from November 1918 through the spring of 1919, the leading actors and institutions varied over time and from one city to another. Workers' and soldiers' councils were almost everywhere the key revolutionary institutions in November; in some areas, however, they were eclipsed by local socialist parties or factory councils as centers for agitation and mobilization. Depending on the city, the vanguard role might have been played by Sparticists, Revolutionary Shop Stewards, USPD activists, DMV militants, or even local SPD officials.[24] Through all such local variations, however, there existed a close association between rank-and-file institutions (whether factory or citywide councils), left-socialist leadership (of some denomination), and popular insurgency. That association cannot be attributed to any widespread enthusiasm for proletarian democracy. Instead, councils won backing and left-wing activists gained leadership roles for want of alternatives; they were the beneficiaries of popular mistrust of the SPD, and they were the only appealing opposition to the government for most industrial workers.[25]

By early 1919 the council movement posed a genuine threat to German political and industrial stability. The claims of workers' councils to municipal and even national power challenged both government control and the position of the SPD within the socialist movement. Demands for extensive industrial powers for factory and workers' councils similarly threatened the authority of both management and unions. And as leading industrialists and army leaders recognized, the SPD and the unions had become the most important bulwarks against the revolutionary flood. In retrospect the agenda for restabilization is clear. Rank-and-file organizations had to be brought under tighter control by the SPD and unions. Curbing council power, however, was a task that neither unions nor employers could manage without state backing—and one that would involve a far-reaching reconstruction of employee representation.

Employee Representation under State Tutelage

The council movement's claim to dual power at the national level was the most easily rebuked. A November 23 decree of the Executive Committee of the Berlin Workers' and Soldiers' Councils (the Vollzugsrat) chided the press and the comrades for ignoring them and reminded workers of their full power "as a provisional controlling body in relation to the government of the Reich. . . . Political power lies in the hands of the workers' and soldiers' councils of the German Socialist [rather than People's] Republic."[26] Members of the provisional government's executive body (the Council of People's Commissars) demurred. Any such claim to executive power on the part of the councils, they argued, was illegitimate and disruptive. At a meeting of the council on November 18, Prime Minister Friedrich Ebert (SPD) denounced recent Vollzugsrat decrees, declaring that he could not "countenance such meddling" and complaining that the Vollzugsrat was "trying to take all authority into its hands."[27] The two sides argued and jockeyed for power in similar conflicts throughout November and December, with the Vollzugsrat making most of the concessions. For example, it agreed not to interfere in foreign affairs or to supervise government ministries directly; in return the Vollzugsrat won largely symbolic assurances of its right to oversee general policy. Its members' reluctance to claim sovereignty reflected in part a realistic appraisal of their prospects. Popular support for council rule was at best untested, and a victory for the committee might have harmed national interests: the Entente deemed the provisional government the only legitimate body for negotiating an armistice.[28] The crucial December 16 congress of workers' and soldiers' councils thus ratified an accomplished fact. Vollzugsrat members had called for proletarian democracy based on a congress of workers' and soldiers' council delegates who would choose a central council to organize the government. The SPD's well-developed local machinery ensured a large majority in favor of National Assembly elections—"middle-class democratic government," in the left's view. The December congress went on to relieve the Vollzugsrat of its self-imposed responsibility as representative of workers' and soldiers' councils in the nation as a whole. The Zentralrat (Central Council) established in its place had no real power and, for good measure, a solid SPD majority.[29]

The bid by workers' and soldiers' councils for political authority at the local level was a good deal more potent. Many such councils claimed control of city governments at the outset of the revolution, although in most cases they exercised little more than a general supervision of existing municipal administrations. With December's move toward parliamentary democracy and National Assembly elections January 18, however, SPD and government leaders argued that the councils would have to renounce their political pretensions. "Once democratic principles have been established in the Reich, the state, and the communities," warned SPD defense minister Gustav Noske, "the workers' councils will have to disappear as political entities."[30] Where SPD members dominated local councils, this view generally prevailed. National Assembly elections, however—ratifying "bourgeois" democracy and leaving socialist parties in the minority—prompted leaders of workers' and soldiers' council in several cities to assert control more forcefully in defense of the revolution. Communists seized control and declared a soviet in Düsseldorf, for example, while the Bremen Council suppressed nonsocialist newspapers and disarmed government troops. Such action seemed to be all the more necessary to council partisans in the light of SPD collaboration with the old military regime (and its counterrevolutionary auxiliary, the Freikorps) in suppressing popular disturbances. The earliest such case occurred on January 5 in Berlin. Under Revolutionary Shop Steward and Sparticist leadership, 400,000 workers took to the streets to protest the government's dismissal of Chief of Police (and USPD member) Emil Eichorn and to assert the Vollzugsrat's authority over such appointments. The government replied with force, and the next four months saw a virtual civil war between insurgent councils and the state. The precise grounds for council action varied from one city to another. The Berlin events sparked sympathetic action in Munich in January; demands for socialization and control through councils led to strikes in Essen and Halle in February; and Ruhr miners struck again in April, echoed (partly in mutual support, partly for local reasons) in Stuttgart, Braunschweig, and Munich. In each case the SPD and its army allies prevailed. The government declared a state of siege and dispatched troops and Freikorps to disband councils. By early May repression of revolutionary city governments throughout Germany was complete.[31]

On the industrial front, reforms rather than coercion proved to be feasible and had a more lasting impact. State policies reinforced union control over rank-and-file organization and in so doing restored management authority and moderated industrial conflict. Because factory councils were an important base for workers' councils and a major target for radicals' organizing efforts, their domestication shored up Weimar political stability as well.

Employers had already taken the initiative in working with unions to control insurgency, joining representatives of the leading socialist, liberal, and Christian unions in the Stinnes-Legien agreement on November 12, 1918.[32] The pact broke sharply with long-standing open shop traditions. Industrialists now recognized unions, endorsed collective bargaining, and accepted local, industrywide, and national joint committees to arbitrate differences. Arrangements for workshop representation steered a middle course between employers' customary support for company unions and radical demands for factory council power. The document called for "workmen's committees" in every establishment of fifty or more employees, and employers guaranteed their independence by pledging not to support or subsidize yellow unions. On the other hand, unions and employers resolved to limit the workplace committees' responsibilities to administering agreements worked out through regular collective bargaining.

Explaining his wholehearted support for parliamentary democracy and cooperation with trade unions, chemicals industrialist Carl Duisberg admitted frankly, "I am an opportunist: I adapt to circumstances."[33] Revolution was the chief circumstance favoring employers' abrupt change of strategy. Unions, old enemies, were now potential allies for containing unrest. Even before the revolution, moreover, the rapprochement between SPD and liberal parties made the Reich much less likely to side with employers in labor conflicts. Here too, self-interest recommended a pact with the devil. Employers also chafed under wartime economic restrictions, and voluntary cooperation with unions seemed to be the best hope for rapid decontrol. Union leaders had their own reasons to compromise with the class enemy. They too feared insurgency in their own ranks, and they shared with employers both an impatience with many state regulations and a willingness to make concessions for the good of economic recovery. Perhaps most important, the modest sacrifices made in the agreement (including some waffling on the eight-hour day and restrictions on the right to strike) seemed to be amply justified by the reward of union recognition.[34]

The November revolution not only changed the calculus of self-interest for employers and unions. It also ruled out restabilization through private agreements alone, for rebellious councils began to challenge union control of the work force—a prerequisite for the success of Stinnes-Legien—as well as state authority. The provisional government weighed in behind union-business collaboration shortly after the revolution, recognizing the joint industrial council (Zentralarbeitsgemeinschaft, or ZAG) established under Stinnes-Legien. On December 23 it backed by decree the basic approach to employee representation agreed to by unions and industrialists. And in the face of continuing agitation on behalf of factory and workers' councils, the

National Assembly made workplace representation, within a larger framework of union rights and collective bargaining, a basic principle of the Weimar constitution. As a result, Cabinet Minister Joseph Koeth predicted, council advocates would be appeased and "trade unions would be vitalized."[35]

Constitutional backing for the principle of industrial democracy at the workplace, local, and national levels signaled the government's determination to go well beyond Stinnes-Legien in regulating employee representation. The form and scope of industrial democracy were fiercely contested. Once workers' councils had been defeated as governing bodies, the USPD elaborated a program for workers' control over a socialized economy through a hierarchy of factory, industry, and national economic councils. For many workers sympathetic to the USPD and supportive of socialism (if only as an alternative to autocratic management), such a system could coexist with parliamentary government.[36] On the employers' side, most hoped to minimize the spread and power of works councils. Even here, however, alternative programs for industrial democracy held some appeal for progressive managers. In the technocratic vision of Walter Rathenau and Wichard von Moellendorff,[37] joint representation through works councils would support labor-management cooperation to rationalize production and form the basic cell for tripartite management of the national economy.[38] Union leaders, by contrast, saw works councils as subversive of their authority, and they endorsed a much more modest agenda at the July 1919 congress of the ADGB. Works councils should be set up only "in cooperation with the trade unions" and should "introduce industrial democracy together with management." "The basis of industrial democracy," in turn, was "the collective agreement with legal force." The SPD, finally, regarded the clamor for industrial democracy as politically disruptive and saw works and workers' councils as breeding grounds for bolshevism.

SPD leaders had cause for alarm other than the precedent of Aleksander Kerensky. Drafting of the Weimar constitution took place amid violent clashes between the government and insurgent strikers and workers' councils. The government's failure to include any provision for councils in an early version of the document sparked widespread counterdemonstrations. Subsequent backsliding from the constitution's implicit recognition of councils as the basis for democratic economic controls brought further protests and in August spurred a new USPD initiative: the party launched its Central Office of German Factory Councils to coordinate local and regional bodies and give substance to the Weimar constitution's promise of workers' control. Noske promptly shut the office, but SPD officials also recognized the need for more constructive measures. From the fall of 1919 through early 1920, accordingly, the government prepared successive drafts of works council legislation for discussion and modification by parliamentary representatives, unions, and employers.[39]

What finally emerged in the Works Council Act of February 4, 1920, nodded in the direction of both socialist ideals of workers' control and the technocratic vision of rationalization through cooperation. Above all, however, it lent state authority to the organization of works councils as purely economic institutions under firm union control. The law required works council elections in all establishments of fifty or more employees, and it endowed them with real powers. Councils could review company records, negotiate certain work rules, consult on the hiring and layoffs of large numbers of employees, and handle grievances over the dismissal of individual employees. Nor were these merely pious recommendations. The act *required* works council elections, and it created substantial legal obstacles to the firing of those elected. More important, the law gave works councils the right to appeal disputes to outside arbitration by union-management and state bodies. These provisions did not satisfy advocates of socialist control, of course, and the law clearly followed the SPD's position that "as regards questions concerned with the economic and technical management of business . . . the works council cannot be given equal rights with the employer, but merely a right of supervision and inspection."[40] Compared to British shop stewards (much less American shop committees), however, the councils had considerable responsibilities and genuine legal backing.

Much of the Works Council Act sought not to empower councils but to subordinate them to trade unions and collective bargaining procedures. The new law abolished councils at variance with union-management agreements, thus helping to eliminate rogue councils in favor of union-controlled ones.[41] Other provisions helped to quell union fears (and left-wing hopes) that the councils might develop into local and national alternatives to the ADGB. Councils were explicitly confined to individual plants and denied any independent funding. The act also emphasized that works councils' duties were subordinate to union-management collective bargaining. For example, the councils could negotiate work rules, but only in areas not covered by existing agreements. If they failed to settle any dispute in direct discussions with management, matters passed into the hands of union officials.[42]

Approval of the Works Council Act occasioned further protests organized by the USPD and communists, and International Labour Office observers found "workers of every shade of opinion" to be "unanimous in regarding the Act . . . as merely an installment, as the first step towards effectual industrial democracy."[43] It proved instead to be the last step, and "effectual industrial democracy" remained limited to collective bargaining. By late 1920 it was clear that the law also had aided unions in regaining control of the councils. Unions' superior organization allowed them to dominate council elections over the summer of 1919, and in October the ADGB summoned a national conference of factory councils to ratify the ultimate authority of the unions. The 1922 ADGB congress capped this victory by requiring works council candidates to be unionists and barring trade union members from running on rival slates.[44]

The Works Council Act was the most important means by which the Weimar government regulated employee representation in the interests of centralized union authority and orderly collective bargaining. It was not the only one. Already in December 1918 the provisional government gave statutory backing to trade agreements and established conciliation boards to handle disputes—with the Demobilization Office reserving the right to impose board decisions on both parties. Effective January 1, 1924, a government decree established a system of district boards to handle appeals and arranged for district and national mediators to assist in resolving disputes. Where mediation failed, the federal minister of labor could impose awards or extend existing ones to recalcitrants within an industry. The government's response to protests against the Works Council Act demonstrated that as a last resort, state coercion would be deployed against rivals to trade union authority.[45]

Government-imposed reconstruction of employee representation played a major role in restabilization after the war and revolution. Politically the works council system undercut a crucial base for left socialist challenges to the SPD and the government. In the economic arena, it helped to defeat the council movement's threat to union control and contributed to a short-lived moderation of industrial conflict. After initial friction where militants worked to expand the scope of works councils and some employers sought to reclaim unilateral authority, relations generally settled down. Even in Red Berlin, by the beginning of 1921 the government inspector could report that "employers are now more willing to negotiate with the councils, and the radicals originally elected to the councils are in many instances being replaced with more conservative members."[46] Although they contested the works council legislation on particular points (notably on access to company records), employers themselves recognized the benefits of the councils for regularizing labor relations within the plants. More grudgingly they also endorsed the system of arbitration that buttressed union power: regular mechanisms for adjusting wages helped to remove a major irritant during the inflationary period. It is for these four years of at least reluctant employer cooperation that the "corporatist" label best fits Weimar industrial relations.[47]

Both inflation and the council movement had been tamed by the end of 1923, and industrialists largely withdrew their cooperation. Where possible, they took advantage of weakened unions to limit works council influence.

They also showed increasing hostility to the arbitration system because it made it difficult to translate employer advantages on the labor market into lower wages.[48] Despite growing employer opposition, however, the policy of statutory works councils and arbitration survived through the 1920s. It did so not because the government or employers feared revolution. That threat had clearly passed. Rather, the SPD retained sufficient political influence to protect Weimar labor policy from attack by employers and their political representatives. As long as this political prerequisite remained secure, so did the Weimar system of employee representation.[49]

BRITAIN

"Once the strike begins, it is imperative that the state should win. Failure to do so would inevitably lead to a Soviet Republic." This March 1919 warning might well have come from Ebert or Noske in the Reich Chancellery amid demands for socialization and threatened strikes by Ruhr miners. It came instead from Prime Minister David Lloyd George, anticipating a walkout by British miners.[50] In retrospect Lloyd George's alarm seems unwarranted: Britain faced no revolutionary crisis in 1919. British workers certainly shared many of their German counterparts' wartime hardships—rapid inflation, rationing of some essentials, overcrowded housing—even if the shortages were not so desperate as in Germany. They shared, too, a keen sense that one class fared better than another in the distribution of the war's profits and sacrifices.[51] But these complaints were not bound up with animosity toward an undemocratic state, and the British government did not face the dilemma of winning the industrial cooperation of a disfranchised working class. The labor policies deemed to be necessary on the home front clashed not with workers' political status but with their industrial rights.[52]

Munitions and Craft Unionism

The war effort required a vast increase in munitions output—the products of the engineering industry above all. Increasing output while conserving skilled labor required more efficient work practices and greater use of less-skilled men and women. Here, however, government needs collided with the well-entrenched work rules and powerful unions of skilled engineers. After considerable haggling, union officials obliged by waiving craft restrictions on war work, and the June 1915 Munitions of War Act made those concessions the law of the land.[53] Workers' freedom (reinforced by acute labor shortages) to switch jobs in search of better wages and to flout workplace regulations and supervisors also jeopardized munitions production. The government responded with provisions in the Munitions of War Act that backed company rules with state authority and required workers to secure a "leaving certificate" from their employers before taking a new job. Violators now had to answer to the state, in the form of local munitions tribunals empowered to hear cases and impose fines.[54] Strikes, too, undermined the war effort, so the Munitions of War Act made unions' voluntary renunciation of strikes legally binding. Disputes that unions and employers could not resolve would be settled instead by government arbitration.

The need for government action on these issues was more pressing in Britain than in Germany because British craft unions and their work rules presented greater obstacles to mass production, as did British employers, who were reluctant to antagonize skilled men.[55] Although the British government demanded greater concessions from unions, however, it also offered a more substantial quid pro quo. In exchange for renouncing craft restrictions, engineering unions won limitations on business profits and government pledges to restore union standards after the war. Officials of key unions also helped to plan and administer labor policy, joining employers and civil servants in local munitions tribunals; the Committee on Production, which set wages; the Ministry of Labour; various advisory committees; and the all-important Ministry of Munitions. Labor's importance to the war economy won recognition in political affairs, too, including Labour Party representation in the Coalition government and a place in Lloyd George's inner War Cabinet.[56]

As craft privileges and worker liberties came under pressure from dilution commissioners and Ministry of Munitions officials, the government and union officials became targets for popular resentments. So did union leaders. National union executives were most vulnerable to reproach as being distant bureaucrats who sided with the government at the expense of their members. Local officials faced the same dilemma, however: the more closely they complied with wartime labor regulations, the more unresponsive they appeared to their constituents. Animosity toward the government and union leaders appeared in Germany as well, but industrial policy was the principal source of friction in Britain. Skilled men had more to give up, and workplace rationalization posed more of a threat to workers organized by craft rather than (as in Germany) by industry.[57] The deep roots of craft unionism in Britain contributed to distinctive wartime tensions in another way. Government and union officials demanded sacrifices and restraint from workers who had long traditions of shop floor organization and activism to back up their growing wartime leverage. The most important result was the Shop Stewards' Movement.

Shop Stewards and Union Authority

Engineering shop stewards had long acted on behalf of their mates to
enforce union rules, negotiate piece rates, and handle grievances, and shop
stewards had found themselves at odds with the union hierarchy even before the war. Officials of the largest engineering craft union, the Amalgamated Society of Engineers (ASE), were committed to certain dispute resolution procedures defined both by the union's own constitution and by an
industrywide collective bargaining agreement. Stewards and their workshop
constituents did not always play by the rules, however, leading to frequent
complaints that local officials "had been ignored until after members had
downed tools. . . . As this . . . happened on several occasions the [District]
Committee naturally resented what appeared to have become a policy."[58] The
war greatly enhanced shop stewards' importance. They enlisted new munitions workers in unions and socialized them into workplace mores, they
negotiated the many details of government dilution plans, and they helped
workers to deal with the new disciplinary apparatus of leaving certificates
and munitions tribunals. Wartime industrial relations also heightened tensions between stewards and union officialdom. In part this was because the
Munitions of War Act obligated union officials to discourage (or at least not
support) strikes and other violations of wartime labor policy. In part the friction resulted from conflicts over authority and jurisdiction. The major engineering unions vested power in residentially based branches and, higher up,
in local district committees. Shop stewards, by contrast, organized engineers
and exercised authority on the basis of workplace ties. Moreover, the leading engineering trade unions segregated workers by craft. Shop stewards of
various trades in a given plant often found it useful to cooperate in disputes
and even to establish regular joint committees to handle matters of common
concern—the more so when district union officials offered only lukewarm
support. By 1916 stewards in many cities had taken the further step of organizing citywide workers' committees. Such organization respected neither
the occupational turf nor the authority of craft unions.[59]

Rank-and-file organization independent of established engineering
unions appeared first in 1915. Militant shop stewards from the largest local
factories organized the Clyde Workers' Committee and led strikes for wage
hikes and against the dilution policies approved by their unions and the
government.[60] Sheffield's Workers' Committee called out 12,000 engineers
in November 1916 to protest the conscription (in apparent connivance with
local employers) of a skilled man who should have been exempt.[61] And when
the government announced plans in April 1917 to limit draft immunities for
skilled engineers and to extend dilution to private work, ASE chairman

Brownlie warned ministry authorities that his "district officials had expressed great difficulty in preventing their members from taking drastic action." At the beginning of May the officials failed: shop stewards led strikes in almost every major engineering center in the country.[62]

As these examples suggest, this was not a revolutionary movement. Engineers most often acted to defend the sectional interests of skilled men on such issues as dilution, draft exemptions, and wage differentials. Nor did the Shop Stewards' Movement press the fundamentally subversive political demands raised by German strikers in 1917 and early 1918. British engineering workers attacked the government's industrial policies, but they did not, for the most part, challenge the war, much less the constitutional foundation of the state.[63] As in Germany, however, rank-and-file organization provided an opening for left-wing leadership: activists from industrial unionist movements, the Socialist Labour Party, and the Industrial Workers of the World figured prominently among the leaders of wartime workers' committees. They did so not because their critique of trade union bureaucracy, craft organization, and capitalist control of industry reflected the views of most rank-and-file engineers. They won support instead because they were willing, as many regular union officials were not, to press demands and coordinate strikes in defiance of the government—strikes that even relatively conservative engineers might join.[64] Quite apart from its ideological leanings, moreover, the Shop Stewards' Movement's challenge to national union authority had important implications for industrial and political stability. Well before World War I, engineering employers had relied on formal agreements with union leaders to codify management rights and to subject workplace conflict to union discipline and the rule of law.[65] These remained the first line of defense against unrest during the war. The state's own efforts to meet production needs and maintain industrial peace also presupposed union authority. Government officials developed labor policies in consultation with union leaders and relied on those leaders to keep their constituents in compliance with wartime policies. It was the indispensability of union authority to employers and government alike that made the Shop Stewards' Movement so profoundly subversive of industrial and political order.[66]

With both statutory restraints and patriotic inhibitions lifted, labor militancy exploded after the war. Indeed, labor troubles in 1919 caused much greater alarm among government and business elites than had wartime conflicts. A wider class consciousness seemed to unite workers previously divided by occupation or workplace, and they seemed to be in rebellion on all fronts. The number and size of strikes rose sharply, the Labour Party (still mistakenly regarded as a threat to government and private property) made strong advances, and local protests erupted against everything from high rents to Allied intervention against Soviet Russia. Combined with continuing news of revolution abroad and reports of disaffection within British army units, it is hardly surprising that elites shared Lloyd George's fear of a miners' victory leading to a Soviet-style republic. Some of the hue and cry over bolshevism served public relations needs, with politicians and employers seeking political advantage by inciting fears of the left. Underneath the rhetoric lay realistic concerns, however, all of them familiar from the war. Union leaders had insufficient control of their members, labor militancy targeted the state, and for both reasons radicals stood to gain popular support.[67]

Engineering once again led the way. When the ASE and Engineering Employers' Federation (EEF) agreed to reduce the standard workweek to forty-four hours, engineers in Glasgow, Belfast, and London rejected the compromise and struck in January for a forty-hour week. Wartime tensions between insurgent organization and district committees had healed, but in other respects the strikes represented a last stand for the Shop Stewards' Movement. Workers' committees joined district officials in leading the strikes, repudiating government efforts to resolve the dispute and defying ASE orders to stay at work. Calls in Glasgow to hand municipal authority over to the Workers' Committee were hardly representative of popular sentiment, but they indicate the continued role of a radical minority in insurgent movements and helped to fuel government fears of a Bolshevik menace.[68]

The lifting of government controls meant that neither the state nor its former union allies bore the brunt of engineering insurgency. In mining and railroads, however, the government remained the boss and thus the target of employee demands. And in the interests of restoring industrial peace and economic competitiveness, government officials continued to intervene in disputes. Industrial conflict thus remained politicized in the immediate aftermath of the war, with unions willing to use their economic clout to force favorable state action—above all in demands, first raised in January 1919, that the government nationalize the mines on pain of a coordinated strike by coal, railroad, and dock unions (the "Triple Alliance"). Beneath the government's exaggerated alarm over bolshevism, then, there was a genuine threat to industrial relations stability. As in the war, the union authority on which employers and the government relied to keep the peace remained either too fragile (as in engineering) or too recalcitrant (as in mining) to do so. "The curse of trade unionism," Churchill complained in February 1919, "was that there was not enough of it."[69]

Voluntarism, Collective Bargaining, and Employee Representation

From the beginning of the war, the British government relied on union leaders to discuss and if possible approve labor policies before enacting them.

As early as 1915 officials recognized that this approach could undermine union authority and with it the government's own policies. Accordingly, the government responded selectively to the Clyde Workers' Committee's resistance to dilution plans. Dilution commissioners worked with moderate local unionists, establishing joint committees to oversee workshop changes, while repressing left-wing newspapers and deporting radical leaders. When shop stewards threatened to gain control of the employees' side of joint armaments committees (set up in major munitions centers to improve productivity), the Ministry of Munitions abolished the committees and centralized labor administration. And when stewards leading the 1917 strikes against dilution and conscription demanded to meet with Minister of Munitions Christopher Addison, he refused, telling parliamentary critics that "to recognize the shop stewards would be nothing short of a betrayal of the trade unions" and "the high road to industrial anarchy."[70]

The government's response to the Shop Stewards' Movement included more constructive measures to avert anarchy, particularly the reform of employee representation to put union authority on a more stable footing. The goal was not simply to squash the movement on behalf of employers. The Ministries of Munitions and Labour had their own interests in curbing industrial conflict and rationalizing production during (and after) the war.[71] It was hoped that employee representation reform would serve these ends. In contrast with Germany, however, even during the war the British state preferred where possible that employers and unions themselves agree on suitable reforms. This voluntaristic rather than corporatist bias became much more pronounced after the war, but the government's underlying commitment to joint regulation of employee representation remained.[72]

In March 1917 a subcommittee of the Ministry of Reconstruction (known, after its chairman, as the Whitley Committee) published its first recommendations for industrial relations reform.[73] The report looked forward to peace, endorsing workplace cooperation as the key to curbing strikes and improving industrial efficiency. Whitley Committee deliberations were also informed by current troubles. The Commission of Enquiry into Industrial Unrest had recently documented widespread dissatisfaction among workers with government-imposed restrictions on their personal freedom, with their trade unions, and with wartime delays in settling disputes.[74] Union members on the committee were especially alarmed by challenges to their authority from the Shop Stewards' Movement. The Whitley report's main recommendations addressed all these concerns. A hierarchy of industrywide, district, and workplace councils should be established, with equal representation for employers and employees, to discuss workshop methods and industrial policy. Ideally these would encourage a more constructive spirit on both sides. More specific recommendations aimed to reform employee representation and consolidate union authority. Works councils should be encouraged but also placed firmly under union control. One early council plan (for the pottery industry), for example, stipulated that "only Trade Unionists shall be eligible to serve on the Operatives' Section of the Committee."[75] At a time when trade union leaders feared that shop stewards and irregular local committees were usurping official powers, the Whitley plan also established a clear pecking order. Works councils could discuss only matters not already covered by regular collective bargaining agreements, and where national agreements existed, "the District Councils or Works Committees should not be allowed to contract out of conditions so laid down, nor, where conditions are determined by local agreements should such power be allowed to Works Committees."[76]

The Whitley recommendations won government approval, and the Ministry of Labour worked to secure their adoption. In this the state gave the lead. In sharp contrast to developments in Germany, however, Whitley's plan was never mandated, and it emphasized that employers and unions should reach agreements on councils with minimal state involvement. The Minister of Labour specifically emphasized this point, reminding employers and unions that "the formation and constitution of the Councils must be principally the work of the industries themselves."[77] Under the plan better-organized trades warranted a lesser state role. Employee representation plans already established through bilateral agreements need not be disturbed; only in industries with weak employer or union organization should the government play a role in setting up the councils, with the state jump-starting negotiations and then withdrawing as soon as possible.[78]

The Whitley scheme proved a disappointment to its champions. An initial flurry of interest led to the formation of joint industrial councils in thirty-three industries by May 1, 1919, with agreements pending in nineteen more. The pace slackened by the end of the year, in part because of cuts in the Ministry of Labour staff assigned to spread the Whitley gospel.[79] The government's growing reluctance to promote the scheme reflected a larger retreat from active intervention in industrial relations. But the postwar history of Whitleyism is in some respects consistent with the original plan in its voluntaristic bias and its deference to union authority. The state's role in setting up joint councils was indeed most prominent in poorly organized trades. In those cases Whitley's grant of sovereignty to industrywide negotiation and agreement was confirmed: not only did joint industrial councils take precedence over works committees, but in many instances unions and employers never set up the latter at all. In contrast to German government officials, moreover, British policymakers refused calls to give even joint industrial council agreements any statutory backing.[80] As for well-organized trades, the failure of Whitleyism to take root demonstrated employer and union fears that works councils would jeopardize their own control.[81] Yet the exclusion of Whitley councils by strongly organized unions and employers was consistent with Whitley's deference to existing collective bargaining agreements. Certainly this was the pattern in engineering. With government prodding, unions and employers in this case devised their own means for reasserting authority over rank-and-file organization.

By late 1917 engineering workers' committees in a number of cities had led major strikes against state policies, and their leaders pressed for recognition by the government as legitimate representatives of rank-and-file workers—the "high road to anarchy" against which Addison warned. Engineering employers were equally alarmed. Long concerned to protect their "right to manage," EEF spokesmen saw the Shop Stewards' Movement as a new threat to their control of production practices. They also regarded shop stewards and workers' committee activists as unreliable, strongly preferring to make agreements with the more "responsible" national union executives. Union leaders had fears of their own. In discussions with Ministry of Munitions officials, ASE representatives stressed that works committees "should be restricted to purely domestic matters and that the Ministry should take no steps which might encourage them to undermine the authority of the trade union executives." Aware of these reservations, ministry officials "hoped that the constitution of officially approved works committees, with functions more or less clearly defined, would help check the more revolutionary tendencies of the shop stewards' movement by bringing it into an ordered scheme."[82]

They had their best opportunity in Coventry. The Coventry Workers' Committee had less influence than its counterparts in Glasgow or Sheffield, but a committee of local unionists—the Coventry Engineering Joint Committee (CEJC)—kept management and district union officials on the defensive. Employers opposed CEJC demands that shop stewards receive recognition and the power to negotiate changes in work practices. The CEJC's plan also preempted district craft union officials' authority over stewards and grievance procedures. Local conferences on shop steward recognition broke down by November 1917, and the CEJC rallied 50,000 munitions workers in an eight-day strike on behalf of its scheme. The strike failed to win a local agreement, but together with Ministry of Munitions pressure it forced national union and EEF leaders to settle on a new plan for employee representation in Coventry and throughout the industry.[83]

The December 20, 1917, Shop Stewards Agreement might not have been signed without government prodding, but it was a bilateral pact between the EEF and major engineering unions. Its overarching purpose, moreover, was to reform employee representation in the interests of union control and industrial relations stability. Employers agreed to recognize stewards, while unions won clear authority over their appointment and affiliation. The scheme further barred stewards from acting at variance with existing collective bargaining arrangements and insisted that disputes that stewards could not resolve would be handed over to union officials. Meanwhile, "no stoppage of work shall take place."[84] The agreement did not prevent further unofficial strikes over conscription and dilution in May 1918, but in the face of these strikes government officials reaffirmed their basic strategy. Minister of Labour John Hodge assured ASE leaders of the government's intention "to help you in maintaining Executive Authority."[85]

The Shop Stewards Agreement had much in common with Whitley's recommendations. Both sought to reconstruct employee representation in the interests of union authority and stable, industrywide collective bargaining. Both relied on voluntary, bilateral agreements rather than (as in Germany) legal mandate. And both assumed employers' willingness to make such agreements. By and large (and in contrast to their counterparts in Germany after 1923 and in the United States at most times), employers obliged, and they continued to do so after the war. In 1919 EEF and ASE negotiators amended the 1917 agreement to provide an additional layer of workshop organization and consultation, once again under close control by unions and collective bargaining procedures.

The government, too, remained committed to backing union authority to marginalize radicals and stabilize industrial relations. Sometimes this called for tough action. During the forty-hour-week strikes in Glasgow, London, and Belfast, government officials refused to mediate and sent tanks through the streets of Glasgow to intimidate strikers. In this the state sided not only with employers but also with the ASE Executive, whose back-to-work orders and suspension of local union officials had failed to break the strike.[86] The government's more conciliatory approach appears in the 1919 Restoration of Prewar Practices Act. Some cabinet ministers and many employers argued that fulfilling wartime commitments to restore craft privileges would damage British industrial competitiveness. The prevailing view, however, was that failure to honor its pledges would undermine the authority of union leaders, men who had accepted dilution and reassured their members that this sacrifice would be temporary. "The upshot," warned David Shackleton of the Ministry of Labour in the overheated rhetoric of the time, "would be the destruction of organised trade unionism, and a great stimulus to extremists."[87] By removing one key grievance among skilled workers, the act also eliminated a major inducement to rank-and-file revolt.

Once again the government's approach largely matched employer strategies. As the postwar economic boom faded, EEF members sought to reverse union gains, and they took special aim at unauthorized local bans on overtime work. When engineers repudiated their union's concessions on these issues in 1922, the EEF began a three-month lockout of 260,000 workers nationwide. In the heat of battle some unionists branded the lockout an attempt to smash organized labor. Employers instead used their victory to tighten existing collective bargaining agreements. The Terms of Settlement, which ended the dispute, reaffirmed managerial prerogatives, but it also formalized procedures through which unions could appeal decisions. The settlement tightened control over shop stewards and local union officials, closing some loopholes in prior agreements, but it did not give managers sovereignty over employee representation. Instead, the pact subordinated workplace representatives and negotiations to union hierarchies and centralized collective bargaining.[88]

The government's strategy presupposed reasonable leadership on both sides of industry: union executives willing to make concessions and restrain their members and employers willing to work with them. These preconditions were not always met. In coal mining union leaders refused to back down from demands for nationalization and, later, industrywide arrangements to support wage levels; mine owners proved to be exceptionally pigheaded in opposing wage claims and industrywide agreements. With no room to maneuver, the government first temporized (setting up a commission in January 1919 to consider nationalization) and then prepared to win a strike should it occur. Even in mining, however, government officials were careful to distinguish between moderates and militants—in this case, being careful to appease the miners' Triple Alliance partners before the October 1920 showdown. In the other major case where the state was unavoidably the target of strike threats—railroads—moderate union leadership and less-benighted employers supported a different approach. National Union of Railwaymen president J. H. Thomas agreed to drop demands for nationalization, and the government helped to resolve the union's dispute with railroad owners on the basis of national wage agreements and state financial support for the industry.[89]

Although the overall goal of reinforcing union authority and collective bargaining continued after the armistice, the Coalition government certainly retreated from its activist wartime role on behalf of those goals.[90] In February 1919, for example, the government convened the National Industrial Conference of union and business leaders to discuss solutions for industrial unrest and recommend legislative measures to implement them. Conference participants reached agreements on a wide range of reforms, including a statutory minimum wage, unemployment relief, and the establishment of an organization to sustain labor-management cooperation at the highest level (the National Industrial Council, or NIC). Lloyd George reneged on his pledge to give legislative backing to most of the conference proposals, however, including the NIC—a clear retreat from state intervention. A comparative perspective, however, highlights what government, employer, and union representatives at the conference all accepted: that industrial relations should be based on "the full and frank acceptance of employers' organisation and trade unions as the recognised organisations to speak and act on behalf of their members."[91]

Labor conflict no longer endangered military efforts after the armistice, thus reducing pressure for state intervention. Changing political alignments also favored decontrol. Some Labourites and Liberals had hoped to adapt war powers to postwar reconstruction, and Lloyd George was particularly adept at exploiting fears of the left to win reforms from his coalition partners or the more obdurate employers. ("The English capitalists, thank God, are frightened," he noted in his diary in March 1919. "This makes them reasonable.")[92] As those threats diminished, so did political support for the prime minister's activist approach. And as Labour's electoral advance undercut Liberal strength and Conservatives became the dominant force in Lloyd George's coalition, the cabinet became more reluctant to depart from laissez-faire principles—especially to the benefit of labor. A similar dynamic occurred within the civil service as the treasury gained influence at the expense of the relatively reformist Labour Ministry.[93] A third element making decontrol possible was the disposition of labor leaders and employers. Both sides hoped to quickly reclaim their prewar freedom of action. As the failure of the NIC showed, both sides also preferred to press their interests through existing industrial relations institutions rather than to experiment with new procedures. Once economic downturn and weakened unions replaced the initial postwar boom and labor militancy, moreover, employers turned especially strongly against what they regarded as pro-union government intervention. What they sought in its place, however, was not a regime of open shops but concessions agreed to and backed up by unions. American employers on a fact-finding trip in early 1919 were surprised to find little support for breaking unions. "The call seemed to be for better organization, coupled with better means for collective bargaining and better methods of enforcing contracts through organizations of employers and employees."[94]

Both the turn to voluntarism and its endorsement by many unions and employers reflected the success of government responses to the wartime labor crisis. Pragmatic measures to meet rank-and-file insurgency strengthened union authority and incorporated workplace labor relations into formal, more centralized agreements. Government-promoted reforms of this kind helped to put industrial relations and workplace unionism on a more stable footing after World War I.[95] The success of these reforms in turn made employers more willing to pursue their interests in deflating wages or regaining managerial prerogatives through negotiation with unions. In contrast to postwar American trends, collective bargaining agreements in Britain covered growing numbers of workers and increasingly subjected employee representation and workplace labor relations to joint regulation.[96] To say that these reforms were successful does not mean that Britain reached the promised land of industrial peace. Conflict continued, but in more constitutional forms and more clearly bound by national agreements and authorities.[97] This in turn made it easier for the government to minimize its involvement in industrial disputes—a disengagement that, by depoliticizing economic conflict, reinforced a broader restabilization of class relations in the 1920s.[98]

Compared to Germany's, Britain's labor crisis, even at its peak, was more of an industrial rebellion than a political upheaval. The difference can be traced back to tensions between the prewar status quo and the demands of modern warfare—tensions that in Britain centered on the rights and authority of craft unions and in Germany focused on working-class political participation. The difference can also be traced forward to the character of restabilization. For Germany this involved continuing intervention by the state, statutory regulation of employee representation, and sustained SPD political leverage. Britain, by contrast, saw a retreat to voluntarism after the war, regulation of employee representation by collective bargaining, and reliance on union discipline to routinize industrial conflict. On one crucial point, however, the German and British outcomes converge: government officials generally agreed that employee representation and workplace labor relations should be conducted through trade unions, and this view prevailed. Unionists and their progressive sympathizers in the United States largely concurred. As chapter 2 shows, government officials championed a different approach.

CHAPTER 2

Reforming Open Shops in the United States

On September 22, 1918, Midvale Steel and Ordnance Company president A. C. Dinkey proclaimed "the right of wage earners to bargain collectively with their employers," and he invited employees to meet with managers for the purposes of "adopting a plan of representation by the employees which shall be thoroughly democratic and entirely free from interference by the companies."[1] Lest workers be unsure how to exercise their rights, Midvale officials presented thirteen elected employee delegates (seven of them foremen) with a plan developed by the company. It allowed workers to choose representatives to discuss grievances with management; it also stipulated who could be chosen as a representative (only company employees of at least one year's standing) and what grievances could be negotiated. The leading industry journal—referring to the plan's repudiation of autocratic rule rather than its exclusion of union representatives—hailed the company for its "willingness to make their industry a safe place for democracy."[2]

Dinkey's new enthusiasm for democracy was widely shared by employers during the final months of World War I. They were joined by many government administrators, political progressives, union leaders, and labor radicals, each championing his or her own vision of industrial democracy. Few saw their ideals realized. The new forms of employee representation flourished above all in the industries that supplied munitions and bore the brunt of labor militancy, and the version of industrial democracy favored there excluded unions and government alike.[3] Yet the democratic reforms undertaken by employers owed a great deal to federal efforts to maintain peace in war industries. Employers often complained that government labor agencies undermined management authority and aided unionization. Wartime militancy and challenges to management control had roots other than Washington's coddling of unions, however, and these were problems for the government as well as for employers. In coping with those problems, government agencies responsible for industrial relations in munitions helped to give management authority and labor peace a more secure foundation.

These agencies did so by reforming open shops, and both the reform and the persistence of open shops deserve emphasis. Shop committee plans installed by the National War Labor Board (NWLB) formed the centerpiece of a larger effort to curb victimization of union members, introduce more systematic grievance procedures, and encourage more consensual forms of workplace governance. These measures improved working conditions and (together with labor shortages) supported a boom in union membership. In striking a balance between the competing claims of employers and organized labor, however, the NWLB's plans also respected open shops. The board's shop committees created alternatives to union recognition and collective bargaining that insulated labor conflict and organization within the factory gates from outside coordination and support. State policies did not dilute unions' wartime strength or membership. Instead, government-promoted reforms of workplace industrial relations helped to consolidate management control and limit broadly based worker mobilization once the war boom subsided. Reconstructed open shops thus made industry safer both for the introduction of "democracy" at work and for democracy in the larger political arena.

The following account serves a twofold comparative purpose. First, it anchors the comparison of the United States to Britain and Germany, for which purposes munitions production is an ideal focus. This was the most important sector of the war economy; it fell under the jurisdiction of the NWLB, the best-known government labor agency; and it became a center for company unionism after the armistice. Second, the chapter offers the first of three industry studies *within* the United States. Whereas the cross-national comparisons presented in part 1 highlight political as well as industrial conditions shaping government policy, the internal comparisons offered in part 2 largely hold political influences constant. They emphasize instead how the prewar balance of power embodied in the labor process and industrial relations strongly influenced the nature of labor's challenge and the options open to government officials in their efforts to restore order. In developing this argument for the munitions industry, chapter 2 thus looks not only across the Atlantic to Britain and Germany but also across town to the offices of the Railroad Administration and the Shipbuilding Labor Adjustment Board.

THE PREWAR STATUS QUO

Few firms specialized in munitions production prior to 1914. The tech-
nologies for doing so were well established in the metal trades, however, and
so was the requisite pool of labor—from machine-tending operatives to highly skilled pattern makers, molders, metal polishers, and machinists. American firms were generally better prepared than British ones to meet the demands of war production. Large-volume manufacturers had already moved
away from craft techniques by 1914.[4] Rather than leave the planning of operations or the routing of work to ornery craftsmen, employers increasingly
assigned these tasks to new management professionals.[5] Furthermore, where
markets justified the investment, employers bought "foolproof" machinery
that let less-skilled workers do much of the production labor.[6] Craftsmen
remained, but in new capacities. In mass-production sectors such as auto-
mobiles and small arms, skilled workers found themselves increasingly
confined to making the tools, constructing the fixtures, and setting up the
machinery that made it possible for operatives to turn out standardized pieces on a repetitive basis.[7] More diversified plants might find skilled men concentrated in certain departments and engaged in small batch production,
while machine tenders predominated elsewhere. This was a common pattern in electrical engineering and heavy armaments.[8]

Whether working in segregated production departments or as toolmak-
ers, craftsmen's ability to disrupt operations gave them considerable clout.
Compared to British workshops, however, U.S. firms relied more on "skilled"
machines and managers in these branches of metalworking. Craft unions
resisted the subversion of customary standards and privileges,[9] but they had
few members and little clout. Approximately 11 percent of machinists (the
largest and most important metal trades craft) belonged to the International Association of Machinists (IAM) between 1901 and the war, barely a third
the union density among British engineers. This level of organization among
machinists matched that of the nation's industrial work force as a whole. For
the skilled trades in which most American unionists worked, however, it was
a poor showing (IAM officials often complained that even the despised hod
carriers were better organized).[10] As for the less skilled, industrial or general unions in Germany and Britain offered these workers some representation. The predominance of craft organization helped to keep them outside
the house of labor in the United States, where the AFL was reluctant to recruit operatives even into separate "federal" unions.[11]

The local union lodge, combining men of a single trade from around a
city, served as the organizational base and nerve center for prewar labor

struggles in the metal trades. Lodge officials (more than the national executives of a union) dictated local trade policy, negotiated agreements with firms, called strikes, and administered benefits. The lodge was also an important center for sociability. Local union minutes often devote far less attention to collective bargaining than they do to family picnics, "smokers" for recruiting new members, and participation in holiday parades.[12] Nevertheless, both above and below the lodge, union organization remained fragile. Most major cities had a metal trades council by World War I, with representatives from the different crafts. Metal trades councils usually lacked authority to coordinate local policy or conduct strikes, however, because constituent lodges would not compromise their own autonomy, and the AFL's Metal Trades Department (which chartered and supervised metal trades councils) would not devolve its own, limited powers. Below the lodge level, the shop steward organization typical of British engineering was much less developed in the U.S. metal trades. Employers often fired any known unionist, so openly organizing at work or serving as a formal union steward were out of the question. Rather, workplace unionism took the form of ad hoc committees formed for the purpose of handling an employee's grievance or—under favorable conditions—presenting what were in fact union demands, even if they were not openly designated as such. But in prewar arms factories, auto plants, or electrical machinery works, these committees usually dissolved once the dispute passed.[13] Metal trades unionists thus entered World War I with few institutionalized links either across trades or between individual shops and citywide union bodies.

Weak unions, exclusive organization, and clandestine, isolated workplace activism were not peculiar to the metal trades, and the reasons for the "exceptional" weakness of American unions have been widely debated.[14] One culprit in the metal trades was the organization of work. Industries where skilled men still monopolized production tasks (as in much construction and printing) were likely to be better unionized.[15] More important, American employers remained dead set against unions at a time when their British counterparts tolerated organized labor.[16] The National Metal Trades Association (NMTA) adopted a belligerent open shop stance, and most local associations of metal trades employers followed suit. In principle open shop managers refused to discriminate either in favor of or against unionists in employment and declared their willingness "to treat with . . . individual employees whenever they felt they had any grievance"—but not with "outside" union representatives.[17] In practice partisans of the open shop fired and blacklisted known union members, sought legislation curbing union rights, and planted spies to help preempt organizing drives. Usually employers prevailed. Large enterprises had the market power and financial reserves to screen out unionists, hire private armies to defeat strikes, and impose working conditions unilaterally. Small companies achieved much the same ends by pooling resources in local associations.[18]

Why were U.S. employers so hostile to unions? The usual explanations recapitulate standard accounts of American exceptionalism in general, including an individualistic and property-conscious culture, a more fluid social structure, and characteristics of the state and legal system.[19] To understand the development of the open shop, however, one must also look at conditions within particular industries. Anti-unionism in the metal trades reflected less a principled aversion to "collectivism" than the close association, in fact and in employers' minds, between open shops and management control. The formation of trade unions and efforts to formalize craft work rules came at a time when rapid technological and managerial innovations were already underway. In 1900 the NMTA experimented with an industry-wide agreement under which unions joined organized employers as allies in a common effort to maximize productivity and curb workplace conflict. British engineering employers adopted this strategy in 1898, and they continued to rely on it through the 1920s. The experiment proved to be short-lived in the United States, where cooperation offered employers fewer benefits and imposed greater costs than in Britain. Within a year employers had redefined craft unions as a threat to their control of both work and workers. In this view unions defended restrictive work rules and fomented strikes, jeopardizing employers' ability to get the maximum benefit from new workplace practices. Management control required open shops.[20]

On the eve of World War I, then, the position of skilled men in U.S. metalworking firms compared poorly to that of British engineers. The establishments that employed them already relied less on craft knowledge and manual skill, the unions that sought to represent them were weak and relatively isolated from the workplace and from other trades, and employers successfully fought off demands for recognition and collective bargaining. These features of the prewar status quo were closely connected. Employers defined their own control of the workplace and the defeat of craft unions as two sides of the same coin. "Unions," the NMTA president reminded conventioneers in 1913, represent "the teachings of class selfishness, the insistence on 'the closed shop,' the curtailment of output, the encouragement of soldiering, [and] the employment of force."[21] And employers' success both in deskilling work and maintaining open shops reflected the basic balance of power in the prewar metal trades. It was above all this link between workplace control and open shop industrial relations that wartime mobilization threatened to break and that government labor policies would help to protect.

WARTIME MOBILIZATION

For those who labored on the home front, war was at once a blessing and a curse. Foreign orders for war materials began pouring in by early 1915, and the country added its own demands for munitions in 1917. Before 1914 six government arsenals and two private ordnance works turned out heavy weapons, and a handful of firms produced small arms and ammunition. By the war's end nearly 8,000 plants were fulfilling ordnance contracts. Boom conditions gave workers the upper hand in the labor market, but war prosperity also had its costs, including scarce housing, runaway inflation, and heightened work pressures. Skilled men also saw further erosion of their crafts as huge orders for standardized products allowed manufacturers to invest in more automatic machinery, subdivide jobs, and hire less-skilled employees to do the work.

Those employees with some prior organizational resources moved quickly to exploit new opportunities. After years in which skilled workers shunned unions out of fear for their jobs, local lodges signed up new members by the hundreds. Cleveland IAM branches counted 200 applications a week by early 1916, and nationally IAM membership shot up from 72,000 in 1915 to over 305,000 in 1918. The International Brotherhood of Electrical Workers, representing another key group of skilled workers in war industry, saw similarly explosive growth, from 41,500 in 1917 to 139,200 by 1920.[22] With their new bargaining power, metalworkers sought concessions on issues old and new. Particularly in 1915 and 1916, they pursued long-standing claims for the eight-hour day and recognition of shop committees to represent unionized employees at work. As inflation accelerated, so did calls for wage hikes. As management "diluted" skilled labor, moreover, unionists demanded that employers accept craft standards in classifying and paying workers. Knowing that employers had full order books and fat profits, munitions workers took the offensive. NMTA members reported five strikes in 1914 and sixty-seven in 1915, but even these figures sharply discounted labor unrest: Bridgeport alone experienced fifty-five strikes during the summer of 1915. Open shop employers insisted that they would not be moved, boasting that "those who fought their strikes all won."[23] In practice, however, demands and strikes gained concessions: employers simply announced wage hikes and shorter hours without meeting union representatives or signing agreements.

The government's initial efforts to manage these conflicts, like its policies in other areas,[24] were uncoordinated and largely ineffective. Nevertheless, early intervention in labor disputes did embody some common principles, most of which would also guide the NWLB after April 1918. First, federal officials relied as far as possible on voluntary compliance.[25] The Department of Labor's Mediation and Conciliation Service was often the first on the scene of disputes, engaging in shuttle diplomacy between the men and employers who refused to deal directly with union representatives. The diplomats had no authority to impose settlements on recalcitrant parties, however, and employers—many of whom regarded the entire Department of Labor as pro-union—viewed them as nothing more than a "mediation service whose good offices they could accept or reject as they might wish."[26] President Wilson's Mediation Commission, organized in September 1917 to investigate ongoing strikes in western copper mines, oil fields, and lumber forests, set other precedents. It held hearings at which contending parties testified, issued formal recommendations for awards, and appointed administrators to oversee them. But the commission had no more authority to enforce decisions than did the Department of Labor.[27]

In munitions production, too, the War Department (which awarded the lion's share of military contracts) relied on Department of Labor conciliators as the first line of defense against labor disputes. Because voluntary measures failed to avert strikes, in the summer of 1917 the War Department began to insert a "labor disputes clause" in its contracts. The clause obligated employers to refer unresolved disputes to the War Department for settlement, and the department organized its Industrial Service Section to handle these cases. Connecticut munitions makers, among others, strenuously protested this interference with the management of their businesses, but Secretary of War Newton Baker stood firm. "When . . . we make a request of the workers that the manufacture be continued under all circumstances and that no strike be called, we must be in a position to state to them that another and more peaceful machinery has been created which will consider and determine the questions formerly decided through the agency of the strike." Voluntarism persisted, however; the War Department rarely invoked the disputes clause, and from early 1918 the department made the clause itself a voluntary addition to war contracts.[28]

Although the Wilson administration proved to be reluctant to infringe on the liberties of either employers or unions, it did establish some guidelines for their wartime rights and obligations. Both were entitled to a voice in policy. That public-spirited employers should help to plan wartime mobilization seemed only natural: the government, after all, had neither the experience nor the staff for economic management. The government's recognition of union leaders as responsible partners in forging labor policy was more startling. Even before America's declaration of war, AFL president Samuel Gompers took his seat on the Council of National Defense's Labor Advisory Committee, a semipublic body appointed by President Wilson to help prepare the nation for war. Specific labor boards established for indi-

vidual industries similarly co-opted leaders from the appropriate unions—
from the building trades on the Cantonment Adjustment Commission, from
the metal trades on the Shipbuilding Labor Adjustment Board, from the International Longshoremen's Association on the Labor Adjustment Commission, and from the International Ladies Garment Workers' Union in agencies responsible for army clothing.[29]

These new public roles came with new obligations to act responsibly.
The crucial guiding principle devised by business and AFL representatives
on the Council of National Defense (CND) was that neither employers nor
employees should "take advantage of the existing abnormal conditions to
change the standards which they were unable to change under normal conditions." There would be lively disagreements about just what these "standards" might be, but from the outset government officials included the
open (and closed) shop. Employers should not discriminate against unionists or interfere with employees' right to join unions. Where an employer
maintained an open shop before the war, however, workers should not take
advantage of their wartime leverage to impose a closed shop or even demand union recognition. Secretary of Labor William Wilson made these
principles explicit in public statements in April 1917; they became part of
the formal agreement guiding industrial relations in coal mining during
the summer and were consistently followed by government boards established that summer for cantonment construction, shipbuilding, and harbor
workers.[30] "Responsibility" also excluded restrictive union work practices.
American officials did not suspend craft standards by edict, but NWLB
guidelines discouraged "methods of work . . . which operate to delay or
limit production."[31]

In practice these seemingly evenhanded guidelines did not impose equal
sacrifices on unions and business. The ban on union-busting tactics facilitated
labor organization and angered many employers. But respect for "existing
standards" also meant that unions had to defer to conditions—the open shop
and the refusal to recognize unions—that employers had been able to impose before the war, even though the balance of power had now shifted in
the unions' favor. Much the same applied to work practices. Unions had
generally been unable to restrict management prerogatives before the war.
Now that the tables had turned, the government declared such restrictions
illegitimate. Meanwhile, employers remained free to dilute labor. The implications of respecting "existing standards" is especially clear in contrast to the
situation in Britain. With trade unionism and craft practices firmly en-
trenched in British metalworking, government officials committed to maximizing munitions output had little choice but to ease restrictive work rules
and to do so in close cooperation with union leaders. The latter won close

to a veto power over labor policy affecting their members and guarantees that advantages relinquished by skilled workers during the war would be restored. American employers needed little assistance from state officials to rationalize manufacturing practices. The adoption of specialized equipment, finely divided job tasks, and less-skilled production workers was well underway even before the war, and craftsmen were usually in no position to block further changes. Because the government rarely demanded of unions any sacrifices in established work practices and occupational privileges, federal officials had little obligation to extend union recognition in return. As War Department labor mediator Louis Wehle recalled, neither he nor Secretary of War Newton Baker deemed compulsory arbitration to be necessary, because "skilled labor was not so highly organized as in Britain."[32] The balance of power at the point of production, then, made it unnecessary for the government to break with the open shop status quo to satisfy its need for munitions. And, unlike in Britain, the government did not give skilled workers any guarantees that advantages lost during the war would be restored.

Demonstrating their patriotism and commitment to the war effort, most national union leaders endorsed the CND's guidelines for wartime industrial relations. Ratifying those principles had an important corollary: union executives should not countenance strikes. The AFL convention in November 1917 endorsed government mediation in lieu of walkouts but still allowed strikes as a last resort. The leadership of key AFL unions went further in the formal agreements that established government labor boards during the summer and fall of 1917. In coal mining, future fuel commissioner Harry Garfield oversaw an agreement between the United Mine Workers and the operators of the Central Competitive Field that imposed penalties for strikes. The United Leather Workers formally agreed not to strike under the terms of the Harness and Saddlery Commission, and the International Longshoremen's Association did so for New York harbor. In establishing procedures for handling disputes on army construction work, Gompers and Secretary of War Baker agreed that there would be no interruption of work if disputes arose, and most building trades unions followed suit in setting up the Cantonment Adjustment Commission. Similar provisions appear in shipbuilding and munitions production.[33]

Thus the basic principles guiding government labor policy had emerged well before the formation of the NWLB in April 1918. There should be no restrictions on war production, whether by work rules or strikes, but management could no longer deal with grievances and disputes autocratically. The open shop could stand, but the worst abuses of open shop employers (such as discrimination against unionists) must stop. As implemented by federal agencies and backed by the national leadership of metal trades unions, this was the context for the development of insurgency in munitions for America's first year of war.

CHALLENGING THE OPEN SHOP ORDER

The emerging character of munitions workers' militancy was a complex product of the war economy, legacies from prewar industrial relations, and early government policies. The war economy fueled unrest by aggravating old grievances and adding new ones. Munitions production accelerated the dilution of skilled work already underway, and skilled craftsmen lost ground relative to semiskilled workers both in wages and in status.[34] Workers of every grade also confronted rapidly rising costs for food and housing, and they had good reason to believe that profits (and "profiteering") were greater than ever. To make matters worse, the idiosyncrasies of geography, local labor markets, and uncoordinated government wage policies gave almost every munitions employee reason to grumble that workers elsewhere who deserved less earned more.[35] At the same time tight labor markets and craftsmen's strategic role in munitions production gave them extraordinary leverage. In the context of heightened grievances and enhanced power, the policies of employers, unions, and government not only added to rank-and-file unrest but also gave it a distinctive shape. Open shop employers' refusal even to meet with union representatives, much less negotiate wages and working conditions, was nothing new. What galvanized many munitions workers was the sense that, finally, they could turn the tables on employers. Moreover, they felt justified in doing so by their nation's war on autocracy. With that goal finally within reach, the policies of national union and government officials tried men's patience. Union executives had agreed to suspend demands for union recognition and to avoid strikes. Munitions workers who sought gains through walkouts thus won no support and frequent censure from their national leaders. IAM vice president John Anderson's criticism in September 1917 was typical: "I am sorry to say our men participate far too often in [unauthorized] strikes, thereby . . . causing employers to lose confidence in us as a reliable organization."[36]

Compared to German or British approaches, U.S. policies were more of a mixed blessing for labor. Uncooperative workers did not face military reprisals from an autocratic state, nor did they see strikes legally banned or dilution imposed by government officials. Federal intervention also helped to neutralize the worst anti-union tactics and gave munitions workers some protection for organizing. On the other hand, munitions workers resented the government's insistence that strikes and demands for union recognition were illegitimate. Although federal labor boards offered employees a mechanism for resolving disputes, they also worked slowly. Walkouts cut red tape. A common lament among union officials was that "it has been a hard job to hold [the men in], due to the fact that so many of them have been of the opinion that they could get quicker action by showing their strength."[37]

Union and government policies thus channeled wartime unrest into insurgent action. America's late entry into the war made an important difference, however. Even before the war boom got underway, British and German union leaders promised to suspend strikes and speed production; government measures enforcing these pledges also took hold early in the war. Restrictive union and government policies did not appear in the United States until mid-1917. By this time munitions workers, and especially craftsmen, had two years of organizing and striking under their belts. National union officials withheld support from insurgents before 1917 in compliance not with government policy but with union constitutions: out of 179 machinists' strikes in 1915, 136 lacked executive approval.[38] Local union officials were much more responsive to workers' desire for immediate results. They provided essential leadership and organization, despite munitions workers' tendency to strike first and join the union later, if at all. As a wave of strikes got underway in Cleveland in October 1915, business agent William Jack would wait outside plants, hold a mass meeting of workers at the end of the shift, and take a strike vote on the spot while pickets from other plants cheered from across the street.[39] Lodge officials in other munitions centers showed a similar willingness to take charge and win recruits among workers new to unions but eager for quick gains.[40] The development of munitions insurgency was accordingly very much a local affair and, after union executives withdrew support, one that often pitted local lodges and their supporters against national officials.

The key to mobilization was the development of workshop organization organically linked to the local labor movement. The distinctive structure of wartime insurgency can be traced to prewar labor relations as well as to the timing of the United States' entry into the war. Britain makes a telling contrast. British engineers from the late nineteenth century on took advantage of their strategic position in the labor process (and relatively tolerant employers) to consolidate workplace unionism. Even before the war, industrywide agreements conceding (in principle) management control and limiting the right to strike encouraged engineers to rely on workplace delegates to defend their interests.[41] As wartime government policies took hold, British engineers thus had not only the incentives but also the institutional resources and traditions of shop floor autonomy to defy their national unions.

In the United States munitions workers were not only free to pursue their interests through local union channels; they also entered the war with few

organizational alternatives. Rather than mobilize independently of established union structures, American metalworkers took advantage of war conditions to build more effective workplace unionism and to forge closer links
between shop floor and citywide bodies. Plentiful jobs and government
checks on employers finally allowed activists to organize shop committees
openly. These committees gave lodges a much stronger base in the plants
from which to monitor conditions, recruit new members, and represent union
interests to employers. At the same time shop committees gained external
support and links to activists in other firms. Changing the common prewar
scenario of ephemeral committees and lodges isolated from the shop floor,
wartime mobilization produced more integrated local labor movements with
unprecedented capacity for coordinated action on behalf of union goals.
Newark's IAM leaders, for example, urged union members to elect committees in preparation for advancing districtwide demands as part of their organizing campaign in early 1918.[42] Their counterparts in the nation's leading munitions center, Bridgeport, pursued a similar strategy. Over 1916 and
1917, officials brought employees of individual firms to lodge headquarters
to elect shop committees; these committees in turn stood ready to receive
"advice from the business agent," present union demands, and call men out
on strike as necessary. The rise to power of militant shop floor activists in
contentious elections for district IAM offices in May 1917 strengthened these
ties between citywide and workplace organization, as did a series of mass
meetings held over the summer to hammer out a common set of demands
to levy on local employers.[43]

Craft union lodges in munitions industries demanded shorter hours and
higher wages to keep up with inflation. Employers often made concessions
on these points, denying all the while that they did so in response to union
pressures. By early 1918, however, workers were also pressing issues that
more seriously challenged the open shop order—above all, demands for
classification, union rights, and the recognition of union shop committees.
Employers rarely budged on these points.

The call for classification originated with craftsmen seeking to enforce
union standards in the face of wartime dilution. Employers argued (as they
had before the war) that employees should be rewarded according to their
individual merit and effort. Unionists demanded instead that managers clas-
sify employees using a small number of standard categories of skill (toolmak-
er, machinist, etc.), each with a minimum rate of pay. Such a scheme limited
employers' discretion to grade and pay workers as they saw fit, and it appealed most to craftsmen. Newark IAM leaders promised that victory in this
area would block employers' efforts "to break down the machinists' classification by bringing untrained men into the shops" and placing them on "some

of the simpler forms of machinists' work at low wages."[44] In key munitions centers such as Newark and Bridgeport, local lodges broke new ground by extending proposals for classification to specialists and machine operators.[45] Doing so threatened to make it much less profitable to replace craftsmen with green hands; it also rallied wider support for classification among munitions workers of different levels of skill. Finally, imposing common union standards throughout a city promised to reinforce broader trade and worker solidarities in local labor movements.

Munitions workers also pressed employers on the issue of union rights. Between April and October 1917 about half of all strikes (of which the metal trades accounted for the great majority) involved demands for union recognition or the closed shop.[46] Open shop employers refused, often invoking the government's policy on "existing conditions" to justify their refusals. They were little more receptive to calls for shop committee recognition.[47] This demand did not in principle violate open shops, because it did not require management to deal with "outside" union representatives. Employers nevertheless realized that what workers sought were *union* committees, acting in concert with (and most likely selected by) local union officials. Saginaw manufacturers protested that "the men who [presented demands] were [not] a committee elected by members of our shops" but instead were "appointed by the President of the Local Machinists' Union." Saginaw unionists in turn insisted on choosing their committeemen as they saw fit and frequently struck on account of "several of the plants discharging committees."[48] At GE-Pittsfield, similarly, general manager Cummings Chesney proclaimed his willingness to meet with groups of employees but refused to "officially receive a committee representing any of the so-called national . . . labor unions" or to sanction "any committee that . . . simply carries out the instructions of some organization."[49] The promise to meet with employees in "groups" did not satisfy GE workers. When the firm introduced yellow-dog contracts in March 1918, Pittsfield's metal trades council demanded recognition of shop committees based on trade union affiliation. Union demands also called for the formation of a conference committee appointed by the council to handle disputes not resolved by craft committees or officials of the corresponding trade union. Under this plan grievance procedures would put union and metal trades council leaders in charge of representing workers—demands, manager Chesney rightly complained, that violated the government's policy protecting open shops.[50] Even where union locals did not demand formal bargaining rights, shop committee recognition was a highly charged issue. For unionists, the committees were a means of consolidating local organization; for employers, they were Trojan horses bringing union control into the workplace.

Neither the form nor the goals of munitions workers were "radical" in the sense of challenging the rights of private property, the legitimacy of the state, or even—in most cases—the prevailing craft organization of the American labor movement. Rank-and-file organization under local leadership and demands for classification and shop committee recognition confronted all three parties with serious challenges, however. National union leaders found their authority defied. Employers faced a threat to open shops—where open shops represented both a means to contain the labor movement and a mechanism of management control. And the bitter conflicts between labor and management disrupted the government's war effort.

For union executives, war conditions heightened familiar problems of internal discipline. Locals struck more often without national sanction, and these wildcats caused the additional embarrassment of violating union commitments to sustain war production and respect existing standards. In many cases insurgents also seemed to be guided by metal trades councils or allied union locals rather than by the constitutional authority of their own national leadership. At GE, for example, the affiliation of Pittsfield machinists to both the city's metal trades council and a multiplant network of GE union activists caused IAM executives considerable alarm.[51] Union tactics in Newark, too, ran up against executive authority and jurisdiction. Local recruitment strategies betrayed IAM president William Johnston's pledge to one Newark firm that the union would not organize production workers.[52] And in July of 1918, 12,000 munitions workers of different skills from plants throughout the city followed a district IAM strike call. They did so after repeated refusals by local employers even to meet with union representatives (as government policies allowed employers to do), snubbing IAM Grand Lodge advice to refer the dispute to government mediators.[53] Bridgeport district officials of the Metal Polishers' and Machinists' unions worked together in July 1917 to keep Remington Arms employees on strike to win equal pay for women and shop committee recognition, despite an agreement arranged by national union executives and federal mediators. Doing so defied both the general principle that war production should not be interrupted and the authority of union and government officials. Further disputes over the closed shop in the first half of 1918 aggravated relations between local and national authorities. Frustrated by a May walkout at numerous firms, Major B. H. Gitchell of the Industrial Service Section attacked business agent Sam Lavit for an "unauthorized strike," and IAM Executive Board (and NWLB) member Tom Savage flatly refused to consider local demands until the men returned to work.[54]

Employers, too, regarded wartime insurgency as a serious challenge to management control and the industrial relations order. The nature of that control and order differed from Britain's, as did the nature of the crisis. British management had long relied on trade agreements and union recognition to cope with their labor problems, a strategy that depended on unions controlling their members. The Shop Stewards' Movement undermined this pillar of the industrial relations order, threatening to free rank-and-file workers from the discipline of union authority and conciliation procedures. In contrast, U.S. employers generally sought to preserve management prerogatives and combat strikes by excluding unions, not by allying with them. Open shops served as mechanisms for securing control over production at a time of rapid—and contested—changes in management and manufacturing techniques. The close association between open shops and management prerogatives at work meant that unionization in itself appeared to threaten employers' control, and demands for classification according to union standards made that threat explicit. Open shops had also contributed to industrial relations stability before World War I by helping to keep industrial conflict relatively episodic (however dramatic some of the episodes) and fragmented. Institutionalizing and coordinating workplace unionism on a wide scale thus presented a major strategic challenge. And both as rivals to management authority and as the basic cells for a more cohesive labor movement, union shop committees stood at the center of the fray. Small wonder that Bethlehem Steel president Eugene Grace repudiated shop committees that so much as "savored" of organization and that NWLB employer representative Herbert Rice defended Grace's position, opining that one should not deal with committees when "right behind them were within sight, spiritually but not visibly . . . the leaders of the unions."[55]

The character of wartime insurgency and the nature of traditional defenses led British employers to distinguish between responsible union leaders and unofficial agitators, strengthening the former. Most American employers vigorously rejected the possibility of recognizing unions as a way to discipline labor unrest. Such a strategy would not work, argued Walter Drew, because "many of the local strikes on war work have been put into effect and maintained in direct opposition to the advice and orders of the international officers." Worse still, unionization would simply give "added power . . . to the radical, the mercenary and the unpatriotic elements of labor."[56] Drew's attack on conservative craft unions as being every bit as threatening as Wobblies and socialists is typical, and it obviously served polemical purposes. It also reflected the fact that U.S. employers had the luxury of not facing a cohesive or potent challenge from industrial unionists and socialists, so that they had no need to choose the AFL as the lesser of labor's evils. Here too, industrial traditions as well as wartime labor politics are important. America's open shop heritage and the absence of an organized, independent rank-

and-file movement allowed employers to lump the AFL together with out-side agitators who fomented strikes and threatened private property—and to oppose both with equal vigilance.

Labor unrest no more subverted state power than it did employers' property rights. While waiting to hear union delegates from Bridgeport, NWLB cochairman William Howard Taft feared the worst: "Isn't there some question here of Bolshevikism [*sic*]?" The answer was clearly no. As even employer representatives on the board reassured Taft, "The men seem[ed] to be a little out of control of their International leaders . . . in Washington," but they posed no challenge to the legitimacy of government policies, much less the state itself.[57] Germany provides the clearest contrast. Workers there, mobilized through factory and workers' councils, not only challenged management rights and union leaders; they also claimed power at the expense of the Social Democratic Party (Sozialdemokratische Partei Deutschlands, or SPD) and governmental authorities. American labor's challenge, on the other hand, was largely contained within the industrial sphere and within established union structures. One reason was that the nation's relatively brief involvement in the war gave U.S. workers less cause for complaints against the state: government controls were lighter, imposed fewer hardships, and ended relatively quickly. Employers, not the government, were visibly responsible for dilution and open shops, and in some respects government agencies proved to be allies of labor in wartime conflicts. Prewar conditions also played an important role. The federal government entered World War I with no tradition of taking responsibility for employment conditions or labor relations and no heritage of excluding workers from full citizenship on the basis of their economic status. These legacies helped to insulate state legitimacy from industrial conflicts.[58]

Interruptions in the flow of munitions, not the specter of bolshevism, caused government administrators the most concern. Given employers' open shop commitments and the crude and uncompromising tactics sometimes used to fight unions, mobilization by even conservative unions threatened continual disruption of production. Strike figures for the first six months of the war make the government's problem clear. Demands for union rights found employers at their least conciliatory. Management refused to compromise in 83 percent of strikes for the closed shop and 76 percent of those for recognition, whereas they stood firm in only 28 percent of strikes for higher wages, shorter hours, or both. Conflicts over union rights thus led to more serious disputes. Walkouts involving these issues accounted for 43.5 percent of the establishments affected by strikes but 69 percent of the workdays lost, and they lasted twice as long as strikes for wages or hours.[59] Local mobilization also undercut pledges made by national unions to avoid strikes and respect open shops. These dilemmas forced the government to devise new methods for stabilizing war industry. At a time of pressing military needs, tight labor markets, and resurgent unionism, management simply could not be allowed to run their shops in the old way.

REFORMING OPEN SHOPS

In munitions production—the most strike-prone of war industries—state responses to labor insurgency were delayed, confused, and contentious. Administrative rivalries and battles between unions and employers share the blame. Only as the NWLB began issuing decisions in May 1918 did something resembling a coherent strategy for stabilizing industrial relations in munitions emerge. The strategy was to reform open shops. NWLB awards helped to rationalize grievance procedures and employment practices, often over firms' objections, but they also sustained management control and made it more difficult for unions to link workplace struggles with labor organization of a wider scope and a broader base. New forms of employee representation were the centerpiece of this strategy. The NWLB plainly did not "defeat" unions. As Melvyn Dubofsky and others have stressed,[60] the board retained and enforced policies that gave union leaders more influence in government and munitions workers more security to organize. Shifting the focus from unions' political clout or numerical strength to their role in industrial relations, however, points to other facets of NWLB intervention. The shop committees introduced by the board came *after* local unions had already developed workplace roots and made little or no independent contribution to shop floor unionism in the short period between their introduction and the end of the war. The committees' role in undermining union control, by contrast, becomes clear almost immediately after the war—as local union activists themselves recognized. In this crucial area NWLB policies gave open shop labor relations a more secure foundation and provided an influential model for employers' own efforts to reimpose order.

The NWLB originated by presidential proclamation on April 8, 1918. A year of war and months of squabbling over guiding principles preceded the proclamation.[61] Formal responsibility for defining those principles fell to the War Labor Conference Board, established by Secretary of Labor Wilson in January 1918 and evenly balanced between appointees of the AFL and the National Industrial Conference Board (NICB). Both sides accepted precedents set by the CND and existing labor adjustment agencies, but each interpreted those precedents to its own advantage. The NICB represented mostly larger companies and espoused relatively enlightened views on industrial relations.[62] Its recommendations aimed to freeze the status quo by banning strikes, guaranteeing labor unions no more than nondiscrimination against their members, and construing "no change in existing standards" to mean that even wages and hours would be frozen unless the government deemed otherwise. AFL proposals included an unqualified right to collective bargaining through any representative chosen by employees, the right to organize, and the right to strike (as a last resort). In the end the two sides agreed simply to affirm that "there should be no strikes or lockouts during the war" and to guarantee both labor's right to organize and bargain collectively and employers' right to maintain open shops. The NWLB would neither treat demands for recognition as legitimate nor allow unions to "use coercive measures of any kind to induce . . . employers to bargain" with them. The joint report also declared workers to be entitled to a "living wage" and women to be entitled to equal pay, and it "discouraged" any practice that would limit the output or raise the costs of war materials.[63] With these agreements reached, President Wilson designated the War Labor Conference Board participants as official members of the new NWLB.

The press quickly dubbed the NWLB a "Supreme Court" for industrial conflict. This was an exaggeration. The NWLB rarely decided disputes in industries covered by other boards, and it failed to standardize government labor policies. More important, the NWLB had limited power. Where the government had established labor boards by direct agreement with unions and employers, awards had the force of contract. The NWLB wielded only moral authority. Unless both sides agreed to let the board settle their dispute, its decisions were mere recommendations.[64] Despite these limitations, the NWLB played the leading role in the wartime munitions industry during 1918. Most major munitions disputes ended up on the board's docket, and where the Department of Labor or Industrial Service Section successfully handled cases, they followed the NWLB's lead. In effect the board formalized existing policies and extended them more widely and publicly. Above all, the board translated broad principles into concrete measures applicable to particular cases.[65] In doing so, the NWLB emerged as the most important agency for defining how the government would meet labor's challenge in munitions.

The board's strategy for reforming employee representation without undermining open shops is clearest in the areas of classification, union rights, and collective bargaining. Demands for classification aimed to replace employers' discretion in assigning and paying employees with union standards—standards that would be common across plants in a community. Employers attacked classification as an illegitimate intrusion on employer prerogatives, certain to undermine discipline and efficiency; business representatives on the board echoed their testimony. Labor spokesmen replied that clear job categories with minimum wage rates protected skilled workers against autocratic management. The board settled on a compromise permitting classification where necessary to curb abusive employment practices but also minimizing union involvement in setting or administering standards. When munitions workers demanded classification in a number of firms in a community (thus mandating union standards across plants), the board refused to go along. Instead it recommended that "shop committees and the management should get together and work out classification on a plant by plant basis."[66] Employees could appeal to the NWLB if plant bargaining failed, but the board lacked a majority in favor of union standards. In four cases, each involving a single firm, the board did grant classification.[67] These decisions did not permit unions to standardize occupational definitions and wages across plants. They nevertheless infringed on management autonomy, showing the board's willingness, where necessary, to discipline rogue employers. At Bethlehem Steel the board replaced the bonus system in the firm's machine shops with hourly wage rates based on craft classifications. The decision followed clear evidence that the old system defied workers' understanding, included incentives for foremen to drive their subordinates, and led to more strikes than occurred in departments with more straightforward wage schemes. In a setting that NWLB examiners decried as "feudal," the board's commitment to industrial peace and production outweighed its respect for management prerogatives—but not for the open shop.[68]

The more direct challenge to open shop industrial relations involved union demands to represent employees in collective bargaining. In all these cases the NWLB strictly followed the principle that firms need not recognize or bargain with a union if they had not done so before the war. The board did not defer to the prewar status quo, however. Instead it enforced the principles that proponents of the open shop espoused but rarely practiced: nondiscrimination against unionists and a willingness to meet with one's own employees to discuss grievances.[69] One celebrated case involved Western Union's long-standing requirement that employees sign a statement forswearing unions. Business representatives on the NWLB defended the practice as part of sacrosanct "existing conditions." Cochairman Taft sided with labor, however, insisting on a more enlightened version of the open shop. Employers need not recognize a union, but they could not deny employees their right to join one. The board accordingly recommended that Western Union reinstate employees fired for organizing and cease discrimination. When the company's president refused to comply (even after a direct appeal from President Wilson), the president took over the wires. Federal control did little to benefit unions, but the episode (and a similar case leading to the takeover of Smith and Wesson) underscored the government's determination to uphold employee rights as well as open shops.[70]

The NWLB's charter also supported workers' right to collective bargaining, and board decisions required management to discuss grievances with employees. The open door had long been offered as a corollary of the open shop: managers proclaimed their willingness to "meet individual employees or committees of employees, to consider suggestions . . . for their betterment."[71] Collective bargaining was another matter, and the NWLB's guidelines raised an obvious question. If unions could not legitimately claim recognition, how could employees deal collectively with employers? The NWLB's answer (following a precedent set by the President's Mediation Commission) was to promote shop committees chosen by employees from their fellow workers.[72] The idea had much to recommend it. As a practical matter, it seemed to be a workable compromise. Employers would not be asked to deal with "outsiders," employees would be given some collective voice, and there would be some mechanism for resolving disputes before they erupted into strikes. Shop committees also seemed to apply the lessons learned in Britain, whose Whitley committees were often cited (and as often misunderstood) by American advocates of employee representation plans. Finally, shop committees appeared to be consistent with practices among "progressive" employers before the war, notably Rockefeller's Colorado Industrial Plan (a company union introduced in 1914).[73]

In championing shop committees as the proper vehicles for collective bargaining, the NWLB entered contested terrain. The President's Mediation Commission had not specified what form and roles those committees should assume, and over 1917 and 1918 factions on both sides of industry staked out opposing positions. The most conservative employers would have nothing to do with collective organization of any kind. Radicals within the labor movement saw shop committees as building blocks for industrial unionism and workers' control. Given labor's wartime power and the government's firm stand against radicalism, neither view gained support among labor administrators. The alternatives offered by AFL unions and mainstream employers had wider appeal and more powerful backing. The former generally viewed shop committees as delegates of the union lodge at work charged with recruiting members, monitoring conditions, and handling the initial stages of disputes. Such practices, familiar enough before 1915, had been impossible to institutionalize where employers maintained open shops; war conditions now made it possible to do so. "Progressive" employers, by contrast, followed the precedent set by Rockefeller. His Colorado plan for employee representation sought to preempt both union recognition and government intervention. The goal, as the company's labor relations adviser put it, was to steer a course between "the extreme[s] of individual agree-ments . . . and an agreement involving recognition of unions," thus restor-ing the company's reputation (badly tarnished by the Ludlow massacre) through "a maximum of publicity with a minimum of interference."[74]

Finding a middle way between mobilized workers and anti-union employ-ers required more interference than many businesses preferred. Unlike the President's Mediation Commission, the NWLB promoted shop committees as a solution to wartime union struggles on a large scale, ordering (or recom-mending) them in over 125 awards.[75] The board also broke new ground—at least for munitions production—by spelling out specific plans for shop com-mittees and then supervising their installation. Even employer representatives on the board saw the virtues of shop committees as a compromise between bona fide collective bargaining and unbridled management authority. Man-dating specific plans for employee representation was another matter. Loyall Osborne, a Westinghouse executive on the board, argued that "it is unwise for us to attempt to put [in] our own particular brand and say that is the only way by which collective bargaining can be reached." Taft's view (and vote) carried the day, however: it would not do to say "just have collective bargaining. . . . Unless you do send somebody to hold the election the first time, you will have all sorts of trouble."[76]

The shop committee plans finally implemented by the board typically had the same constituencies, powers, and industrial relations roles. And in each of these areas, the board's employee representation scheme offered a nonunion model for workplace labor relations. Under the typical NWLB plan, elections in each department allowed employees to pick one or more co-workers to represent them on a shop committee; these committee mem-bers in turn chose a few delegates for a plantwide council. This liberal mod-el of representation recognized the individual citizen of the firm, not mem-bers of a union, craft, or class that extended beyond the factory gates. The board's electoral procedure, moreover, had impeccable democratic creden-tials. It extended rights to all employees, not just the union members who initiated the dispute, and unionists who criticized departmental elections would appear to be only selfish and parochial. Responding to the shop com-mittee scheme contained in the Ordnance Department's August 12, 1918, award (later upheld by the NWLB), Newark machinists argued that "we should be left entirely alone in this matter and free to select representatives who are true to the cause they represent."[77] Bridgeport's IAM business agent echoed the point late in September, several weeks after the NWLB's call for shop committees in local plants. He asked the board to confine its award to the skilled crafts that had brought the original complaint, thus producing "a workers' committee of tried and true men and women who have been tested and found to be capable of truly representing the workers."[78] On the other side, employers' commitment to democratic values probably does not explain why they "usually preferred representation according to physical divisions of the plant . . . whereas the employees favored representation according to craft."[79] At a time when unionism was based on trade and the strongest worker identities were those of craft, organizing employee representation along departmental rather than occupational lines diluted trade union strength. Some government investigators expected as much. In September an Ordnance Department examiner advised NWLB secretary Jett Lauck that the board's plan for elections at Bethlehem Steel would likely result in unionists controlling committees in the machine shops, but elsewhere one would expect representatives "not so susceptible to trade union organization." The examiner's prediction proved to be accurate.[80]

Early on the board took more of a middle ground on the fractious issue of where to hold elections. At GE-Pittsfield, the first dispute where the NWLB had to deal with this issue, the local examiner reported that management "refused to allow the men to elect their committees in the Union Hall, taking the ground that nonunion men would not go to the Union Hall." At stake was not just the likely outcome of elections but also rival principles of representation. Employers held that the basic electoral unit should be the individual employee. Many workers instead sought representation rights as members of a union. As board examiner William Stoddard acknowledged, "They object to holding their elections in the plant, as the management desires, because they believe that they have the right to elect whom they choose and where they choose."[81] The board's July 31, 1918, award offered the obvious compromise, elections on neutral ground. Other early awards followed this precedent. Outside elections had a low turnout, however, and board members assumed that they favored union representation. By early October the board's examiners and employer members had altered the policy, beginning once more in Pittsfield. Stoddard advised his superiors in Washington that outside elections were "very inconvenient," and the board's chief examiner replied on October 9 that "it will be all right to hold elections in shop."[82] The board's October 24 award for GE's Lynn plant was the first formally to recognize the possibility of inside elections, ratifying the common practice of examiners. Board member and IAM president William Johnston sought to overturn that practice at the end of November, and Frank Walsh ridiculed the employers' position ("I would be willing to make a compromise that the matter be submitted to the employees as to where the manufacturer's [sic] association should meet. They are interested in seeing that . . . no bad fellows get in"). A deadlocked board let the change to in-plant elections stand.[83]

These electoral constituencies and procedures did not prevent unionists from gaining committee seats—at least while board supervision of in-plant elections remained vigilant—but board members emphasized that committees represented employees, not unions. This principle occupied center stage in another crucial early case, that of Bethlehem Steel. At the firm's enormous Bethlehem plant, some 3,000 machinists struck in April and again in May 1918, demanding, among other things, that management meet with grievance committees.[84] Company president Eugene Grace proclaimed his willingness to do so—unless the committees in any way "savored of organization." Herbert Rice, a GE executive on the board, defended the company by distinguishing between a committee of employees and a union committee. The latter acted as "representatives of organized men . . . [and] had other affiliations and was dictated to in some respect" by unions. Employee committees, by contrast, had no such corrupting ties. Even the labor members of the board accepted Grace's right to ignore union committees, and their award in this case (as in others) made shop committee members responsible only to employees.[85]

Shop committees had some recourse. If unable to settle a dispute with management, they could appeal to local NWLB examiners or to the full board. This right of appeal clearly distinguished wartime shop committees from company unions entirely at the mercy of employers, and employees benefited from this check on factory despotism. Unions, however, did not. Collective bargaining agreements typically called for initial negotiations between union committees and management. Unresolved conflicts then passed to union officials in consultation with employers—a procedure the government ratified in wartime coal-mining, cantonment construction, and railroad operations. The NWLB scheme for handling grievances, by contrast, bypassed union representatives. The scheme introduced at Bethlehem Steel, as in most cases, routed disputes from shop to plantwide committees and from there to the board. Union officials had no formal role in the process, and when the company's elected department representatives chose three union officials (none of them employees) for the plant appeals committee, it was not only the company that protested. Richard Gregg, the board's prolabor examiner in the case, also recognized the impropriety of the choice. Back in Washington, the top administrator of NWLB awards, E. B. Woods, went further. Woods declared that Bethlehem's vice president was "entirely within his rights in refusing, on behalf of the Company, to deal with a group of men from outside the plant."[86] Ordnance Department and NWLB administrators also shared with company executives an ideal that "the interests directly concerned solve their own problems as far as possible."[87]

The board's award for Bridgeport, where most metal trades firms in the

city appeared in a single docket, added an unusual twist to customary procedures. Disputes not settled within a plant could be referred to a local board
of mediation, with three labor representatives chosen in citywide elections
in September 1918, three delegates from the Manufacturers' Association, and
a chairman to be appointed by the War Department. When union officials
won election to the local board, it appeared that in Bridgeport, at least, unions
would have some real role in NWLB-sponsored labor relations procedures.
In fact, the War Department never installed a tie-breaking chair—an oversight that at least one Ordnance Department mediator considered to be
"somewhat more than an accident."[88] The difficulties of pressing union interests through this system of bargaining caused enormous frustration. As
early as September IAM business agent and local board member Sam Lavit
complained "that advancing demands through a balanced committee of six,
with a powerless head, to the deadlocked War Labor Board will profit us
nothing."[89] Labor members abandoned the charade and resigned from the
local board the following March.

NWLB shop committees did not drain unions of their members, but they
offered an alternative to employee representation based on union constituencies and unionized industrial relations. This compromise between open
shops and union power put shop committees in a precarious position. To the
extent that they enjoyed some independence from management pressures
and some rights of appeal over management heads, they did so only while
the NWLB, rather than unions, would back them up. In such key cases as
Bethlehem Steel and Bridgeport, the board was unwilling or unable to do
so. The NWLB's reforms had a larger significance, too, against the backdrop
of a wartime crisis in the open shop order. That crisis involved both management prerogatives at work and the character of labor mobilization in
industry. In both areas NWLB policies contributed to restabilization.

Within the workplace employee representation plans helped to rationalize and consolidate a nonunion internal state.[90] By the end of 1918 increasing numbers of employers embraced the virtues of more open communication and more rule-bound authority at work. What commentators often
referred to as the "square deal" had many advocates, including enlightened
industrial engineers, welfare workers, and newly professionalized personnel
managers. As a practical matter, more judicious employment management also
helped to retain scarce labor during the war.[91] The board's intervention in
workplace representation was another significant force stimulating the adoption of more systematic and constitutional methods for "managing men" at
firms such as Bethlehem Steel, notorious for autocratic supervision. Even
Frank Walsh, a sharp critic of employers generally, considered Bethlehem
Steel an exception, "one of those concerns that is entirely out of harmony with

the National Manufacturers' Association [*sic*] and with Mr. Emery. . . . This is one of those concerns that . . . will have no dealing even with the poor representation that men can have from getting their own fellows to represent them."[92]

The board's July 31, 1918, award promised a square deal by abolishing the firm's capricious piecework system and introducing committees to represent employees. As usual, there was no question of recognizing the union. What the NWLB demanded was a minimum of fair play in working conditions and the handling of grievances. The firm and the board bickered over details of the shop committee scheme, but ultimately the firm recognized the importance of a workplace rule of law. Its substitute plan followed the board's principles by assuring employees that they could join unions and serve on committees without discrimination, by organizing elections by department rather than occupation, and by establishing a hierarchy of appeals leading to a plantwide joint committee. The plan (approved by the board in early 1919) thus implemented systematic procedures for organizing representation and handling disputes without union or government oversight. Bethlehem employees and management, board member Johnston allowed, would now "work out their own salvation" alone.[93]

Open shops not only managed labor on the job; they also balkanized labor protest. Here too, NWLB employee representation plans introduced significant reforms. The forging of links between rebellious union locals and committees of union activists within the plants posed the key challenge to the open shop order. Employers repeatedly stressed their opposition to committees in any way affiliated with or coordinated by outside unions. As a leading Bridgeport manufacturer warned an IAM shop steward, he "would be glad to have the men represented, but not if they had anything to do with the machinists' union. . . . If the shop committee was appointed by the union to take up any grievance he could not consider the matter." Bethlehem Steel's Eugene Grace and his defenders on the board concurred, repudiating any committee that "was dictated to . . . [or] advised" by a union.[94] The importance of the board's alternative approach is illustrated by the resolution of wartime conflicts at GE and in Bridgeport.

Late in November 1918 representatives from the five GE plants formed the Electrical Manufacturing Industry Labor Federation (EF). The initiative came largely from radical leaders connected with Schenectady's metal trades council and Erie's IAM local, but the affiliation of all five plants raised the specter of united action against the company by employees of almost every trade and skill level. National union leaders as well as GE management and NWLB officials raised the alarm. The EF, like other wartime insurgent organizations, pitted local union activists against their own national executives.

In this case the most important of these executives was William Johnston, president of the IAM and member of the NWLB. His concern both for national authority and for the sanctity of craft organization led him to oppose the new electrical industry union.[95]

In mid-December the EF led 30,000 workers from the Erie, Schenectady, Fort Wayne, and Pittsfield facilities in a strike against wage cuts, layoffs, and Erie management's efforts to force employees to join a newly minted company union.[96] IAM and IBEW leaders refused to support the strike, but neither the NWLB nor GE relied on union sanctions to end the walkout. Instead, NWLB officials broke the strike by isolating workers at individual plants from EF leadership. They began with the weakest link, Lynn. Board members threatened to withdraw wage increases and shop committees recently awarded to Lynn workers if they joined the strike; in a letter to one Lynn organizer, secretary Lauck added that a strike would be "in violation of the principles of the War Labor Board." The threats worked. Attention then turned to Pittsfield, where similar warnings led employees to abandon the strike on January 3, 1919, in return for the face-saving promise that the board would look into local grievances. With Lynn and Pittsfield back and individual defections growing elsewhere, the EF called off the strike on January 6.[97] GE managers then ensured the demise of multiplant unionism. At each plant the firm used its victory to purge EF and other union militants. Although management declined to accept any further government meddling in its internal labor relations, it retained NWLB committees—in form if not always in personnel—after the strike. A board examiner in February found that "department committees are almost daily adjusting grievances with the management, and the Appeals Committee meets each week." He added that management's attitude was "entirely friendly and favorable," despite the fact that committees still included many unionists. Management's new disposition reflected the fact that even committee members carrying union cards were "considered representative of union, non-union and other interests."[98] By this time, too, plant delegates were effectively cut off from companywide union organization of any kind. It was this severing of links across plants *combined with* employee representation reforms inside them that typified postwar stabilization. The NWLB's shop committee scheme and its handling of the December strike deserve much of the credit for this outcome at GE.

The EF had unified workers of different skills, trades, and plants in a common battle against GE. Bridgeport's IAM leadership forged a similar coalition among employees in firms throughout the city, and here too, NWLB intervention undermined their ability to coordinate local militancy. The board's August 28 award, denying classification and substituting its own plan for shop committees and a local board of mediation, prompted 7,000 machinists to strike in defiance of the NWLB and their national leaders. The men returned only after President Wilson threatened to blacklist and draft them—and urged them to give the new system of collective bargaining a try.[99] The new system discouraged united action of the kind undertaken in August. The award took the key issue of classification out of the hands of the city's union leaders and assigned it to shop committees in individual plants, where the opportunities for unionists to win their demands, much less to impose craft standards throughout the city, were nil. As business agent Sam Lavit complained, by not providing "such machinery that we can immediately press home [demands for classification] . . . for the whole community," the board reinforced open shop control within the workplace.[100] Nor did unionists find much to recommend the NWLB plan for employee representation. Lavit criticized the board's procedures for electing delegates to the citywide Local Board of Mediation. "Organized workers should have been asked to furnish through their own machinery the spokesmen for labor" instead of going along with the board's departmental elections.[101]

Shop committee elections in each plant got underway in December, and at first Lavit expressed optimism. Departing from the long reign of open shops, these committees promised "for the first time in Bridgeport . . . the right of collective bargaining." At this point, too, Lavit could still hope that the board's examiner would "surely adjust any mistakes . . . bound to arise in the elections."[102] By March local union leaders had turned firmly against the board's plan. In several cases examiners had approved shop committees installed solely by management before the board's award took effect; elsewhere the new shop committees preempted workplace bodies previously organized by unionists. Nor did unions do as well as hoped in shop committee elections, winning only about 15 percent of the slots from constituencies that crosscut trade affiliations. Local union officials might have used their position on the Local Board of Mediation to coordinate labor action across the city, but the board's paralysis made it ineffective as a base for union leadership. In a further blow to union influence, NWLB staff excluded local officials from the implementation of other aspects of the award.[103] Marginalizing local labor leaders reinforced the atrophy of union roots within the factory gates. Denied support from either unions or a functioning local board, shop committees had no protection against discrimination and no right of appeal beyond employers. "I wish the whole National War Labor Board would go out of business," Lavit complained. "Then we could organize. This way, we are encumbered."[104] The local union newspaper reached a similar conclusion. Bridgeport workers, it declared, "will never again allow anyone to step in to adjust their grievances, for they have learned a lesson that it is only through One Hundred Per Cent Organization that they can ever expect to get any justice."[105]

Unionists elsewhere learned the same lesson and moved quickly from guarded support to open opposition. It was generally local union leaders, those most active in cultivating workplace unionism and coordinating workplace militancy, who first turned against the board's plan. As early as August 1918 Newark machinists protested an Ordnance Department shop committee scheme that followed the board's principles, objecting that it interfered with "how we should select our representatives." A February 1919 NWLB investigation of Bethlehem Steel's Lebanon plant, where the firm had installed a plan similar to the one in Bethlehem, found widespread agreement among unionists that it was "a method adopted by the company for destroying the local union."[106] National union leaders, by contrast, were more committed to the government's war program and wary of militant local officials. By the middle of 1919, however, AFL leaders also recognized how the board's shop committees and their successors made trade unions marginal to postwar industrial relations. Gompers thus refused to accept proposals at the First Industrial Conference for collective bargaining through employee organizations and in-plant negotiations, and at its 1919 convention the AFL denounced employee representation as "a delusion and a snare." Employers, meanwhile, quickly discovered the virtues of industrial democracy—especially where, as in NWLB plans, elections took place along "more democratic" lines than those of craft or union affiliation.[107]

The NWLB's employee representation reforms thus pointed in a very different direction than those in Germany and Britain. In the latter cases government policies encouraged the subordination of shop committees to union authority and collective bargaining procedures. Reconstructed shop committees would serve not as the basis for rank-and-file rebellion but as the agents of union discipline and as a first step in industrywide consultation between unions and management. The NWLB approach, by contrast, made shop committees independent of unions in their constituencies and industrial relations roles—an approach that also helped to contain rank-and-file challenges. Under the board's scheme, unions found it more difficult to sink roots in individual shops, and employee committees faced management with diminished support from external labor institutions.[108] It should be remembered that government policies also benefited workers in key respects. Protection of the right to organize facilitated union recruitment of new members, and where Neanderthal employers jeopardized labor peace, the government intervened forcefully on labor's behalf. Such intervention rarely occurred before the war. These new policies testify to both labor's wartime clout and the state's wartime needs. Contrasting the United States with Germany also highlights the importance of new political alignments. In both cases the emergence of a dominant center-labor political bloc made possible unprecedented moves to accommodate labor. Rapprochement between the German SPD and liberal parties in 1916 created a political bloc sympathetic to industrial relations reform and union recognition. The army's need to win labor support for the war effort made that bloc an influential one, even over the objections of heavy industry.

In the United States, too, organized labor gained political influence during the war. Historians commonly point to the U.S. government's "normal" bias against organized labor between the late nineteenth century and 1932, tracing this to electoral considerations and to the power and legal norms of the judiciary.[109] Wartime developments briefly neutralized this bias. The war emergency itself tipped the constitutional balance of power from the courts to the executive branch. The Wilson administration in turn proved to be more receptive to trade union influence, an acknowledgement of AFL contributions both to the war economy and to Wilson's 1912 and 1916 electoral victories. Employers, accustomed to very different federal priorities, viewed the president as prolabor; Wilson, one industry journal claimed, "has never failed in a single instance since he has been President to yield completely to any demand which organized labor has made, however unreasonable and outrageous."[110] The result for wartime labor policy was liberating. Without labor's improved political and economic bargaining position, it is unlikely that federal labor administrators would have been willing to act decisively against such extremist open shop employers as Smith and Wesson, Western Union, and Bethlehem Steel.

As the contrast with Britain makes clear, however, favorable political conditions do not guarantee that any particular approach to employee representation reform will prevail. Among policies that had become politically feasible, the legacies of prewar industrial relations selected particular approaches. They did so in part by defining what was at stake. In Britain the character of prewar labor relations led to wartime mobilization against government and union policies by rank-and-file engineering workers under at best tenuous union control. Labor posed a different problem in the United States. Unions' sturdier roots in individual workplaces enabled local militants to lead a more broadly based, concerted assault on the open shop order. The obvious solutions—tightening or loosening union control over employee representatives—were made plausible by other typical characteristics of British and American industry. State officials naturally drew on prewar precedents to cope with wartime labor problems. The 1917 Shop Stewards' Agreement did not set a new course for industrial relations in Britain. Instead, it amended procedures for settling disputes that dated back to 1898. No such instruments for restoring order existed in U.S. munitions. More important, the industrial relations status quo helped to define what government policies would work. As the Whitley Committee clearly recognized, any suggestion that shop committees should be introduced without union participation and outside of bilateral agreements was likely to antagonize unions *and* employers, in part by further fueling breakaway movements. In the United States munitions employers fiercely resisted any government plans that would have required them to negotiate wages and working conditions with unions,[111] and wartime insurgency was largely allied with rather than independent of local union leadership. Under these circumstances, the strategy rejected by Whitley served the constructive purpose of fragmenting American labor's challenge and putting open shops on a more stable footing.

THE STATE AND EMPLOYEE REPRESENTATION FROM WAR TO PEACE

The political conditions that permitted government intervention to defend basic labor rights against hostile employers disappeared rapidly from late 1918. After the armistice President Wilson could no longer invoke a war emergency to legitimate common sacrifices; after the November 1918 elections he could no longer muster a congressional majority for policies benefiting organized labor. Employers who had grudgingly tolerated government restrictions and union incursions at a time of national crisis (and lucrative war contracts) now mobilized to reverse union gains.

A wave of labor unrest after World War I fueled both the political lurch to the right and employers' counterattack on organized labor. Nearly a quarter of the nation's work force took part in strikes in 1919, including groups (such as telephone operators, police, and actors) not previously known for their militancy. Many of the walkouts disregarded AFL executives' authority and pleas for moderation; the luridly publicized Seattle general strike seemed to exemplify labor militancy unchecked by responsible union leaders. As in Britain and Germany, government officials feared the worst. In March Labor Secretary Wilson warned the nation's mayors that recent strikes in Seattle, Patterson, Butte, and Lawrence represented "a deliberate attempt . . . to create a social and political revolution that would establish the soviet form of government in the United States and put into effect the economic theories of the Bolshevik of Russia."[112] Such rhetoric would become commonplace during the 1919–20 Red Scare, but it was even more fanciful in the United States than in Britain. The postwar strike wave pressed the same demands that had motivated wartime disputes, above all wage hikes to catch up with inflation, shorter hours, and collective bargaining through union representatives. The latter was the most contentious, as workers, liberated from wartime constraints, squared off against employers eager to reassert control. The largest and best-known battle began in September 1919 in steel—the leading mass-production industry and bastion of the open shop—but smaller conflicts broke out immediately after the armistice.[113]

Almost everywhere unions lost. The combination of rapid decontrol and renewed employer hegemony stands in sharp contrast to labor relations under the NWLB, when federal checks on management supported impressive union growth. But it would be a mistake to conclude that the victory of open shops in metalworking industries represented a return to the prewar status quo or that employers' triumph and federal control were mutually exclusive. Focusing on workplace industrial relations rather than on the rise and fall of union membership leads to a different assessment. The approach to employee representation championed by the NWLB became an essential pillar of industrial relations in the 1920s, one widely adopted to reform open shops. The government no longer regulated shop committees. This withdrawal of state supervision consolidated rather than departed from wartime innovations in nonunion labor relations, however. Both the continuing commitment of employers to new forms of employee representation and the lasting contributions of NWLB policies to these open shop reforms deserve more emphasis.

By late 1918 a common view among leading metal trades firms was that shop committees offered a potent antidote for excessive turnover, festering grievances, and old-fashioned "bullying" foremen—as well as for unionism. In recommending shop committees in 1919, the National Metal Trades Association assured its members that "when the management attempts to carry out the system in good faith and gives close attention to it, the hostility of organized labor has been practically ineffective."[114] Contemporary surveys confirmed the NMTA's optimism. Studies of shop committee plans in 1919 (most of them in metalworking firms other than shipbuilding) conducted by the NICB and the Shipping Board's Emergency Fleet Corporation found wide agreement that employee representation offered a means to address employee grievances and improve communication without the "class feeling" and adversarial attitudes that managers associated with unions. A sizable minority of the employers surveyed opposed shop committees, but rarely on the grounds that committees allowed employees to take their first steps towards bona fide trade unionism.[115]

Enthusiasm for shop and plant committees grew rapidly. Only a handful of firms had committee plans in January 1918; an NICB study in 1919 found 225 such plans, involving 500,000 employees. Two-thirds of these were in metal trades other than shipbuilding, and two-thirds had been introduced without NWLB involvement. The number of plans increased another three-fold by 1922[116] and continued to spread through the mid-1920s. With 1,400,000 employees covered in 1926, the movement directly affected only a minority of American workers. The significance of company unions exceeded their sheer numbers, however. They were concentrated in strategic sectors of the economy (large manufacturing firms in mass-production industries) and of the labor movement (the highly strike-prone metal trades). The impact of the movement is best gauged by noting that in 1926, one out of every three "organized" workers belonged to a company union. The contrast to German developments is striking. Employee representation arrangements mandated by the German government helped to eliminate yellow unions, which claimed barely 3 percent of organized workers in 1925. And while union density in both Germany and Britain stabilized during the 1920s at roughly twice the prewar norm, in the United States it dropped back to levels equal to or slightly less than before the war.[117]

Whether in the form of full-blown company unions or more modest departmental grievance committees, employee representation in the 1920s had much in common with NWLB plans. Widely trumpeted as a form of industrial democracy and voluntary cooperation, the plans enabled employers to present their larger postwar open shop drive as an "American" alternative to the AFL's un-American closed shops and class warfare.[118] Like their NWLB predecessors, however, postwar schemes represented a compromise between union control and unreconstructed employer authority. In both periods employee representation plans typically included rule-bound grievance procedures, a hierarchy of departmental and plantwide assemblies, certain safeguards for committee elections and members, and regular meetings between employee delegates and management. And company unions, even more than NWLB committees, were bound up with other open shop reforms in the 1920s. The decade saw growing numbers of employers formalize disciplinary procedures, codify techniques for hiring and allocating personnel, and endorse regular communication and cooperation as means to streamline operations and resolve conflicts at an early stage. In many cases these were probably cynical ploys to fend off unions. Yet by addressing long standing dissatisfactions over arbitrary and abusive supervision through more rationalized industrial jurisprudence, company unions gave management control a more secure foundation. Indeed, this was one of the most common arguments employers made on behalf of shop committees and company unions. "Any reasonable plan of Employee Representation," Bridgeport manufacturers opined, "voluntarily adopted by the Management and fairly . . . operated in connection with an open shop policy free from discrimination constitutes, for large plants with complex problems, the best known remedy for the present labor unrest."[119] This middle ground between "militant, closed-shop unionism on the one hand and the stand-pat, run-my-own business type of employer on the other" was what progressive employers such as Standard Oil chairman A. C. Bedford and GE's Owen Young resolved to defend at the October 1919 Industrial Conference convened by President Wilson. Bedford wrote Young that employers must stand together behind the principle of "providing adequate machinery for adjusting grievances within each plant," adding, "We therefore urge the Conference to give greater attention to plant organization as the most effective means of adjusting controversies."[120] The conference failed to bridge the gap between employers and the AFL. Business representatives who championed employee representation against the "closed shop," however, affirmed their commitment to the guiding principles of NWLB reform: workers had a right to join unions and bargain collectively.[121]

Company unions also paralleled NWLB committees in their political role, limiting the organizational vehicles for broadly based labor mobilization. British outcomes stand in sharp contrast. Industrial relations reforms there put workplace representation under tighter control by national union leaders—a soothing influence if, as most employers assumed, national officials acted more responsibly than shop stewards. Postwar representation plans in the United States, even more than NWLB committees, sealed off workplace labor relations from outside interference. These hermetic arrangements for handling industrial conflict made it more difficult for local or national union officers to coordinate policy and action. The implications of these contrasting strategies are apparent from strike patterns. Industrywide stoppages accounted for roughly 80 percent of working days lost in Britain between 1919 and 1926; although directly comparable figures are unavailable for the United States, the percentage of all strikes that involved only a single establishment rose from 63 percent in 1919 to about 80 percent during 1922–26.[122]

Champions of company unions also hoped that such bodies would cultivate a workplace identity at the expense of more encompassing (and more union-prone) class or craft solidarities. Employee representation plans of the 1920s, like NWLB committees, invariably organized workers along departmental or arbitrary numerical lines rather than by craft. Moreover, it was extremely rare for company unions to link workers with their counterparts in other factories owned by the same firm.[123] Employers recognized the need for constructive measures that would "transfer the allegiance from the unions to the employing organization,"[124] and company unions seemed to answer this need. At least one leading open shop spokesman credited wartime government labor policy with showing employers the way: "Under the guidance of the National War Labor Board and through a broader recognition by the employers of the necessity for group co-operation," management had

learned "that intra-factory organization of employees produces greater loyalty and solidarity between the management and the employees and thereby makes the men less susceptible to the appeal of militancy."[125] The fact that
managers deemed employee representation to be especially suitable for
skilled men made this strategy particularly potent. Craftsmen, after all, had
strong occupational identities reaching beyond the workplace, and during
the war they played leadership roles in all-grades militancy. Employee representation during the 1920s, as Gompers recognized, instead "organize[d]
them away from each other."[126]

Continuities between wartime and postwar employee representation do
not prove that the former influenced the latter. Company unions in the 1920s,
moreover, differed from NWLB shop committees in several respects. They
often came packaged with labor practices that the NWLB had done little to
promote, including "Americanization" programs and welfare benefits. They
sometimes had different constitutions and even narrower responsibilities
than their NWLB predecessors. Most important, they always had complete
independence from government control—indeed, company unionism spread
most rapidly after federal controls ended. The links between wartime government labor policies and postwar employee representation are still clear.
The most direct connections are also the least common: few shop committees
introduced by the NWLB survived unchanged into the 1920s.[127] More often
employers launched their own plans in the hope of preempting government
interference and retained these plans after the war. After reviewing NWLB
principles, the American Anti-Boycott Association recommended the "method of collective bargaining by shop committees." The association pointed out
several advantages. For one thing, introducing shop committees demonstrated an employer's public spirit: "Adjustments made directly with the employees . . . constitute a patriotic service, since they relieve the already overbur-
dened War Labor Board." Perhaps more important, employee representation
plans avoided intervention by third parties and the possibility of public
hearings, "which tend to widen the gulf between employer and his employees and in many instances inevitably encourage the employees to rely on
outside leadership."[128] Bethlehem Steel took the same tack. Faced with
NWLB sanctions at their Bethlehem plant, company officials developed a
committee system at their other facilities that, they assured board members,
was "in accordance with the principles as you have declared them."[129]
Bridgeport's Manufacturers' Association similarly urged its members to
adopt employee representation plans before the board intervened, and several major firms followed that advice. Midvale Steel, International Harvester, and Goodyear also adopted reforms that largely satisfied NWLB guidelines in order to avoid government intervention.[130]

Perhaps the major impact of NWLB shop committees was as a model for employers' own postwar initiatives. As late as 1935, 27 percent of existing company unions had originated in 1915–19, when government shop committee plans had the greatest influence.[131] Bridgeport, the most famous home to NWLB shop committee plans, was one mecca for reform-minded employers in late 1918 and early 1919.[132] When the NWLB's formal authority came to an end in April 1919, local employers had ready their own "Bridgeport Plan for Employee Representation." The scheme closely followed the government's precedent, except that it omitted the last vestige of citywide coordination, the Local Board of Mediation. Willard Aborn, the NWLB staffer who helped the Manufacturers' Association to develop its new plan, acknowledged union fears that "this system of negotiation between employer and employee robs the union of its basic function." What the Bridgeport plan offered instead, Aborn claimed, was "in plant cooperation" to adjust grievances before they caused troubles and "to hear employee suggestions for improving operating methods." Like the NWLB scheme, the employers' plan affirmed management's ultimate control while creating more systematic opportunities to air complaints and appeal decisions. Whereas the board had excluded appeals to union representatives, however, the Bridgeport plan excluded appeals to the government as well.[133]

The nonunion character of employee representation reforms both during and after World War I clearly distinguishes restabilization in the United States from outcomes in Britain and Germany. Comparing British and U.S. policies *during* the war highlights the influence of employer dispositions and prewar industrial relations on government strategy. What changed *after* the armistice was not the nature of open shop reform so much as the state's refusal to check employers' authority in any way. This retreat stands in especially sharp contrast to Germany's intervention and testifies to America's "exceptional" political alignments. Both German and U.S. labor gained political legitimacy and influence during the war, but their fortunes diverged after 1918. Germany's revolution brought the SPD into government, and the party retained at least veto power through most of the 1920s. The AFL, having tied its political fortunes to the Democratic Party, went down with the ship: Republican victories in the 1918 congressional and 1920 presidential elections left the AFL politically marginalized and with few allies in government.[134] These contrasting political alignments favored very different policy outcomes. In Germany a highly politicized rank-and-file movement posed a common threat to unions, the state, and employers; within the state the political position of the SPD (which had its own interest in stamping out challenges from the left) ensured both a direct government role in employee representation reform and policies supportive of union authority.[135] The

United States lacked Germany's statist traditions, but more immediate political realignments closed off opportunities for government-sponsored reforms favorable to trade unions. The labor movement never generated a political challenge sufficient to frighten liberals (much less employers or Republicans) into accepting the use of state power on behalf of union authority. On the government's side, Progressive advocates of using the state's enhanced powers to engineer a better society after the war had never been more than one faction within the Wilson administration.[136] After November 1918 such ideals of reconstruction stood no chance against Wilson's congressional opponents. In early December the NWLB stopped taking new cases; by early 1919 its limited authority lapsed altogether.[137] At the same time as Germany moved to state-guaranteed works councils under union control, the U.S. government turned shop committees over to the unilateral authority of employers.

Employers joined congressional Republicans and SPD ministers in bringing about these divergent outcomes, and juxtaposing America and Germany highlights the political considerations that shaped management strategies. By late 1918 leaders of German industry embraced unions as partners in a common quest for economic stability, and for a time many business leaders also supported state measures to ensure union control over factory councils. Their American counterparts denied any such role to unions and after the armistice insisted that the government abandon its wartime responsibility for employee representation. German firms (especially in heavy industry) had been no less hostile to unions before the war than had American open shoppers. Revolutionary challenges to employers' political power and property rights, however, appeared to be far more threatening than collective bargaining. By this time, too, political realignments had made the state a much less reliable backer of employers. The alternative for industrialists was to ally with unions against revolution, as they did in the 1918 Stinnes-Legien agreement, and collective agreements grew rapidly during the early 1920s. By the end of 1923 the upheavals of revolution, occupation, and inflation had passed. Heavy industry's immediate needs—for lower labor costs, longer hours, and greater fiscal restraint—now opposed state support for union authority in employee representation and industrial relations. But here too, the SPD's political influence overrode business interests in shaping policy during the 1920s. By the end of the decade close to three-quarters of German employees remained covered by collective contracts, and an increasing number of these had been extended by government order.[138] Union agreements in the United States at about the same time covered all of 7 percent of the work force and less than 3 percent in metalworking.[139]

Progressive voices in America certainly made the argument German industrialists found so compelling in 1918: only unions could save the nation from radicalism and disorder.[140] Furthermore, at least some U.S. employers (and politicians) in 1919 believed that revolution was at hand—a belief we should not discount simply because it was false. American and German alarmists differed not in their acumen but in their perceived options. German employers, however well-founded their fears, clearly distinguished revolutionary from responsible labor leaders. U.S. business made no such distinctions between the AFL and the radical left. *Iron Age* was typical in denouncing postwar strikes (most of them centered on union recognition and wages) as "un-American" efforts "to override the Government and control industry" and in celebrating their defeat as a "decisive check to the revolutionary forces in unionism."[141] Objective conditions made this undiscriminating view of labor possible: no left challenge forced employers to choose a partnership with unions as the lesser of two evils. With the electoral center of gravity shifting rapidly to the right, moreover, there was no political counterweight to prevent employers from regaining control of labor relations immediately after the war.

By late 1918 political shifts as well as employer hostility guaranteed a rapid return to unfettered open shops—but open shops significantly transformed by wartime government intervention.[142] This argument implies a counterfactual: had *both* political alignments and industrial relations differed, government policies might have been more supportive of a union role in workplace representation. This can be shown with more confidence than most counterfactuals allow. The Wilson administration's Progressive and union base enlarged the political space for intervention favorable to organized labor. Government policies in munitions nevertheless fortified the open shop because of that industry's characteristic production relations and employer strategies. These characteristics typified American industry, but there were exceptions. The goal of part 2 is to show that while Wilsonian progressivism survived, different industrial relations practices yielded more "European" approaches to employee representation reform.

PART 2

Internal Contrasts

Introduction:
The Logic of U.S. Case Studies

All three belligerents saw the pre-1914 order fracture under the stresses of war, and in each case government-sponsored reforms in employee representation contributed to new structures of stability in the 1920s. Germany mandated works councils under union control, turning back the revolutionary assault on employer and state authority. Britain encouraged organized labor and employers to regulate workplace unionism jointly, undercutting a rank-and-file threat to industrial order. Both nations anchored postwar stability in unions. The United States, by contrast, met wartime upheaval with a nonunion plan for employee representation, one that put open shops on a more stable footing. Comparing the United States with Germany highlights the political origins of government strategies. Of these two nations, only Germany saw an independent radical movement seriously contest state authority, and only there was labor's political power sufficient to sustain pro-union government policies in the face of a postwar employer backlash. Playing off the United States against Britain points to the influence of industrial relations. British employers regulated management prerogatives and workplace conflict through collective bargaining, not open shops. The character of wartime insurgency in Britain, but not in the United States, gave employers, labor leaders, and government officials a common interest in reinforcing union authority. Both layers of explanation involve a similar causal sequence. Prewar class relations shaped the nature of the wartime crisis (particularly the politicization and autonomy of rank-and-file rebellion) and the possibilities for restabilization (specifically the disposition of employers and the political weight of labor). The end points of these causal trajectories were particular approaches to industrial relations reform. Both layers are essential for understanding American outcomes.

Part 2 shifts the point of comparative reference from countries abroad to industries within the United States. As the comparative focus changes, so does the explanatory emphasis. By comparing policies applied to different American industries, I hold national politics "constant" and highlight industry characteristics that "explain the variance" in government strategies. The language of social science is misleading, however, because the causal impact of political and industrial forces varies with time and setting. As part 1 shows, political factors seem to be decisive for explaining certain cross-national differences in government policy after the war. During the war, however, political alignments and state institutions played a lesser role in shaping labor administration. Political conditions expanded the menu of possible responses to labor insurgency, but the characteristics of particular industries determined which of these possibilities prevailed. Although the explanatory burden thus rests on individual industries, the state's "permissiveness" is important and of two kinds. First, enduring features of American political institutions and culture made it difficult to formulate and impose any unified approach to the wartime labor problem. Second, immediate (and short-lived) political alignments, along with the wartime industrial balance of power, neutralized the federal government's normal bias against labor.

The United States, like all participants in World War I, entered the war without clear plans for managing the home front, and it jury-rigged solutions to problems as they arose. America's later entry into the war also left little time to learn from mistakes or to systematize war administration. The government's inability to direct the nation's labor policy in any coherent fashion also had deeper institutional and ideological roots. In comparative perspective the American state had long been fragmented in its powers (among the federal executive, courts, parties, and state governments) and underdeveloped in its administration (institutionally and in terms of a trained class of civil servants).[1] Robert Cuff and John Lombardi have shown what this meant for wartime labor policy. The absence of suitable administrative mechanisms and relentless infighting among political fiefdoms consistently frustrated efforts to develop and implement uniform national labor policies.[2] Even had the administrative means existed, the political will might have been wanting. Government leaders during the war, from Woodrow Wilson down through key labor administrators, generally shared voluntaristic ideals and a minimalist view of state responsibilities. The state might aid and cajole private interests into meeting public needs, but it should never coerce them.[3] Both administrative incapacity and voluntaristic commitments ensured that government policy-making would rely on and defer to private interests (whether business executives on loan to government agencies, responsible labor leaders, or social work "professionals").

These features of American politics were of long standing. The political leverage exercised by organized labor was new and short-lived. Wilson probably owed his 1916 election to AFL support, and he repaid the debt with policies and appointments favorable to labor. Even among those not beholden to Samuel Gompers, the AFL's wartime contributions won it unprecedented support within the federal government. The temporary shift in political forces is suggested by the willingness of the conservative former president William Taft to side with labor representatives on the NWLB in defending basic union rights and a minimum of fair play in the board's collective bargaining plan—at least while the war emergency lasted. It is suggested, too, by the willingness of Secretary of War Newton Baker to override munitions makers' objections to federal intervention in labor disputes.[4]

Political conditions made an unusually broad range of policies feasible, but work practices, industrial relations, and the character of labor's challenge in munitions favored only one of them: the reform of open shops. Part 2 examines cases where production methods, labor relations, and wartime conflicts took different forms and led to different government policies. The cases examined are railroad shops and shipbuilding. Both were essential to the war effort. Both shared with munitions plants the same key occupations (such as machinists, boilermakers, and electrical workers) represented by the same international unions (the International Association of Machinists, the International Brotherhood of Boilermakers, etc.) and at least similar joint associations (from the AFL's Railway Employees' Department and Metal Trades Department at the top to system federations and metal trades councils at the local level). Although unions and employers in the munitions, railroad, and shipbuilding industries all dealt with the same federal government, they fell under the jurisdiction of distinct and independent regulatory agencies—the NWLB for most munitions producers, the Railroad Administration, and the Shipbuilding Labor Adjustment Board. None of these industries began the war with "British" levels of craft union power or industrywide trade agreements. Compared to one another rather than to Britain, however, they display strikingly different prewar work practices and labor relations.

Railroad shops—the roundhouses and other facilities devoted to maintaining and repairing locomotives and rolling stock—distinguished themselves from most other metalworking sectors by their relatively traditional manufacturing methods, their stronger unions, and their greater acceptance of collective bargaining. The railroad industry's history of federal regulation

complicates the comparison. Even before the war, federal legislation subjected railroad transportation to rate controls and (under the 1898 Erdman Act
and the 1913 Newlands Act) established mechanisms for voluntary arbitration of railroad labor disputes. Beginning in January 1918 government control gave Washington bureaucrats final authority over railroad operations,
including the conduct of labor relations. The government returned railroads
to private ownership in 1920, but some federal regulation continued through
the decade. These regulatory measures reflected political leaders' concern for
"the public interest," as they defined it, rather than any particular features
of railroad industrial relations, a rationale not applicable in other metal
trades. Such complications do not undermine the usefulness of railroad shop
crafts as a comparative case, however. Prewar repair shop labor relations
were largely unaffected by federal intervention, because the government did
little more than offer to mediate disputes. The operating brotherhoods and
the carriers occasionally exercised this option; shop craft unions and management did not. Wartime regulation was far more intrusive, but the simple existence of government controls did not dictate what specific labor
policies would be followed.

Shipbuilding resembled railroad shop work more than munitions manufacture in its bespoke character and its reliance on large numbers of skilled
craftsmen. World War I created enormous pressures for rapid expansion in
ship production, and the combination of craft privileges and abrupt change
in wartime labor processes made for a much more explosive—and potent—
challenge than in either railroad shops or munitions plants. Shipbuilding is
also notable for its diversity. Munitions were most often produced and railroad equipment repaired in firms with long-standing labor relations practices, and these practices bore enough of a family resemblance that one can
speak of the unionization or work rules "typical" of each sector. The wartime shipbuilding industry, by contrast, was mostly new growth. Firms (including some with no prior shipbuilding experience) built yards, installed
managers, and recruited workers at breakneck speed after 1915. Varying local
standards rather than industrywide traditions shaped labor relations, and
these variations make local case studies of wartime shipbuilding both necessary and valuable—necessary, because the sharp differences in starting
points strongly influenced what impact the government's shipbuilding program had and how workers mobilized in response; valuable, because these
differences, combined with decentralized shipbuilding administration, led
to contrasting government reforms of employee representation even in this
single industry. The government's strategy for bringing stability to Bay Area
labor relations (chap. 4) resembled that adopted by the Railroad Administration. Labor policies in Great Lakes shipbuilding (chap. 5) looked more like

those seen in munitions production. Juxtaposing local patterns within a single industry as well as different industries builds a strong case for the influence of prewar labor relations on wartime government reforms of employee representation.

CHAPTER 3

Corporatism, Voluntarism, and Collective Bargaining in Railroad Shops

A railroad shop craft worker comparing notes with a munitions factory employee would have reported very different experiences on the job, with the state, and in the labor movement. The wartime government intervened much more closely in railroad labor relations than any federal agency did in munitions production, and it proved to be far more supportive of craft privileges and unions there. Railroad labor unrest, too, followed a different trajectory from other metalworking sectors. Few disputes erupted among shop craft workers between 1915 and 1918; conflict intensified only after the war, peaking relatively late (1922); and unrest finally took the form of a centrally coordinated national strike. The 1922 shop crafts strike was in some ways the concluding act in a political drama, one in which a resurgent Republican Party and an anti-union backlash steadily eroded federal support for organized labor and industrywide collective bargaining. During the war, however, government policies owed less to political alignments than to the legacies of prewar railroad labor relations. Even after 1919 these inherited constraints appeared in the industry's split between open shop and union sectors, with their divergent plans for employee representation.

RAILROAD LABOR RELATIONS BEFORE WORLD WAR I

"Any engineer or shop man who has ever visited a railroad shop cannot have failed to take away with him the impression of a journey back into the dark ages of machine shop practice. Archaic machine tools, inadequate equipment, poor tools, obsolete methods, ingenious but expensive make-shifts can all be found in any railroad shop."[1] Railroad shop practices offend-ed enlightened editors of *American Machinist* as late as 1922 because these shops were in the business of repair and maintenance, not mass production. Carmen, the largest single trade in railroad repair shops (accounting for about half of the nation's 350,000 shop craft employees in 1916), mended freight and passenger cars and locomotive cabs; machinists (together with their helpers and apprentices, roughly another quarter of shop craft employ-ees) worked on mechanical equipment such as locomotive power trains and brakes; and boilermakers, sheet metal workers, blacksmiths, and electrical workers applied their skills to other train parts.[2] Because these tasks varied from one job to another, specialized tools and an extensive division of labor were rarely economical.

The central role of skilled workers in railroad shops supported relative-ly high levels of unionization, with trade unions in turn helping to enforce craft work rules. Neither union membership nor shop floor power reached British norms, but compared to other U.S. metal trades employees, railroad shopmen more often won recognition for their shop committees, limitations on the use of less-skilled workers, and acceptance of customary apprentice-ship ratios.[3] On the eve of World War I, 30 percent of shop craft workers belonged to trade unions, almost three times the level of the machine trades as a whole.[4] Shop craft employees also outpaced their metalworking coun-terparts elsewhere in the United States by developing effective mechanisms for concerted action. Whether because of their often isolated work settings or the impact of highly mobile activists ("boomers"),[5] shop craft employees of different trades began forming "system federations" on railroad lines in 1908. The spread of these organizations reflected a shared identity as "rail-road men" and a general recognition of practical imperatives: "Our employ-ers are combined on one common ground; why should we not be the same?"[6] Representatives of different trades organized "federated" shop committees in individual roundhouses to take up grievances involving more than one craft. Representatives in system federations in turn aimed to negotiate con-tracts and handle disputes for all the shop craft employees of a particular carrier. Regional alliances and a "federation of federations," finally, sought to coordinate trade policies, handle jurisdictional problems, and manage strikes on a still larger scale.[7]

The early system federations appeared to both union leaders and railroad managers as dangerous insurgencies. Union executives denounced them as incompatible with craft organization and national authority. Railroad offi-cials feared a new American Railway Union. Illinois Central president

Charles Markham warned that "if the system federation once became established it would . . . overshadow the international unions and deprive them of their power. . . . The next step would . . . [be] the organization of a national system federation . . . [which] could order strikes on one road or on every road in North America. The railroads would be at the mercy of such an organization."[8] By 1916, however, system federations had become domesticated residents in the house of labor, constitutionally obligated to respect the authority of craft unions and of the Railway Employees' Department (RED) in drawing jurisdictional boundaries and calling strikes.[9] Yet within these limits, system federations institutionalized joint action among different trades in a single industry, an accomplishment unparalleled in other metalworking industries.

Strategic skills and effective organization gave shop craft workers the clout to persuade many railroad lines to accept collective bargaining before the war. The extent of union recognition in railway shops may appear unimpressive compared to that of the country's best-organized industries. Many northeastern carriers and the midwestern Harriman lines, for example, recognized only the unions of their operating employees[10] and continued to harass organizers and blacklist strikers.[11] The Pennsylvania Railroad took more constructive measures to secure the undivided loyalties of its employees. Among the carrier's several experiments with company unions was the Brotherhood of Railway Mechanics (1911), denounced by AFL organizers as existing "solely for the purpose of maintaining the company's authority over its employees and to prevent them from . . . representing their interests in any independent way."[12] Juxtaposing railroad shops with U.S. auto, small arms, or machine tool firms affords a different perspective, however. Even where railroad managers refused to sign formal agreements with shop craft unions, they more often gave de facto recognition to union demands by posting work regulations consistent with craft standards.[13] Such rules (and union contracts to back them up) became increasingly common after 1910, as system federations gained strength. A Boilermakers' organizer boasted in 1916 that railroad men—unlike wartime newcomers to the labor movement—had "yearly negotiated for new terms, and as a consequence naturally familiarized themselves in handling grievances or breach of contract without conflict or suspension of work."[14] Increasingly, too, railroad managers accepted system federations as legitimate representatives for all shop craft workers, and "federated" agreements replaced separate contracts arranged with individual unions.[15] Unions and managers in the southeast took the next step in 1916, signing a master agreement between railroad lines and an alliance of system federations representing 35,000 shopmen throughout the region.[16]

THE IMPACT OF WAR

On January 1, 1918, the federal government took control of the nation's railroads. President Wilson's decision was forced in part by a transportation crisis threatening the flow of soldiers and munitions to Europe. Railroad management divided among competing lines seemed to be incapable of setting priorities and coordinating traffic, and by the end of 1917 there were 150,000 more freight loadings needing transport than there were cars to carry them.[17] Nor did carriers seem likely to resolve a growing labor crisis. Even as demand grew for labor to repair equipment, many railroad men joined the military or left for higher paying jobs in other war industries. One estimate put the industry's labor force at 12.5 percent less than needed in December 1917. At the same time major strikes loomed. Shop craft employees on some lines planned to walk out for higher wages; western shopmen scheduled a January 14 vote on whether to down tools for a regional agreement.[18] Federal control thus appeared to be the only way to coordinate railroad transportation and avoid costly work stoppages. Railroad managers and workers alike became employees of the United States Railroad Administration, under the direction of William McAdoo. Carriers profited handsomely from the arrangement, with the federal treasury guaranteeing their earnings and assuming the costs of improvements and wage hikes. Railroad executives, moreover, maintained day-to-day operational control and staffed the major managerial positions within the Railroad Administration. In contrast to the NWLB's limited authority over munitions firms, however, federal operation of the railroads gave the government full power to regulate and adjust labor relations.[19]

The most pressing need was to fend off work stoppages by addressing wage demands. Director General McAdoo did so in January by establishing the Railroad Administration's Wage Commission, with union representation, to investigate wages and recommend increases; during the same month he met with RED president Arthur Wharton and agreed to enhanced overtime pay and a minimum wage for all employees. Although the Wage Commission's April award did not fully satisfy shopmen, the Railroad Administration continued to formally recognize the representative role of national union executives in dealing with wage disputes. Union representatives took half the seats on the Board of Railroad Wages and Working Conditions, organized in April to consider all demands for improved conditions.[20]

Dilution was another contentious issue. In an effort to keep equipment rolling with fewer skilled workers, McAdoo asked Wharton to shorten apprenticeships by one year, increase the ratio of apprentices to journeymen, and allow some mechanics' helpers to do skilled work. Wharton struck a hard bargain. His counteroffer permitted three-year apprenticeships but refused to alter the ratio of apprentices to journeymen. Wharton also laid down strict conditions for accepting the promotion of helpers. Only those with at least five years' experience were eligible, promotions had to be approved by union shop committees, and for each trade only one promoted helper per five mechanics would be permitted. Carriers, Wharton added, had to supply union officials with complete records of these departures from craft standards and had to set back all promoted helpers before discharging any mechanics. The RED, in short, insisted that dilution be limited, temporary, and hedged by safeguards for skilled men. McAdoo accepted these terms in the interests of easing the labor shortage and placating railroad shop craft unions. Under General Order Number 8 Wharton's counteroffer became official policy for the industry as a whole.[21] Subsequent Railroad Administration decrees gave skilled workers further protection. An order issued July 25 set forth job classifications for shop craft employees and barred handymen or unpromoted helpers from doing mechanics' work, thus making the most favorable prewar union contracts the national standard. At the end of the year, McAdoo accepted the abolition of piecework, thus eliminating in a single stroke one of craftsmen's oldest and keenest grievances against shop management.[22]

Within the first two months of operation, then, the Railroad Administration had laid down basic policies for dealing with wage disputes and personnel policy. Union leaders won formal representation in both areas, and the Railroad Administration made significant concessions to union interests to win their cooperation. Much the same pattern appears in the Railroad Administration's efforts to develop mechanisms for the routine handling of labor disputes. McAdoo established the Division of Labor in January to formulate general policies, and he appointed union officials to most of the key positions—including W. S. Carter (president of the Brotherhood of Locomotive Firemen) as director and J. A. Franklin (president of the Boilermakers' union) as second in command. Within the Division of Labor, railway boards of adjustment for the basic employee groups (the operating crafts, the mechanical trades, and the maintenance of way and clerical workers) handled all controversies arising from the interpretation of awards or agreements and all disputes not settled locally by unions and management. Equal numbers of carrier and union representatives sat on each board, and their decision was final. Not surprisingly Board of Adjustment Number 2 (for the mechanical trades) often deadlocked between management and labor delegates, but unions could count on a sympathetic audience in these cases. Unresolved disputes went to the director of labor, who made recommendations for a final decision to McAdoo.[23]

The initial handling of railroad dilution and labor unrest clearly differed from policies seen in the munitions industry. The Railroad Administration intervened much more closely in the details of production practices than the government did in arms manufacturing, but it also safeguarded craft interests by introducing only modest deskilling, guaranteeing that union concessions would apply solely for the war, and giving organized labor privileged representation in policy-making. These corporatist arrangements reflected in part the influence of progressivism on key Railroad Administration figures such as McAdoo, his adviser Jett Lauck, and future director general Walker Hines. For these men government control provided an opportunity to show that a partnership among business, labor, and disinterested experts and public servants could achieve efficiency and social harmony.[24] Early government labor policies, however, owed less to administrators' philosophies than to the organization of railroad work and the character of railroad labor relations. The nature of shop craft work limited both the pressures and the potential for dilution. Whereas the government sought to vastly expand the output of ships and munitions, its primary concern in railway transportation was to keep equipment in operating condition. Repair work also limited the possibilities for rationalizing shop practices. The problem was to cope with a shortage of craftsmen in the context of a still traditional labor process. Because of the strength of craft unions, railroad administrators could not count on regional and local managers to introduce necessary changes unilaterally. Manpower policy had to be negotiated with union officials who had the power to block unfavorable changes, and in these negotiations unionists further limited the scope of dilution. Moreover, because the Railroad Administration had to have the cooperation of shop craft unions, the latter could expect—and were in a position to demand—a direct role in wartime labor management.

Federal reliance on union leaders to handle railroad labor also built on prewar industrial relations practices. Many carriers already accepted adjustment boards, with equal representation for unionists and management, to settle disputes and regulate conditions.[25] Even after the Railroad Administration displaced private employers, it drew on prior traditions of voluntary collective bargaining. The administration's regional directors (selected from carrier management) and the heads of the shop craft unions negotiated the terms of Board of Adjustment Number 2, with Director General McAdoo simply approving the pact. Much of the 1919 National Agreement between the Railroad Administration and union executives was also the product of bilateral bargaining.[26] Where early Railroad Administration intervention broke with the past was in making collective bargaining and agreements governing working conditions national in scope and compulsory in character.

The Railroad Administration's deal with national union officials angered open shop carriers, but most managers either accepted the government's approach or were willing to bide their time. Federal policies also had costs for rank-and-file shopmen, who proved to be less patient. Over 1916 and 1917 shopmen had taken advantage of a buoyant economy to seek higher pay (eroded by inflation and falling behind other metal trades) and more uniform wage standards across crafts and shops. The Railroad Administration inherited these demands, and its initial response made matters worse. The Wage Commission's April award offered only modest pay increases, with the best-paid employees getting no hike at all. The award also left railroad men behind their counterparts in other war industries. Lastly, by awarding increases as a percentage of 1915 earnings, the decision both canceled out advances won by many craftsmen since 1915 and reintroduced differentials that unions had fought hard to eliminate. Shopmen voiced their dissatisfaction through wildcat strikes, prompting McAdoo to establish the Board of Railroad Wages and Working Conditions and to approve further increases in July. Despite those new increases, railroad wages continued to lag behind inflation and other metal trades.[27]

By incorporating union executives in a centralized apparatus for managing railroad labor, the government also ran the risk of losing control over impatient and well-organized shopmen. Shop craft employees were accustomed to handling their affairs through local representatives and negotiations, and especially in the prosperous two years before U.S. entry into the war, these methods brought results. Local freedom of action was now sharply limited, as key decisions were made—slowly—by railroad administrators and union leaders in Washington. The loss of local autonomy rankled. Walker Hines, McAdoo's successor as Railroad Administration director, recalled that government procedures "had the effect in many instances of raising a question as to the authority of the local officials and caused some discouragement on the part of some of them."[28] RED officials repeatedly reminded shopmen of the proper channels for handling disputes and invoked patriotic themes to discourage them from taking matters into their own hands: "Surely none of our members are of the German type—an agreement being only a scrap of paper to be torn at will."[29] Still, union executives' close identification with the distant Railroad Administration and its cumbersome procedures undercut their ability to hold members in line. Local shop craft committees repeatedly sought to bypass official procedures, usually by taking grievances directly to the Railroad Administration rather than going through intermediate layers of union and company officials and occasionally by striking in defiance of union authority. In these disputes local federated committees often found themselves at odds with national union executives, the RED, and the once-insurgent system federations, all now incorporated into wartime grievance procedures.

These tensions came to a head by the summer of 1919. Wage increases won the previous July had not satisfied shopmen, and continued inflation and the growing wage gap between railway workers and those in other war industries led shop craft unions to demand substantial increases in January 1919. The Board of Railroad Wages and Working Conditions did not begin hearings on the request until March. A deadlock between labor and management board members continued the delay through June. Shopmen also experienced frustrations in their quest for a national agreement. The idea of national standards for job classifications, apprenticeships, seniority, working hours, overtime, and other conditions had tremendous appeal for shop craft employees. It would fulfill the promise of prewar struggles for regional agreements, bring all employees up to union standards, and symbolize the new status of railroad labor in the war economy. Federal control made such an agreement seem to be well within reach. Between January and May 1919 a RED committee met regularly with representatives of the regional railroad directors in an effort to settle the terms of such an agreement. The two sides agreed on 91 rules and referred 115 still-contested ones to the Board of Railroad Wages and Working Conditions on May 6. By this time, however, the railroads' impending return to private ownership made federal officials reluctant to make—and carrier representatives on the board reluctant to accept—any new commitments to labor. As a result unresolved disputes over work rules and wage claims languished on the board's docket.[30]

Shopmen left RED and Railroad Administration officials in no doubt as to their impatience with these delays. A mass meeting in Kansas City resolved to send the director general a telegram demanding "to have National Agreement decision made at once"—pointed instructions that were repeated in many other communications.[31] RED leaders also acknowledged the "many hundred letters, telegrams and resolutions protesting delay in negotiations for National Agreement and further wage increase." Union leaders could do little but reassure members that action would eventually be taken and urge them not to take matters into their own hands. "Nothing could do your cause more harm now than a demonstration that these organizations were composed of a membership which would not abide by laws that they themselves had made and approved."[32] During June and July most shopmen obliged. Some locals struck on June 15 to speed consideration of their demands.[33] Additional wildcats followed in mid-July when the Board of Wages and Working Conditions announced its deadlock. Only by "canceling charters and memberships, unless the members returned to work," could

RED president Bert Jewell contain these rebellions.[34] At the end of July Director General Hines referred the wage issue to President Wilson, arguing that the imminent end of federal control made any wage award inappropriate. President Wilson passed the buck to Congress, requesting that it establish machinery for dealing with wage disputes once the railroads returned to private control. In the meantime, he urged, shopmen should patiently await a decline in the cost of living. This was the last straw. Faced with indefinite delays in securing a wage hike and the clear failure of RED officials to take action,[35] 200,000 shopmen walked out at the beginning of August. National union executives issued the usual denunciations (their members refused "to accept the advice from headquarters," International Association of Machinists [IAM] officials complained, instead following "the advice of certain local leaders")[36] and ordered the men back to work. President Wilson and Director General Hines added their condemnations and declined to give the men's grievances further consideration until they ended the strike.

The stoppage did bring results. Hines gave shop craft workers a modest wage increase after they returned to work on August 18, and the evident restiveness of shopmen helped to persuade him to sign the National Agreement in September. But the August wildcat also dramatized a more general problem confronting the Railroad Administration in 1918 and 1919. Close cooperation between national unions and the government would not secure labor peace if union leaders lost authority over their members. Railway management also appreciated the dilemma. "The government has encouraged railway employees to organize in order that it might have responsible unions to deal with. If, however, the men will not be led by their 'leaders' and strike in violation of their agreement with the government, their agreements become mere 'scraps of paper.'"[37] It was precisely the Railroad Administration's cooperation with AFL officials, combined with delays in addressing popular grievances, that undermined union leaders' ability to enforce agreements. By mid-1919, a Boilermakers' official lamented, "the mere fact of one being connected with the International staff, served as an acknowledgement of their worthlessness, so that their presence seemed a source of annoyance."[38] The August 1919 strike also demonstrated the potential scope of rank-and-file rebellion. Popular demands for higher pay and standard work rules were quite moderate. But because the organization of railroad employees' organization effectively linked them across trades, shops, and carriers, even action on "conservative" issues could rapidly escalate into a national and immensely disruptive strike. This was the essential dilemma facing the government in its efforts to stabilize labor relations in railroad shops.

CENTRALIZING UNION REPRESENTATION

An *Iron Age* editorial during the August strike noted that President Wilson, in promising to discuss shopmen's demands, had "committed the Government to a policy of dealing with international union officers as against local representatives."[39] Wilson was not alone, nor was he the first. Procedures worked out for boards of adjustment, provisions of the National Agreement, and the joint labor-management committees introduced late in the Railroad Administration's tenure all shored up national union control over workplace representation. In each area Railroad Administration officials hoped that the reforms would quell shop craft labor unrest.

The boards of adjustment organized in May 1918 provided the basic mechanisms for handling disputes between shopmen and management, and they followed industry precedents. If a worker and the foreman could not resolve difficulties, either the federated committee (if an agreement existed between the carrier and its system federation) or the trade union committee took up the issue with management. One major change introduced by the boards of adjustment was to make this standard procedure for *all* shops, even those that had refused to deal with union representatives before the war. A variety of cases came before the board where railroad managers failed to cooperate with union shop committees.[40] In almost all these cases, the board of adjustment sided with employees, removing most obstacles to their rights of representation through union shop committees. Having mandated representation through local committees, board procedures also placed those committees under firm national union control. Grievances not resolved locally had to be channeled through and approved by the international union or the RED before the board would hear it. Local committees or system federations submitting grievances independently were informed that "until such time as approved copies of the case are received from the Chief Executive officers of the Organization, it will, of course, be impossible to give the matter consideration."[41] Nor could local committees easily sidestep national procedures. Shortly after the establishment of Board of Adjustment Number 2, McAdoo learned of a case where employees and railroad officials had turned to local arbitration to settle a dispute. He promptly issued a circular insisting that "no agreement should be reached between officials and employees of any railroad to adjust their differences in any other manner than prescribed in Order[s] 13 and 29."[42] Thus, in the adjustment of industrial conflict, the Railroad Administration gave national union officials a monopoly on labor representation.[43]

The National Agreement—a formal contract between the Railroad Administration and the AFL's Railway Employees' Department—also strengthened the role of local committees in railroad labor relations and reinforced centralized union control over them. The agreement itself, making favorable work rules the standard for all shop craft workers, may have been intended to bolster union authority at a time of rank-and-file disenchantment with the alliance between government and labor organizations. Boilermakers' officials stressed that "while this agreement brings to the men benefits and privileges, it also imposes obligations upon them. . . . Precipitate strikes must be discontinued."[44] As for employee representation, the National Agreement required management to meet "the duly authorized committee" to discuss grievances and guaranteed committeemen necessary leaves of absence, free transportation, and protection from discrimination. A few carriers continued to question whether these had to be *union* committees. Director General Hines set them straight, ruling that "'the duly authorized local committee or their representative' means the committee or representative of the organizations signatory to this agreement."[45] Hines's interpretation made it clear that the regular craft unions—not management or employees themselves—determined what was a legitimate shop committee. The agreement further enhanced union control over employee representation by assigning local committees a regular (but restricted) role in shop labor relations. Their role was to serve as the first stage of grievance procedures. The restrictions were twofold: unresolved disputes once again had to be submitted to the RED, and shopmen had to remain at work while negotiations proceeded.

Between the boards of adjustment and the National Agreement, the Railroad Administration put unions firmly in charge of both shop committees and the channels for negotiating grievances. This monopoly over employee representation enabled union leaders in railroad shops (unlike in munitions factories) to prevent employers from undermining union control. It also fortified union defenses against the "dual organizations, not represented on any Boards of Adjustment," that RED president Jewell feared "stood ready to organize the men if we canceled their charters" for failure to comply with executive authority.[46] These changes thus served the interests both of the Railroad Administration in maintaining labor peace and of union officials in preserving their own dominion. They also won the approval of many railway managers alarmed by widespread labor insurgency in 1919. "Recent developments throughout a large part of the world have indicated that strong and ably led labor unions will prove to be civilization's principal safeguard against the ruin and crimes of bolshevism Future efforts of railway managements should be directed, not toward destroying the unions, either old or new, but toward reaching understandings with them."[47]

Whatever the value of union discipline in fighting bolshevism, it made no direct contribution to another Railroad Administration goal: speeding the

pace and cutting the (government-borne) costs of repair work. Late in 1919
Director General Hines accordingly proposed the creation of new committees composed of employee and management representatives to focus on
improving operations. Railroad Administration officials hoped that the committees would yield more harmonious and productive relations between
labor and management by involving both sides in joint discussions of shop
problems (such as the proper storage of materials, maintenance of tools,
scheduling of work, and methods of repair).[48] Shop committees had a similar appeal among NWLB staffers. The development of plans for railroad joint
committees, however, took a very different path from that of government
committees in the munitions industry. From the start Hines and his assistants
emphasized that unions were to have responsibility for choosing labor representatives on the committees and that those committees would in no way
undercut the position and responsibilities of regular unions. Division of
Labor assistant director Franklin (a former Boilermakers' president) urged
Hines to involve shop craft union leaders in developing the plan *before* it was
submitted to railroad managers. Jewell also insisted on higher-level union
involvement in the scheme. "No system of cooperation, in our opinion, will
bring forth the desired results, unless the National and System scope is considered, rather than the local." Accordingly joint committees should report
to system federation officers and schedule meetings when system officials
could attend. Regular reviews of the fruits of cooperation, Jewell added,
should be presented to the RED.[49]

Hines's final proposal reflected these concerns. It called for separate joint
committees to distance them from the more adversarial relations between
management and grievance committees, but it left the selection of labor representatives to local union and system federation officers. Hines also cau-
tioned railroad managers that grievances still had to be handled solely by
regular union committees and in accordance with procedures laid down by
the relevant board of adjustment and the National Agreement. "Cooperation" would not mean cutting unions out of shop floor labor relations. Echo-
ing Jewell's advice, Hines reminded railroad directors that "in putting this
plan into effect, joint meetings should be arranged between the general chairmen of the organisations and the . . . railroad officials for the purpose of
explaining fully their plan and enlisting [their] cooperation."[50] With these
safeguards in place, Jewell endorsed the proposal. In a letter to all system
federation officials, he assured them that the RED had been involved in developing the scheme and had "agreed to the plan provided our General
Chairmen and Shop Committees were consulted in all matters considered."[51]
With federal control scheduled to end in April 1920, the new committees
made little headway. The insistence on systemwide and national union in-

volvement in workplace cooperation, however, matched the Railroad Administration's general policy of enhancing union control over employee representation. The proposal would also serve as a model for the "Baltimore and Ohio" (B. and O.) plan for union cooperation after 1922.[52]

These methods for regulating workplace labor relations conformed to prewar precedents in the unionized sector of the industry. Craft and federated committees existed long before federal control, and union agreements commonly gave them a formal role in grievance procedures. The Railroad Administration made use of these inherited models of employee representation instead of creating new ones. These were institutions and procedures, moreover, that a majority of carriers as well as union officials recognized. Many regulations in the National Agreement would become flash points for disagreements among managers, unionists, and the board of adjustment, but rule 35, governing grievance procedures, aroused little controversy on either side.[53] Where the government did introduce important changes was in mandating these arrangements on a national scale—even in formerly open shop carriers—and limiting their independence from national union control. The shift from local union pacts to a national agreement with the RED itself heightened executive authority. Changes introduced by the government also reflected the basic character of wartime challenges to industrial relations stability in railroads, challenges that themselves developed out of the Railroad Administration's initial labor policy. By incorporating union leaders into Railroad Administration boards and bureaus, McAdoo and his advisers hoped to win their cooperation in managing wartime labor. Shopmen, however, were well organized locally and chafed at wartime inflation, delays, and restrictions on their freedom of action. Their independence threatened to scotch the deal between federal regulators and union executives. The corporatist strategy of both mandating and subordinating workshop organization sought to avoid this potential collapse of union (and thus government) control.

Usually the strategy worked. Compared to their counterparts in munitions production or most of shipbuilding, railroad shopmen engaged in relatively few work stoppages in 1918 and 1919. Walker Hines exaggerated only slightly in claiming that there were "virtually no strikes" under federal control, and amid the intense industrial conflict of 1919, the Railroad Administration's Division of Labor recorded only sixteen small disputes involving shopmen.[54] In addition to those small disputes, of course, there was a big one: the national walkout in August, which dwarfed most munitions and shipbuilding strikes. The pattern of scattered skirmishes punctuated by infrequent but massive walkouts points to another contrast between railroad shops and most others. The former saw little development of organized insurgency at odds with union officialdom. Resentment of union executives was widespread, but it did not develop into an independent *movement* comparable to those in Seattle, the Bay Area, or Bridgeport. Shopmen remained far more "disciplined" than their counterparts in munitions plants or shipyards, loyal to their local unions and system federations, and generally willing to abide by union rules and procedures. Under federal control that discipline usually translated into obedience to national union executives and the Railroad Administration, but it could also be turned to massive defiance of national authority. The density and solidarity of local and regional organization ensured that *if* shopmen acted against government decisions (or indecision), the action would be coordinated and broadly based.

Reforms in employee representation were not the only factor dampening railroad insurgency. In munitions production and shipbuilding the rapid influx of workers new to unions and union discipline contributed to unofficial action. Shipyard employment, to take the extreme case, surged more than fourfold between October 1917 and October 1918. Railroad shop employment, by contrast, grew only 15 percent from January 1918 to January 1919,[55] and the prevalence of seniority rules probably minimized the movement of employees from one shop to another. Moreover, many government policies benefited all shopmen, whether old hand or greenhorn. Boilermakers at the Altoona shops of the Pennsylvania Railroad had good reasons to christen their new lodge "William G. McAdoo Lodge no. 536."[56] On those lines hostile to unionization before the war (including the Pennsylvania), the Railroad Administration gave shopmen the protections needed to organize.[57] The government also abolished the hated piecework system and extended to all shopmen the seniority rights, overtime rules, and occupational classifications won by the strongest system federations before the war. Unionists recognized the benefits—"the men are better protected on the railroads than they are on the outside"—and some claimed to "have more regard for the railroad rules and the working conditions than . . . the money [the workers were] getting."[58]

Work rules and representation rights issued by the Railroad Administration thus gave shopmen little reason to turn against the union executives who cooperated closely with the government. Procedural rather than substantive issues—delays in wage awards, limits on local autonomy—were what strained relations between shopmen and union leaders. It is here that the government's industrial relations reforms were especially significant. The local and shop organizations that in other settings developed in opposition to established unions were instead strengthened and more closely regulated by Railroad Administration officials in cooperation with national union leaders. The fact that these bodies organized solidarity across trades and employers, as the August 1919 wildcat showed, created the potential for a disciplined, broadly based rebellion. But government policies reduced this possibility in another way. Carmen Sirianni's survey of wartime movements for workers' control points out that rank-and-file revolts against unions occurred most often when commitments to class solidarity ran up against sectional craft organization.[59] In the United States federated committees and system federations already institutionalized solidarities across trades (if not classes). Railroad Administration intervention both reinforced the role of these institutions and shifted power up the organizational ladder from local committees to system federations and, above all, to the RED.

Railroad managers also benefited from these policies. One system federation chair reported that managers on his line often "call[ed] on our committee for help," and he boasted of several cases where federation officers "kept down trouble among the more radical men in the organization."[60] Union officials profited as well. On the rare occasion when they did face challenges from below (as in Chicago, where dissidents threatened to organize a dual movement during the August 1919 strike), they could rely on the Railroad Administration to warn insurgents that the government would not "deal directly with local representatives. . . . The Federated Shop Crafts have designated certain officers to conduct their negotiations with whom we must deal in order to prevent irregularities and chaos."[61]

FROM WAR CORPORATISM TO POSTWAR VOLUNTARISM

On February 28, 1920, the nation's railroads returned to private control. In the usual view what followed was a sharp reversal of fortunes for shopmen at the hands of the state and employers.[62] The latter, organized in the Association of Railway Executives (ARE), mobilized to abolish gains made by shopmen during the war. In place of the nurturing Railroad Administration, the Railroad Labor Board established by the Transportation Act of 1920 imposed most of the carriers' goals: cuts in wages, abolition of the National Agreement, and abrogation of union rights. When shop craft unions, their backs to the wall, finally struck in 1922, the Railroad Labor Board and the Harding administration helped hostile railroad employers to finish them off.

This is a selective interpretation, relying on only one contrast. Comparing time periods shows a clear retreat from the government's wartime support for national union power after 1920. Comparing industries after the war suggests a different evaluation, however. When the NWLB closed its doors in early 1919, unionists in munitions firms lost all federal protections from the depredations of open shoppers. Government oversight of railway labor relations, by contrast, helped to sustain union influence and standards for three more years, even on those lines that would ultimately impose open shops. This latter comparison avoids the simplified view that federal policies between 1919 and 1922 switched from strengthening to attacking unions. The change appears instead as a movement from mandating union representation on a national scale to supporting collective bargaining on a voluntaristic and decentralized basis. Carriers that refused to accept the authority of either unions or the Railroad Labor Board itself were not forced to do so. Nevertheless, until the 1922 strike, the board gave management both the tools and the encouragement to work with shop craft unions.

This evolution in state policy reflected political realignments. In the struggles over postwar federal regulation, ascendant Republicans in Congress ensured that shop craft unions won neither statutory recognition nor industrywide collective bargaining. The turnabout continued under the Harding administration, particularly through appointments to the Railroad Labor Board that decisively shifted the balance against shop craft unions.[63] These changes in policy and political setting clearly freed open shop carriers from many wartime restraints on union busting. Compared to what it did in other metal trades, however, postwar federal regulation helped unions in a substantial sector of the railroad industry to maintain collective bargaining and union-dominated workplace labor relations—accommodations that would survive the 1922 shop crafts strike. Nor did government officials or unionized carriers simply revert to the prewar status quo in this period of decontrol. The Railroad Labor Board's continued intervention in the minutiae of employee representation and work rules had more in common with the Railroad Administration than with federal oversight of shop craft industrial relations before 1917. And carriers that dealt with unions in the 1920s (like open shop metal trades firms) retained or adapted government-fostered employee representation reforms under postwar conditions.

Voluntarism was certainly not railroad unions' preference. In the latter half of 1919, shop craft and operating employee unions led a coalition of labor and radical forces on behalf of the Plumb Plan, a proposal for outright nationalization of the railroads and their operation by representatives of workers, shippers, and the public. Amid the general repudiation of wartime government controls, however, and with support for railroad nationalization weak even among liberal Democrats, reprivatization was never in doubt.[64] Railroad union leaders turned reluctantly to the task of getting the best possible deal in legislation regulating the industry. The outcome of lobbying struggles among labor, management, shipping interests, and government representatives was the Transportation Act of 1920.[65]

Rather than leave labor matters to the discretion of management, the act provided state sanction for—but did not mandate—bilateral collective bargaining. In doing so Congress developed a series of compromises between compulsory and entirely voluntary frameworks for railroad industrial relations. Legislation approved in the Senate (the Cummins bill) and supported by railroad owners banned strikes and established boards made up of labor and management representatives to make final rulings on wages and grievances. The House (in the Esch bill) opted for a much more voluntaristic approach. This proposal preserved labor's right to strike and made board decisions mere recommendations. With the energetic support of railroad labor unions (whose executives, for the purpose of defeating the Cummins bill, suddenly rediscovered the virtues of free collective bargaining), House conferees prevailed on their Senate counterparts to accept the right to strike and renounce compulsory arbitration. The initial bill emerging from House and Senate conferences also stipulated that unions and the ARE choose representatives for boards of adjustment with jurisdiction over the major classes of railway employees. The final version of the Transportation Act continued the shift toward voluntarism by urging carriers and unions to negotiate their own adjustment boards. As a last court of appeal, the act also established the United States Railroad Labor Board to hear unresolved disputes and render decisions. Unlike in earlier legislative drafts, however, this board's power to enforce its decisions consisted of nothing more than bringing the weight of "public opinion" to bear on recalcitrants.[66]

The Transportation Act carried public supervision of railway labor relations into the postwar era, and it assumed and encouraged collective bargaining. Some of these provisions had precedents in prewar railroad regulation, but those precedents rarely involved the shop crafts. Now shopmen were the primary objects of federal labor policy. The act recognized organized labor and employers by giving unions and the ARE responsibility for nominating representatives on the tripartite labor board. The provisions governing boards of adjustment did not similarly stipulate that railroad *unions* would be responsible for choosing board members and handling disputes, but in persuading the House and Senate conference committee not to write such arrangements into the law, Walker Hines specifically endorsed collective bargaining as the proper means for establishing boards. If collective bargaining failed, he reminded the committee, then the government's labor board stood ready to assume jurisdiction. "These matters have been worked out in a satisfactory way by voluntary action in the past and I believe can be so worked out in the future, although of course it would be highly desirable to have cases which remain unadjusted by those voluntary methods appealed to and passed upon by the tribunal."[67] Railroad Labor Board decisions also clearly supported a role for unions in defining work standards and organizing employee representation (in some cases over the objections of employers). More often than not, collective bargaining and union-controlled employee representation proceeded within this framework from the end of federal control until the 1922 shop crafts strike.

The Railroad Labor Board's abandonment of centralized, industrywide bargaining is clearest in the controversies over boards of adjustment and the National Agreement. Section 302 of the Transportation Act called for adjustment boards to handle disputes, but it did not stipulate whether these should be national, regional, or systemwide boards. Railroad labor unions insisted on a national board organized along the lines of wartime arrangements. Such a system, they believed, would help to maintain uniformity and limit the ability of hostile carriers to evade union standards. At first it appeared that the ARE would go along: its Committee on Labor approved the principle of national boards in April 1920, arguing that without such an institution the Railroad Labor Board itself would be paralyzed by unresolved grievances. Pennsylvania Railroad vice president W. W. Atterbury, however, persuaded a majority of the ARE to reject the committee's recommendation. By a vote of sixty to forty-one—with the majority including both anti-union carriers like the Pennsylvania Railroad and those who accepted unions but rejected industrywide bargaining—ARE delegates decided to grant only local boards of adjustment. The Railroad Labor Board's refusal to impose any particular form of adjustment board (while offering its services in helping carriers and unions to reach agreements on their own) sealed the fate of national boards.[68]

In controversies over the National Agreement, the Railroad Labor Board played a more active role in promoting decentralized collective bargaining. ARE representatives made it clear in a March 1920 conference with union officials that they would not renew the National Agreement after federal control lapsed. The dispute reached the Railroad Labor Board in April. When hearings finally began in January 1921, testimony before the board divided along predictable lines. RED president Jewell accused the carriers of refusing to bargain in good faith and violating the existing agreement. Jewell added that provisions of the agreement differed little from prewar customs and contracts and provided for both good service and the protection of employees. ARE chairman E. T. Whiter attacked these same provisions as incompatible with efficient operations and with the varied circumstances of different lines.[69] The board's Decision Number 119, handed down in April 1921, abolished the National Agreement effective July 1 and called on individual carriers and union representatives to negotiate new terms. The ruling thus endorsed management's call for decentralization. Board members recognized that "agreements might not be arrived at." To encourage bargaining in good faith, the board reminded both sides that disputes not settled through negotiations would be decided by the board and threatened that if either side "unduly delay[ed] the progress of the negotiations," the date for terminating the National Agreement would be adjusted to their disadvantage.[70]

Shopmen placed enormous value on the industrywide bargaining and agreements that they had enjoyed under the Railroad Administration, and they bitterly resented the labor board's insistence on decentralization. Still, compared to government policy in other industries, the board's actions continued to support a union role in railroad labor relations. This support is apparent from the board's decisions on work rules, union rights, and the details of employee representation.

In abrogating the National Agreement, the labor board outlined basic standards to be included in local settlements. Although not as generous to workers as Railroad Administration rules, these standards went much further in protecting union conditions than the government had been willing to go in wartime munitions plants. Agreements, the board directed, should protect seniority rights, include job classifications, and provide for apprenticeship. In dealing with the many cases where unions and carriers failed to reach agreement on all points, the board mandated additional rules, including guidelines for hiring and laying off employees, stipulations that only duly qualified mechanics perform work customarily done by craftsmen, and provisions for union committees to handle grievances. In each case the terms of the National Agreement were modified to accommodate carriers, and on many other issues the board ruled against unions. Shopmen, as the 1922 strike would demonstrate, especially resented the restoration of piecework and limits on overtime payments. Spokesmen for both sides recognized that the decisions made concessions to carriers and unions alike, however. *Railway Age* and *Traffic World* editorials claimed victories for management but acknowledged union safeguards, and Bert Jewell proclaimed that the rules announced in Decision 119 "mark the real beginning of industrial law."[71]

In the area of union rights, too, shopmen preferred their cozy relations with the Railroad Administration to the labor board's more qualified support. Yet the board's endorsement of collective bargaining is striking when compared either to the NWLB's unwillingness to endorse union representation or to the government's refusal to defend union rights in other industries after the war. The labor board continued as a minimum standard the principle (common enough during World War I) that "the right of railway employees to organize for lawful object shall not be denied." The board added that they could act "through representatives of [their] own choice, whether employees of a particular carrier or otherwise," and that they were entitled "to be consulted prior to a decision of management" affecting wages and working conditions.[72] The precise application of these reassuring principles proved to be more contentious. Some carriers sought to evade Railroad Labor Board rulings by subcontracting work to nonunion firms or by choosing which representatives they would admit to the conferences required by the board. These were tougher tests of government support for union rights, and on both the board sided with labor. It ruled that employees of a contractor were covered by the board's authority and all its decisions regarding wages, conditions, and bargaining rights. Shopmen discharged in favor of subcontractors, moreover, were entitled to reinstatement.[73] The board's rulings on collective bargaining rights came earlier and seem to have had more effect. Several carriers, proclaiming their willingness to negotiate with unions, nevertheless sought to divide labor ranks by bargaining only with individual unions rather than with system federations. The board's majority replied that system federations, if chosen by the employees to represent them, could insist on a common agreement. *Railroad Democracy's* June 25, 1921, praise for the ruling ("Decision Nullifies Attempt to Breakup Unions and Destroy Real Bargaining") shows that shop craft unions still had some confidence in the board.[74]

These decisions placed the board squarely behind the principle of collective bargaining through union representatives—a principle the government had not applied to munitions factories even during the war. The board followed the same logic in its decisions on employee representation *within* the shops, giving employees the right to form union committees to take up grievances and bargain on their behalf. The forms of representation sanctioned by the board also differed from the shop committee plans authorized by the NWLB and implemented by many metal trades firms: shopmen could organize the craft and federated committees typical of railroad workplace unionism. The links between these committees and local union structures also received the board's protection. As a general rule, shopmen were entitled to choose representatives who were not employees; the grievance procedures promulgated by the board also allowed employees to bring in outside representatives to take up disputes with management.[75] Carriers could challenge the right of union officials and committees to negotiate on behalf of employees.[76] Unlike wartime shop committee elections in munitions plants, however, representation elections held by the board put a union slate on the ballot. When unions won (as they usually did), the board ruled that managers could neither refuse to meet with them nor insist on dealing solely with their own employees. Most carriers complied.[77]

Carriers determined to break with unions and substitute their own plans for employee representation could do so. The example of the Pennsylvania Railroad is the best known. It is so well known, indeed, that it obscures other cases where employers ultimately complied with labor board rulings and even found it advantageous to do so. Consider the Pullman Company. As befits its tradition of paternalism, Pullman was one of the first railroad firms to launch a company union, announcing its "Plan of Employee Representation" barely a month after the lapse of Railroad Administration authority. The plan resembled shop committee schemes in munitions production. Employees grouped by department rather than trade elected delegates to joint labor-management committees, unresolved complaints passed from a local to a companywide joint committee, and final decisions rested with the firm's Bureau of Industrial Relations.[78]

Pullman shop craft workers took the lead in fighting the plan. General Chairman W. T. Bennet of the Buffalo plant's federated committee denounced the scheme as "autocratic and an outlaw plan, contrary to American ideas and principles," and in violation of the Transportation Act. "What are you going to be," he asked in a notice posted in the shops, "a Citizen of the Pullman Company or a Citizen of the United States?" Corporate officials had an answer: they fired Bennet for his "act of insubordination and unwarranted attack on the Pullman Company."[79] Other employees appealed to the board to protect union representatives. Edward Costello, an electrician at the company's St. Louis works, wrote the board demanding to know "why it is that the Pullman Company can violate the Act and . . . get away with it. They are firing our Chairmen all over the System also a lot of Committeemen. . . . Also they are trying to install a Union of their own against our will. . . . I can't see why the U.S. Labor Board can't stop this Company from violating our Agreements."[80]

The RED brought the case before the board, charging the company with denying employees the right to choose their own representatives, discharging committee members, and refusing union requests for conferences to reach a new agreement. Pullman defended the plan as the choice of employees. According to them, only the interference of "certain Union officers, not in our employ [and] not as desirous as we are to see the co-operative spirit established," had incited complaints about the plan.[81] Officers of the company's system federation, especially Chairman Harry Smith, proved to be especially galling to the company. Industrial relations supervisor F. L. Simmons blamed Smith for calling men out on strike at several Pullman shops.[82] On this point the company and the RED had a common problem, however. Pullman employees were fed up with the company's actions and irritated by the RED's insistence on constitutional procedures. "You talk of complying with the laws of your organizations," fumed a St. Louis machinist in a letter to Jewell. "If a man spits in your face do you ask him to wait while you go get a cop or do you try to knock his block off. If your [sic] the man I hope you are I think you'd choose the latter course.

That is the way with us we have been stepped on the face and called in the law [the labor board] now we're fighting."[83] RED officials found Chairman Smith guilty of condoning such illegal action, culminating in his May 31, 1921, circular to system federation members asking them to vote on a strike against the firm. Jewell promptly advised members that the vote was unconstitutional, that a strike would not get union support, and that the "officers of [their] System Federation have . . . knowingly violated the laws of their respective organizations."[84]

The Railroad Labor Board ratified Pullman employees' choice of System Federation 122 as their representative and went on to order the company to negotiate a new agreement. The board's ruling, combined with Pullman's trouble with local union officials, brought the company around. Three days after the board's decision, Pullman officials contacted Jewell and expressed their willingness to hold conferences with the RED, but *not* with system federation officials. Jewell readily agreed. He solicited from Smith and his fellow officers formal authorization to have the RED represent Pullman employees in negotiations with the company and exclude system federation officials both from conferences and from the signing of an agreement with Pullman. The RED representatives involved in these maneuvers later assured Pullman vice president L. S. Hungerford that the federation delegates would not "have any duties to perform that will in any way affect the administration of the Agreement."[85] This outcome, *Labor* crowed, was not only the company's first agreement with organized labor and a ratification of the terms of the National Agreement; it also "supplant[ed] a 'company union' recently formed as a blockade to the recognition of regular unions, and which was dismissed by the Labor Board as denying workers proper representation."[86]

The Pullman case illustrates the Railroad Labor Board's ability to influence even recalcitrant employers and to defend employees' rights to union representation. The labor board's role in the Pullman affair was also consistent with the general pattern of postwar railroad labor policy, giving unions the added leverage needed to reach a voluntary agreement with management but not mandating a solution to the conflict. Much like wartime policies, this arrangement had advantages for employers as well: unions, empowered by the labor board, proved to be useful in disciplining "irresponsible" employee representatives at the local level.

VOLUNTARISM AND INDUSTRIAL SCHISM

In contrast to their experience in munitions plants, then, union officials in railroad shops trying to maintain representation rights and collective bargaining between 1919 and 1922 still found an ally in the federal government, albeit a less reliable and powerful one. Relatively favorable state policies in the area of employee representation and the persistence of collective bargaining in much of the industry also testify to railroad labor's continued clout. From before the war, unions had deeper roots in shop crafts than in other metal trades, and the disruptive cycle of rapid expansion and sudden contraction typical of other war industries mostly spared railroad shops. The nature of repair work also gave skilled workers a continuing foothold that craftsmen in munitions production lacked. And with their extensive shop and systemwide organization, shopmen had the capacity to mount highly disruptive strikes, as they had shown in the national wildcat of 1919.

Craft strength and state policies led to an industrial schism not seen in most other postwar metal trades. Confronted by strong unions and the government's qualified support for union representation, some members of the ARE argued that only collective bargaining and adjustment boards could stabilize railroad shop industrial relations. These employers accepted unions as useful tools for maintaining labor peace and assigned them a corresponding role in workplace labor relations. The leeway afforded by voluntaristic federal policies, however, allowed determined opponents of unions to pursue a different approach to industrial order. Carriers aligned with the Pennsylvania Railroad viewed unions as an obstacle to cost cutting and labor discipline. For these managers, employee representation plans similar to those in munitions factories promised to ease the transition to a union-free environment. The split reflected differing assessments of the prospects for union busting more than an ethical commitment to rival principles: carriers in both blocs were perfectly willing to recognize and bargain with the more powerful unions of operating employees, and they agreed to establish regional rather than system-based boards to deal with them.[87] This division appeared before 1922, most prominently in the Pennsylvania Railroad's refusal to allow labor board interference with its nonunion employee association plan.[88] Company unionism and collective bargaining as competing frameworks for employee representation would be consolidated in the aftermath of the 1922 shop crafts strike.

On July 1, 1922, 400,000 shopmen struck rather than accept a wage cut awarded to employers by the Railroad Labor Board. The storm had been building for some time. This was the third wage cut in a year,[89] and it closely followed the expiration of the National Agreement as ordered by the board the previous August. The board's decisions on work rules eliminated much of what shopmen had accomplished under federal control in areas such as piecework, seniority rights, and occupational classifications. For those who had been especially well organized before the war, these rulings undid what unionists had achieved by their own efforts—"taking away," complained an RED official (with some exaggeration), "conditions we have had for fifty years."[90] Shopmen were further angered by a double standard. Board decisions lowering labor standards were dutifully carried out by employers, whereas some carriers flouted rulings against company unions and subcontracting.

Striking shopmen put on an impressive display of solidarity and discipline under official leadership, testimony both to the joint organizations built by railroad shop workers and to the legacies of government policies designed to strengthen those organizations on a national scale. Federated organization made it possible to coordinate strike action, picketing, and relief efforts in railroad centers throughout the country. Where railroad lines converged in one city, shopmen from different carriers took the additional step of fusing their executive committees into a single body to run joint meetings and make common decisions on strategy.[91] For all their unity and discipline, however, the shopmen proved to be no match for an alliance of hostile employers and anti-union factions within the Harding administration. Railroad Labor Board chairman Ben Hooper promptly branded the strikers "outlaws" and extended to strikebreakers the "benefits of the outstanding wage and rule decisions of the Railroad Labor Board." The Pennsylvania Railroad seized on this resolution to claim that strikers had forfeited their seniority rights, and some other lines followed suit. These resolutions hardened battle lines at the outset of the dispute. Other forms of state intervention turned the battle in the carriers' favor. Officials at all levels of government dispatched local police, state troops, and U.S. marshals to protect scabs, and a flurry of injunctions curbed picketing. Washington's efforts to end the strike culminated in Attorney General Daugherty's request for a restraining order to combat what he labeled "a conspiracy worthy of Lenin and Zinoviev."[92] The federal injunction issued September 1 in effect banned picketing, prohibited any action that might hinder the repair of railroad equipment, and barred union leaders from issuing instructions or using funds to support the walkout.

The labor board's response to the strike, the general willingness of government officials to apply force on behalf of carriers, and the Harding administration's injunction all paved the way for an open shop solution to labor unrest—a solution little different from that seen in the munitions industry. Much like munitions firms, open shop carriers led by the Pennsylvania Railroad took advantage of postwar political opportunities to reinforce open shops with shop committee plans for employee representation. They did so with the apparent approval of Hooper, whose "outlaw" resolution recommended that new employees "take steps as soon as possible to perfect on each carrier such organization as may be deemed necessary" to represent them before the labor board.[93] By 1926, out of about two hundred railroad lines surveyed, sixty had company unions, and these accounted for approximately one-quarter of all employees covered by company unions in that year.[94]

The shop craft strike clearly failed to win back lost wages, working conditions, or industrywide collective bargaining, but the narrative of unions broken, jobs lost, and open shops triumphant is only half the story. Immediately following the September 1 injunction, the RED settled the strike with fifty-two carriers, with more signing on over the next months. The agreement provided some protection for strikers' seniority rights, leaving other issues to be worked out in conferences. On these lines, accounting for about half the industry, union recognition and collective bargaining survived.[95] The settlement had been anticipated earlier in the strike, and federal officials played some role in bringing it about. President Harding met with shop craft union leaders at the end of July and won their approval for a proposal under which strikers would return to work with their seniority intact and carriers would abide by Railroad Labor Board decisions (including those on contracting out and employee representation). At about the same time the presidents of the giant Baltimore and Ohio and Seaboard Railroads opened negotiations with their system federations. The RED, still hoping for a national settlement, called off negotiations at these firms; the ARE rejected Harding's proposal. Another month on strike combined with the federal injunction, however, persuaded union leaders and their constituents to enter into agreements with individual lines. Those settlements resembled Harding's proposal and fit the general model of decentralized collective bargaining supported earlier by the Railroad Labor Board.[96]

New forms of employee representation played important roles in the industrial relations strategies of unionized carriers, as they did for open shop lines, and once again government policies anticipated and encouraged reforms. Most important was the "Baltimore and Ohio plan" for union-management cooperation. The B. and O. plan closely followed recommendations made by Otto Beyer, an industrial engineer who had introduced similar plans in government arsenals during the war. Beyer, like many other devotees of industrial democracy, proposed to involve workers more closely in shop management through joint committees.[97] These committees would give employees regular opportunities to bring their ideas for improvements to the attention of management; managers in turn could use the committees to solicit employees' help in resolving production problems. Partly to win the confidence of workers (who might be reluctant to suggest laborsaving innovations to their bosses), the joint committees also considered means to stabilize employment. Unlike committees to promote harmony and efficiency in the open shop sector, however, those created through Beyer's plan worked with rather than against unions and won support from IAM president William Johnston and the RED's Bert Jewell. Johnston and Beyer began meeting sympathetic railroad officials in the spring of 1922 and, following the settlement of the shop crafts strike, won their first agreement with the B. and O. in the fall. The success of the plan on the B. and O., as measured by shop efficiency, declining numbers of grievances, and increased employment security, led to broader support within the RED and among unionized carriers. By 1926 cooperative committees operated on four major railroad systems and other smaller lines in the United States and Canada, accounting for over one-sixth of the mileage in the two countries.[98] Cooperative committees reinforced collective bargaining by bolstering union authority over workplace organization. The B. and O. plan followed Railroad Administration precedents in safeguarding union control over joint committees, stipulating that employee representatives would be either drawn from or appointed by members of federated shop committees. As in the Railroad Administration's proposal (and the Whitley scheme), moreover, issues normally dealt with in agreements between unions and the carrier were excluded from joint committee discussions. These provisions ensured that cooperation complemented collective bargaining instead of competing with it.[99]

The B. and O. plan promised employers more productive and tractable workers. Given the continued indispensability of skill, cooperative rather than autocratic management seemed to be the most promising way to elicit the best efforts of shopmen.[100] And by strengthening union control over workplace representation, the B. and O. plan bolstered union executives' ability to enforce collective bargaining agreements and curb dissent among their members. In some cases fears that trade standards would be diluted and jobs lost made shopmen reluctant to "cooperate" in improving shop methods.[101] Opposition also came from radicals who rejected cooperation as class collaboration. In Beyer's alarmist inventory, this category included "Foster, the One Big Union, American Federation of Railway Workers and other destructive and extreme left elements in the labor movement." Jewell expanded the list to include those "who are direct actionists and who are opposed to the maintenance of agreement and reasonable methods of negotiation."[102] Carriers welcomed shop craft unions' commitment to disciplining opponents of cooperation, regardless of whether political principle or concern for jobs motivated the opposition. The plan's contribution to union authority thus benefited union executives and management alike.

In both the union and open shop sectors of the industry, then, new forms of employee representation played key roles in the larger "solution" to labor unrest. Shop committee plans such as that of the Pennsylvania Railroad provided a mechanism for organizing representation on a nonunion basis and insulating the work force from union influence or ties to workers outside their own shops. The B. and O. plan, by contrast, extended union recognition and reinforced union control over workplace labor relations in return for a disciplinary role for union executives. The two forms of employee representation made open shops and collective bargaining more workable than these industrial relations strategies had been before the war. Neither approach guaranteed success. In 1925, for example, railway company unions held a convention in St. Louis. Convention organizers (mainly from the Pennsylvania Railroad) designed the gathering to marshal opposition to proposed changes in railway labor legislation. Some delegates found time to mull over the possibility of federating company unions, however, a scheme at odds with the principle of "direct dealing" between employees and management. In the other camp the system federation on the Chicago, Milwaukee, St. Paul and Pacific Railroad (a "cooperative" carrier) complained in 1926 that company officials occasionally violated the principles of the B. and O. plan by unilaterally selecting individuals "to act as representatives of employees, without the knowledge or approval or consent of the employees." Yet in these cases—as in most during the 1920s—the contrast between the two models of employee representation held. The St. Louis convention disavowed federation, and a number of carriers had in any event refused to allow company union representatives to attend. In the other case a reminder to company officials from the system federation about their contributions to the line—including "overcoming tremendous obstacles, such as the One Big Union Idea, the I.W.W., and several movements of kindred kind"—helped to win an agreement that representatives from each craft organization would henceforth serve on joint committees.[103]

The federal government helped to bring about these accommodations, both directly and indirectly. The role played by union officials in managing labor unrest had been mandated by the Railroad Administration on a national scale, and most features of the B. and O. plan can be found in Hines's 1919 proposal to the regional directors. Between 1920 and 1922 the Railroad Labor Board continued to support union authority in workplace labor relations and employee representation, but subject to voluntary agreements with carriers rather than direct state regulation. Both Railroad Administration and labor board policies can be traced in turn back to long-standing features of railroad shop labor processes and industrial relations. For the railroad company unions of the 1920s, by contrast, there are no precedents within the Railroad Administration. The government's role in spreading new forms of employee representation in this sector of the industry was mainly permissive. Before 1922 the labor board opposed such innovations but could not block them; with the 1922 strike the board gave open shop employers a green light. Changed political realignments largely account for this break with wartime policy.

Only with new legislation in 1934 (providing more authoritative mediation and requiring a national board of adjustment) would government policy back union authority over employer opposition, a change in policy closely tied to New Deal electoral politics. Until that time the industry remained divided between the two resolutions of the 1922 strike. The division in effect represented a contrast between "British" and "American" settlements, and it paralleled the contrast between employee representation in wartime railroad shops and wartime munitions plants. This split emerged in the railroad industry only after the government loosened wartime controls. Similar contrasts in the development of employee representation appear in shipbuilding. They appear during the war itself, however, and as a matter of government policy.

CHAPTER 4

State Policy and Union Authority
in Bay Area Shipbuilding

AMERICA'S SHIPBUILDING PROGRAM

The United States entered World War I with neither the blueprints nor the industry to construct "a bridge to France." American shipbuilding declined rapidly after 1870, having failed to make the transition from wood to steel construction. By World War I advocates of "preparedness" were especially frustrated by the nation's limited capacity to build the large steel vessels that were essential for transporting troops and supplies.[1] Congress created the United States Shipping Board (USSB) at the end of 1916 to expand the country's merchant marine, but the government's shipbuilding program did not begin in earnest until April 1917, with the organization of the Emergency Fleet Corporation (EFC) within the USSB. The EFC promptly flooded the nation's shipyards with orders, stimulating older firms to expand and attracting investment in new yards. The number of nonnavy yards quadrupled between January 1917 and August 1918, and shipyard employment surged from 90,000 in October 1917 to 375,000 a year later. In less than two years the nation launched 3,385,000 tons of ships under EFC contracts; between 1900 and 1915 annual output had never exceeded 375,000 tons.[2]

Such phenomenal expansion could hardly have been managed without fundamental changes in shipyard production methods and labor relations. Three months before U.S. entry into the war, an *Iron Age* survey found little in common between the "American system" of manufacture and shipbuilding, dismissing the latter as "a huge job-shop proposition."[3] The comparison to a general machine shop was apt. Shipyards built vessels in small numbers, usually on a special order basis; skilled labor used relatively simple machinery to make component parts and fit them together. Erecting a ship also demanded close coordination among many crafts—carpenters preparing shipways, molders producing castings, boilermakers making large engine parts, machinists turning out ship fittings, riveters joining ship plates, and caulkers filling hull gaps. Orchestrating these activities put a premium on systematic yard administration, but prewar practices fell far short of "scientific" management. Many yards left supervision to subcontractors or gang leaders, and only one yard in the country operated an employment department to select and train workers.[4]

EFC and navy officials responsible for quickly producing large numbers of ships sought to overcome these bottlenecks in three ways. The EFC encouraged standardization by developing uniform specifications for a small number of ship types and having yards specialize in only one or two of them. Henry Ford's vision of assembly-line shipbuilding never materialized, but war orders made it possible to produce some interchangeable ship fittings on a manufacturing basis and to prefabricate ship sections prior to their erection at the docks. More routinized production methods complemented efforts to upgrade inexperienced workers more quickly. Shipbuilding craftsmen generally learned their trades through lengthy apprenticeships or stints as helpers, a system that kept skilled labor scarce. The EFC's Industrial Relations Division introduced programs to quickly teach green hands specialized shipbuilding skills, graduating 80,000 fresh shipyard mechanics from thirty-seven training centers by April 1919. Finally, the EFC sought to educate supervisors in the arts of modern management through educational propaganda, university-based training courses, and the appointment of representatives in most large yards to monitor conditions and offer advice.[5]

The government's shipbuilding program required new mechanisms for handling industrial relations as well as new production methods. Ships could not be built at the pace or cost planned if disputes interrupted production and scarce labor drove up wages. As the EFC opened for business in Philadelphia during the summer of 1917, however, major shipyard strikes loomed in yards around New York City, along the Delaware River, and on the West Coast. To safeguard ship production, representatives of the EFC and the AFL's Metal Trades Department (MTD) agreed to establish the Shipbuilding Labor Adjustment Board (SLAB). All disputes involving EFC work were to be decided by this board, whose three members were appointed by the EFC, the AFL, and the president of the United States. The agreement also provided for local "examiners" to adjust disputes and administer awards. SLAB administrators appointed these examiners in close consultation with local employers and labor leaders, hoping to win the confidence of both sides.[6]

With the formation of the SLAB, EFC officials faced a question common to all war industries: what role should labor unions play in administering industrial relations? Sharp disagreements existed within the EFC. Chairman Edward Hurley was among those advocating "the stiff arm for dealing with organized labor," but most others recommended the inclusion of unions.[7] With strikes underway or pending in key districts, the government had to rely on national union authority to keep shipbuilding workers on the job. A wildcat strike in New York in July, for example, grew to involve 11,000 shipyard employees and nearly spread to navy facilities before officials of the MTD, the International Association of Machinists (IAM), and the local Marine Trades Council regained control.[8] Referring to the strike of 40,000 West Coast shipbuilders in September, SLAB chairman Everit Macy noted that "while the union leaders seem capable and conscientious men, they are unable to control their membership and constant strikes are occurring." In coping with these strikes, Macy called attention to the "very important service rendered by the international presidents. . . . Without their very active service it would have been utterly impossible for us to have gotten the men back in Portland and Seattle."[9] Union executives rendered another service. The large volume and great urgency of EFC ship orders demanded rapid hiring and promotion of new employees; AFL officials obliged by waiving restrictions on the number and length of apprenticeships.[10]

National union leaders could hardly be expected to discipline their members and make concessions on work rules to the government without some compensation. What they won in exchange was an institutionalized voice in labor policy at the national level. In contrast to the situation in munitions (and as in railroads), in shipbuilding the constitution of wartime industrial relations was subject to negotiation and formal agreement between unions and government, and a union representative (MTD secretary Albert Berres) assumed an equal role with presidential and EFC appointees (Macy and L. A. Coolidge) in controlling shipbuilding labor conditions. The specific terms of wartime collaboration required some dickering. Labor leaders negotiating with the EFC sought government sanction for union shops and union standards. Louis Wehle of the EFC insisted that the National War Labor Conference Board's call to respect "existing standards" barred government imposition of the closed shop where such an arrangement had not prevailed before the war. Union leaders conceded the point. They agreed not to contest a firm's refusal either to recognize unions or to close their shops to nonunion workers, provided that they remained free to organize.[11] The EFC gave more ground on union standards. The August 20 agreement made local (rather than union) conditions the benchmark for SLAB decisions governing wages and working conditions. December's revised agreement, however, pegged wage rates to those "established through agreements between employers and employees" in each district.[12]

Although unions gained official standing in wartime labor administration, different levels of the union hierarchy were not empowered equally. The original agreement guaranteed local involvement in SLAB proceedings. As a first step in resolving disputes, district EFC officers had to confer with local union delegates. For cases heard in Washington, a representative of the workers and employer involved joined the board as temporary members with voting power. The experience of the board and of union presidents in dealing with the West Coast strikes persuaded them to centralize procedures, however. EFC and national union officials revised their agreement in December to abandon local representation on the board and to drop the requirement for consultation with local unionists. SLAB administrators Henry Seager and Willard Hotchkiss emphasized how these changes "placed upon the international officers the authority to represent labor in cases having a local significance."[13] The formal pact was not changed again, but MTD officials and SLAB chairman Macy agreed in May 1918 that further curbs should be placed on local union involvement. MTD president James O'Connell urged the board to heed only those requests for conferences or hearings that came from national union officials, adding that at these hearings "local prejudices, the local situation, and local representation" should be "avoided as far as possible." Such an arrangement, he argued, would expedite hearings and guarantee "the full support and authority of the international organizations to carry into effect the awards rendered." Macy concurred.[14] Union leaders' new authority in formulating labor policy and handling disputes was complemented by new responsibilities for preventing strikes. Although the SLAB agreement did not include an explicit ban on walkouts, it did specify a mandatory mechanism for the final settlement of all disputes. SLAB members routinely called on union heads to force their members back to work, and they regarded the centralization of SLAB procedures as a means to make union discipline more effective. Metal trades officials, for their part, regarded the prevention of strikes as their contractual as well as patriotic responsibility under the SLAB agreement.[15]

The EFC's programs for modernizing production practices and managing industrial relations were intended to speed ship construction, but they also fueled labor unrest. New shipbuilding methods had their greatest impact on craftsmen whose pay and status depended on their monopoly of scarce skills and strategic occupations. Employers' efforts to accelerate production threatened that monopoly by shortening training periods and "dis-

carding entirely former practice and regulations as to the number and qualifications of the men being broken in as tradesmen."[16] Shipyard workers did
not see employers as the only culprits. Union leaders had agreed to relax
apprenticeship regulations, and the EFC took an active role in training green
hands to perform "skilled" shipyard work.[17] Wage awards providing for
"first-" and "second-class" mechanics (with first- and second-class pay rates)
proved to be especially irksome. The board first introduced these two classes in a February 1918 decision covering Delaware River shipyards. One goal
was to encourage the upgrading of green hands by creating a ladder of wage
rates (however short); another was to standardize the complicated and id-
iosyncratic classification systems in effect around the country. In the eyes of
skilled shipbuilding workers, however, the second-class designation com-
promised craft standards. It gave employers the government's blessing to
rank fully qualified men at lower rates, and it acted as a Trojan horse for the
substitution of less-qualified men on skilled jobs at reduced pay. A machinist at Bethlehem Steel's Sparrow Point shipyard, having himself been reduced
to second-class status, reported that the men in the yard "criticized and accused the Company of double-dealing with the Government at the expense
of the workers." Local union representatives around the country endorsed
the sentiment.[18]

Dissatisfaction with wartime industrial relations procedures, like discon-
tent over workplace management, focused on both the government and
unions. As did employees in every other war industry, shipyard workers
complained of postponed hearings, delayed decisions, and unenforced
awards. What made wartime rules for industrial relations especially galling,
however, was the gap between what the men believed they could accomplish
through independent action and what formal channels allowed. Shipbuilding employees had never before been in such a strong bargaining position.
Yard owners, flush with war orders, were desperate to attract and retain
personnel, but the new rules of the game severely limited workers' freedom
to deploy this power. Strikes met immediate censure from government and
union leaders. Demands for union recognition, which the men finally had
the strength to win, were denied a hearing. Even if they renounced strikes
and confined themselves to "legitimate" demands, wartime procedures concentrated bargaining and decision making in the hands of national officials
at the expense of local participation.[19] Discontents often flared up in wildcat strikes and denunciations of union leaders, the SLAB, or both. Local leaders in Los Angeles, for example, resolved to strike for union recognition in
defiance of government and union instructions. According to the SLAB examiner, "They do not care whether their international association upholds
them in the strike."[20] Representatives from Seattle went so far as to repudi-

ate the entire framework of wartime labor relations, charging that no *local* organizations had "agreed to abide by the decisions of their internationals or the Wage Adjustment Board." "Until such time as the Wage Adjustment Board sees fit to consult the parties interested," they added, "we fail to see where any possible advantage can be gained by the Internationals signing a memorandum."[21]

These labor problems afflicted shipyards throughout the country. The development of shipbuilding labor protest and EFC strategies to restore order are more local than national stories, however. At the national level one can point to the spread of unionization (the Boilermakers' union, for example, tripled its membership between 1917 and 1920, with shipyard employees accounting for most of the newcomers), the rising tide of shipbuilding strikes (27 in 1916, 101 in 1917, and 138 in 1918), or the rapid decline of militancy as shipbuilding's boom collapsed.[22] Nonetheless, a much clearer and more varied picture of labor mobilization and state intervention emerges from an examination of specific shipbuilding districts. These differed sharply. Shipbuilding was an established local industry in some areas and a new growth in others. Shipbuilders in certain districts had made more progress toward "fabricated ship" techniques than had those in other regions. The districts differed, too, in the condition of the labor movement. Shipyard workers might be strongly unionized or largely unorganized, and they might be closely tied to common labor institutions or relatively isolated. Relations between labor and management also varied. In some districts collective bargaining and industrywide agreements on wages and working conditions were the norm, while in others open shops prevailed. From such divergent starting points, war led to very different patterns of labor insurgency.

More surprising is the way that SLAB policies varied from one district to another, particularly in the role assigned to unions in shipyard employee representation and dispute settlement. These variations were possible because the SLAB issued awards on a regional basis and allowed district administrators considerable leeway in implementing those awards. Many disputes never came to the SLAB's attention; they were resolved by examiners on the basis of local conditions.[23] This decentralized approach, combined with the sharp differences in local industrial relations, produced distinct regional patterns of labor unrest, state intervention, and restabilization. Two case studies show these regional differences in some detail. The San Francisco Bay Area entered the war with predominantly bespoke metal trades, a powerful labor movement, and industrywide collective bargaining. Mass-production techniques (including fabricated shipbuilding), a weak and divided labor movement, and open shop employers typified Cleveland and Lorain (and Great Lakes shipbuilding more generally). Contrasting prewar backgrounds led to different patterns of wartime mobilization and government intervention. Only after the war did the two cases begin to converge, as political and national influences came to outweigh industrial and regional ones in shaping both government policy and local labor relations.

Industry, Unions, and Politics before the War

Prewar San Francisco labor relations seem un-American. At a time when most unions were either on the defensive or nonexistent, San Francisco trade unions thrived. While the country's labor movement was divided along craft lines, San Francisco's trade unions organized themselves into unusually effective city- and industrywide federations. Elsewhere employers generally enforced open shops; here they engaged in industrywide collective bargaining. And while unionists in many other cities split between supporters of the Socialist Party and those hewing to the AFL's policy of nonpartisanship, San Francisco labor formed a relatively cohesive, powerful, nonsocialist political bloc. Always influential, between 1905 and 1911 this bloc controlled municipal administration through an independent labor party.

San Francisco attracted apostles of the open shop like missionaries to Sodom, hoping to redeem the fallen. The city's industrial and labor history condemned most of these efforts to failure.[24] Small firms and geographic isolation left businesses with neither the corporate resources nor the independence from local markets to fight unions. San Francisco's remote location also made it difficult to import scabs in sufficient time and numbers to defeat strikers. On labor's side, the prevalence of small-scale production and construction meant that skilled workers formed a large proportion of the local work force, and at this time craftsmen were the pillars of organized labor. The city's relative isolation also limited ethnic diversity among these workers, thus removing a common American obstacle to labor solidarity. One major racial cleavage did run through San Francisco's working class: white versus Asian. Far from dividing potential unionists, however, Asians—concentrated in the least desirable and least-skilled occupations—became a common enemy that united skilled and semiskilled white workers in defense of job controls.[25]

San Francisco unionists also forged unusually effective institutions for joint action. The San Francisco Labor Council brought together unions throughout the city and played an active role in organizing mutual support, coordinating wage offensives or strikes, and planning local labor strategy. Councils in particular industries had even more influence. The Building Trades Council exercised nearly absolute control over labor relations in construction and allowed little room for independent action by member locals.[26] With a far lighter hand the Marine Federation and the Iron Trades Council (ITC) played similar roles around the docks and in the metal trades. The authority of citywide organizations over local unions, and the loyalty of unionists to these bodies, could cause trouble with national officials. The Boilermakers' union, for example, expelled San Francisco's shipbuilding lodge when the latter followed ITC rather than union orders in a 1907 strike. Across the bay Oakland's Central Labor Council met the same fate at the AFL's hands when it refused to unseat a renegade faction of the Electrical Workers union.[27] Local unionists remained defiant. West Coast labor conditions, they felt, were too distinct to entrust to eastern leaders; Bay Area unionists had instead to rely on one another. Following an unofficial strike in 1904, Boilermakers' president John McNeil chided District Lodge 6 for repudiating his efforts to settle the dispute. "We were compelled to absolutely refuse," the lodge president retorted, "as we could not trust our interests to him, as he could not possibly understand the conditions in this part of the country as he has never been here. . . . Consequently we decided to take care of our affairs ourselves."[28]

This commitment to local solidarity and autonomy, combined with the sheer density of union organization in San Francisco, made the city unusual by American labor standards. Industrywide collective bargaining also set San Francisco apart. Employers recognized unions in the metal trades (usually an open shop industry) as early as 1903, and four years later the California Metal Trades Association and the ITC signed their first agreement regulating wages, working conditions, and grievance procedures throughout the city. Trade agreements made sense for San Francisco employers. Over two hundred metal trades firms in the city employed, on the average, ten workers each.[29] Labor contracts standardizing wages and hours offered these employers some protection from the perils of market competition. Cooperating with unions was in any case usually more attractive than fighting them. The prevalence of craft production limited employers' opportunities to replace skilled workers with more tractable labor, and the men had powerful unions and a developed system of mutual support.[30] Nor, finally, could San Francisco employers count on city government to take their side in battles against unions, for labor was a leading player in local politics.

Labor's influence in municipal government reflected pragmatic more than ideological commitments. The leaders of San Francisco's peak labor associations—the San Francisco Labor Council, the Building Trades Council, and the ITC—were conservative men. They urged caution and moderation on their constituents, denounced Wobblies as hotheads who would destroy the labor movement, and defended AFL craft unionism against even such moderate socialists as Max Hayes, "the noisy little microbe from Cleveland."[31] Unsympathetic to the ideals of the labor left, San Francisco union leaders had a more practical reason to involve themselves in electoral politics: it paid. It literally enriched a few labor officials, as the 1911 investigation into municipal graft would show. It benefited far larger numbers of workers by guaranteeing city policies favorable to unions, providing municipal jobs at union standards, and ensuring that the police would be at least neutral during strikes.[32]

Building from cohesive working-class neighborhoods and strong central organizations, labor achieved greater political influence in San Francisco than in most American cities. The means by which the labor movement did so changed over time. Some workers ran for office on regular party tickets. Between 1892 and 1910, of 120 assemblymen for whom information is available, 49 were laborers, semiskilled workers, or craftsmen—almost as many as lawyers (23) and business and professional men (31) combined.[33] Beginning in 1904 working-class political participation took the form of independent party organization, and in 1905 the Union Labor Party (ULP) swept municipal elections. It remained in power until 1911, when a Progressive ticket campaigning for clean government turned out the scandal-ridden ULP. Rather than go down with the ship, however, unionists abandoned the idea of a separate labor party and forged an alliance with middle-class Progressives. This strategic shift preserved unions' political influence, but at a cost. Without an independent party base, labor's voice in municipal government fell hostage to the political fortunes of Progressive allies. This weakness would prove to be fatal after World War I.[34]

San Francisco was not the whole Bay Area, however. Industrial development came to East Bay cities later than it did to San Francisco, and so did labor organization. East Bay industry's most rapid growth occurred after 1906, as the region rebuilt from the 1906 earthquake and as some San Francisco firms sought refuge across the bay.[35] By this time local employers were not as isolated or unorganized as they had been during the formative years of San Francisco's labor movement. Oakland (the East Bay's largest city) thus lagged well behind San Francisco in union density and the prevalence of trade agreements. Much of unionism's wartime expansion in the East Bay, accordingly, would be new growth; across the bay the war found unions and employers well organized and settled in their relations.

The Impact of War

The Bay Area's war boom, based on a flood of shipbuilding contracts, got underway in the middle of 1915 and accelerated over the next three years. Shipbuilding employment in 1914 in all of California stood at 6,000; by 1919

Bay Area yards alone employed 55,000, making it the nation's largest shipbuilding center. Most of this growth came from a frenetic expansion of existing companies such as Oakland's Moore Shipbuilding Company (250
employees in 1915; 13,000 in 1919) rather than any launching of new ones.[36]
Metal trades union membership soared along with the local economy as
organizers took advantage of tight labor markets. Among San Francisco
craftsmen new members joined well-established labor institutions, the most
important of which were IAM Lodge 68 and Boilermakers and Iron Shipbuilders' Lodge 6. But the spread of unionism was most dramatic and innovative among less-skilled metal trades workers in San Francisco and among
all skill groups in the East Bay.

Organization of less-skilled workers began in earnest in 1916 with laborers and helpers, led by the Industrial Workers of the World (IWW), striking
for higher wages. San Francisco labor leaders had for many years been relatively supportive of unionization by less-skilled workers, and they soon
preempted the IWW in the metal trades. Organization proceeded along two
lines. The Shipyard Laborers' Union (SLU, chartered as an AFL federal union
in early 1917) led the charge during the war, winning wage increases and de
facto recognition by mid-1917 and enlisting members at a pace that made it
the largest labor organization in the Bay Area early the following year (with
2,500 members in the East Bay alone). In San Francisco, craft unions also
admitted less-skilled workers, if only in self-defense. As the SLU extended
its recruitment to include shipyard helpers and apprentices, Boilermakers'
Lodge 6 began enrolling the latter to maintain control over all those who
stood in the line of advancement toward journeyman boilermaker. As the
SLU began organizing semiskilled workers in local machine shops and engine factories, Lodge 68 stepped in to bring those specialists into the IAM.[37]
Wartime labor organization spread most rapidly among previously nonunion East Bay craftsmen as well as laborers. Union membership in Alameda County doubled during the war, and shipbuilding craftsmen accounted
for most of that increase. IAM Lodge 284, only 600 strong before the war,
enrolled 2,400 by mid-1918. East Bay boilermakers with union cards num-
bered fewer than 100 in 1914; Oakland-based Boilermakers' Lodge 233, chartered in 1917, claimed 4,700 members in September 1918.[38]

This influx of workers new to unions subverted both conservative union
leaders and settled industrial relations. Early government intervention further undermined labor relations stability. SLAB procedures departed sharply
from local conventions. Wages and working conditions had long been subjects for agreement between the California Metal Trades Association and the
ITC; during the war the SLAB had final say in these matters. Disputes had
been settled by direct negotiation between employer and union representa-

tives; now each side dealt with a third, outside agency. Collective bargaining agreements before the war applied throughout the San Francisco metal trades; EFC intervention and awards covered only shipbuilding, thus introducing different standards for different branches of the industry. Finally, up until the fall of 1917, shipbuilding workers could down tools if all else failed; the SLAB required arbitration.

Bay Area unionists, like their counterparts elsewhere, chafed at the loss of customary rights to handle their own affairs as they saw fit (including, if necessary, through strikes). And like shipbuilding workers in other districts, they resented the government's delays in making decisions and enforcing awards on recalcitrant employers. Two circumstances made these grievances especially galling in San Francisco. First, workers knew that local union power (combined with employers' lucrative contracts) could have won them better wages and faster decisions than the SLAB allowed. Second, many Bay Area unionists questioned the legitimacy of the SLAB agreement because it had been negotiated without regard for or participation by western unionists.[39] Specific SLAB policies reinforced the sense that government intervention violated local rights and interests. Beginning with the February 1918 awards, the SLAB introduced its two-tier system for classifying skilled workers. Employers in many districts refused to recognize craft classifications at all; they rewarded workers on their individual merit (as judged by often capricious foremen). In these cases recognizing only first- and second-class machinists or boilermakers benefited many workers. In San Francisco, however, prewar trade agreements largely ratified strict craft standards for classification and pay. The SLAB's two-tier system thus not only diluted craft standards but also gave San Francisco employers a victory that, acting alone, they never could have won from local unions. A second policy that inflamed Bay Area labor relations concerned union recognition and closed shops. Following general government policy, the SLAB would not entertain worker demands on these issues unless they could demonstrate prewar precedents. Closed shops already existed for skilled shipyard employees in San Francisco. Newly organized workers, however—both those of lesser skill and those in the East Bay—felt themselves entitled to (and capable of achieving) similar conditions. Only the government's insistence on "existing standards" seemed to stand in their way.[40]

Many of these local circumstances and tensions figured prominently in the opening shot of the Bay Area's wartime labor conflict. On September 17, 1917, San Francisco's ITC launched a general strike against Bay Area shipyards and machinery firms. The strike coincided with walkouts in Seattle and Portland (40,000 West Coast shipbuilding workers in all), but it had local origins and guidance. The ITC's contract with the California Metal Trades

Association had expired on September 15. Negotiations underway since the middle of August had stalled. Local employers accepted many terms laid down by labor, including union shops, the eight-hour day, and representation of employees by business agents (with the latter having free access to shops and yards). These were all familiar features of previous agreements. On two major points, however, employers balked. They wanted the EFC to compensate them for the increased costs of the ITC's wage scale, and as of September 14 EFC general manager W. L. Capps declined to do so. Employers also opposed the provision allowing unionists to refuse to work on materials made by "unfair" (nonunion) businesses. Capps relented on the wage issue the day after the strike began, agreeing to pick up half the bill for any pay raises ordered by the SLAB. The right to boycott nonunion materials proved to be less tractable. Officials of a majority of ITC unions, under considerable pressure from their national executives, conceded the point for the war period; EFC officials in turn tactfully agreed not to put this concession in writing. Rank-and-file boilermakers, however, refused to compromise on the issue of nonunion components, and they insisted that their local officials reject the settlement. The issue was of special concern to the more recently organized employees of Oakland's Moore and Scott shipyard, which used boilers from a nonunion firm in Portland. Work remained at a standstill because ITC unions had decided that no one would return to work until all trades agreed to do so. It took several more days of arm-twisting before all unions accepted the agreement and returned to work. Even then, the men refused to honor their unions' promise to work on unfair materials.[41]

The September strike demonstrates the advanced development of San Francisco's labor movement at the outset of the war. Not only were workers more densely organized in San Francisco than in most American cities, but they were organized in different ways. Metal trades councils at this time rarely had much clout with constituent unions. The ITC, by contrast, coordinated and handled negotiations for an industrywide strike. It also enforced the principle that no union's members would return to work until all unions agreed to do so. This local solidarity across craft lines was sustained despite efforts by national union executives to force their locals back to work. Institutionalized solidarity in the Bay Area also departed from American norms by including less-skilled workers. Through the newly organized Shipyard Laborers' Union, even laborers had a voice in central labor councils and the ITC. Nor was this mere lip service. In September's negotiations, for example, the ITC Conference Committee demanded larger pay hikes for less-skilled employees than those sought for craftsmen.[42] Common organization throughout the Bay Area also made it possible for workers in different plants, in several cities, and in quite different industrial sectors (shipbuilding, small machine shops, and large engine factories) to act together in preparing demands, walking out, and accepting a settlement. Metalworkers reaffirmed their identification with a citywide labor movement three months later. The September strike had ended with a provisional settlement on most issues and an agreement to leave the final decision on wages to the SLAB. The board's jurisdiction extended only to shipyards, however, and other metal trades firms declined to pay the same scale. Under ITC leadership 10,000 metal tradesmen struck on December 26 to enforce the scale throughout the Bay Area. Employers might denounce the "unreasonable and unpatriotic attitude of organized labor," but in the end they conceded the point. The strike thus preserved for workers both common conditions and a united front in the city's metal trades.[43]

Labor's Local Revolt

At the war's outset existing labor organization generally served San Francisco and East Bay metalworkers well. Local leaders aggressively pursued rank-and-file demands despite national union and government pleas for restraint. The ITC's contribution to joint action among members of different unions also minimized the tensions between popular insurgency and sectional organization that proved to be so disruptive in other cities. By the beginning of 1918 this situation had changed. ITC officials deferred to the authority and procedures of the SLAB, including those provisions that concentrated power in the hands of national union executives. Following the September strike, moreover, the ITC and California Metal Trades Association signed a new agreement that (like its predecessors) restricted the ITC's freedom of action in changing working conditions or calling strikes. Most officials of San Francisco's craft lodges accepted these constraints as part of responsible collective bargaining. For shipyard workers trying to pursue old battles over unfair work or to keep wages in line with rapid inflation, however, "responsibility" looked like a sellout. It was particularly East Bay and less-skilled workers—newly empowered by organization and by wartime labor markets and with the most ground to make up—who felt the keenest grievances against the ITC and national union executives. On September 6, 1918, San Francisco–based SLAB examiner R. H. Brotherton wired Macy to request help in dealing with East Bay metal workers, noting his fear of "constant trouble from [the] Oakland organization."[44] It was not the first time Brotherton had raised the alarm. East Bay boilermakers, machinists, and semiskilled workers (organized in Boilermakers' Lodge 233, IAM Local 284, and the Shipyard Laborers' Union) had been involved in almost constant disputes since January. Job classifications, working hours, and conditions in "outside" (nonshipyard) shops provided most of the fuel for strikes, and over the course of the year East Bay workers defied all the institutions pledged to industrial peace: the ITC, international unions, trade agreements with the California Metal Trades Association, and the SLAB itself.

The confrontation over job classification began in January 1918, even before the SLAB's wage award allowing for both second- and first-class mechanics. Lodge 233 secretary E. B. Wolfe complained at that time of employers "laying off skilled ship builders, substituting in their places green men and paying these men a much less scale than was agreed upon." Those laid off, he added, were often the most active unionists.[45] The battle lines grew more complicated as the dispute developed. In February President M. J. McGuire of Boilermakers' District Lodge 6 (based in San Francisco) reached an agreement with Bethlehem Steel designed to regulate the upgrading of less-skilled men. Helpers could be put on mechanics' work for six months (a shorter probationary period than was customary) on a sliding scale of pay; at the end of the period they would get the full minimum skilled rate. The SLAB and the ITC approved the pact and extended it to all local shipyards.[46]

McGuire's agreement angered many craftsmen because it gave shipbuilders license to accelerate the upgrading of less-skilled men and to do so at lower pay. The agreement also discriminated against the East Bay, where shipyard expansion was more rapid and unions less able to control job classification. Lastly, it appeared to be inconsistent with the SLAB's West Coast award, which provided for second-class mechanics but said nothing about lower probationary rates. The SLAB award gave East Bay activists an excellent opportunity, however. By demanding that all yards pay the SLAB minima for everyone doing mechanics' work—regardless of prior experience—leaders such as Wolfe could rally a powerful coalition of craftsmen and less-skilled labor. The latter stood to gain higher wages as soon as they were promoted. Craftsmen new to the Bay Area gained some protection against being classified below their real skill, while older craftsmen fearful for traditional union standards saw employers denied one incentive for dilution. The demand had the additional virtue of appearing to affirm rather than repudiate government authority. The men asked only that the Macy agreement be honored "in letter and spirit."[47]

The ITC stood by McGuire's pact, as did the national Boilermakers' leadership. Shipyard employers, having the backing of the Bay Area's responsible union leadership, refused Lodge 233's demands. Continued appeals by East Bay labor officials eventually won SLAB promises to apply the minimum rates. Some employers refused to go along, however, prompting a July 14 mass meeting of Lodge 233 members to declare a strike. The next day 3,500 boilermakers at the three major East Bay yards answered the call, demanding that yard owners agree to pay the proper rates, to do so retroactively, and to give local union officials free access to shipyards. The action came despite opposition from the ITC, the San Francisco Labor Council, and their national union executives.[48]

SLAB assurances that classifications and minima would be enforced brought the strikers back to work in two days. The next wave of unrest proved to be more intractable and more of a challenge to the EFC itself. In an effort to bring East Bay standards up to the level of the best-organized yards along the coast, Oakland Boilermakers and Shipyard Laborers locals announced demands in June for a wage increase, a forty-four-hour week (eight hours per weekday and a Saturday "half-holiday"), and the closed shop. These terms originated with the Pacific Coast District Council of Boilermakers and received some support from Boilermakers' lodges up and down the coast. The ITC and International Boilermakers' leadership, however, disavowed the proposal on the grounds that "the half holiday and the union control of hiring . . . conflict with the Macey [*sic*] agreement."[49]

East Bay workers moved on two fronts. Within the shipyards, boilermakers focused on the Saturday half-holiday. On Saturday, September 7, Lodge 233 members refused to work past 1 P.M., prompting the ITC to declare the action illegal and Boilermakers' president Louis Weyand to warn Wolfe that "radical action and force will place our organization in [a] bad light with [the] Government."[50] These pressures got men back to work, but similar walkouts occurred in October and November. ITC leaders regarded the strikes as violating not only ITC authority but also agreements with the California Metal Trades Association. The SLAB's Brotherton, in turn, bemoaned the "tendency to break away from agreements"—including that guiding the SLAB itself—and the breakdown in union discipline. The Oakland Boilermakers, Brotherton claimed, "stated frankly they do not care for the support of their international organization[,] believing they are strong enough to go it alone." In the short term they were right. By mid-December the last holdout, Bethlehem Shipbuilding, conceded the forty-four-hour week.[51]

The controversy moved beyond the yards in early 1919, as Bay Area unions resumed their efforts to bring outside shops up to the level mandated for shipbuilding. The ITC took a strike vote in January, and several unions (including San Francisco's IAM Lodge 68, as well as East Bay locals) set a February 1 deadline for employers to grant SLAB wages and the forty-four-hour week. A compromise worked out by the ITC and California Metal Trades Association, extending the Macy scale but not the forty-four-hour week to outside shops, promised to defuse the situation. Despite agitation to walk out in support of the Seattle General Strike, the *Labor Clarion* (the San Francisco Labor Council's official paper) expressed confidence that "the unions here can not be induced to follow the lead of the Northwest in violation of their agreements."[52] Not all local unions lived up to the *Labor Clarion*'s expectations, however. San Francisco and East Bay machinists began taking the Saturday half-holiday unilaterally (at shipyards as well as outside shops), and on February 7 Oakland Boilermakers, Bay Area machinists, and Shipyard Laborers struck to enforce the Macy scale and a forty-four-hour week. The usual cast of characters weighed in against the strike. The EFC suspended shipbuilding contracts in January, pending the locals' strike vote; the ITC threatened to expel wayward affiliates; IAM president William Johnston ordered machinists back to work in a telegram read to (and voted down by) 3,000 machinists; and the California Metal Trades Association on several occasions warned of a lockout and the withdrawal of its offer to make the Macy scale retroactive. IAM locals, Lodge 233, and the Shipyard Laborers' Union, with the support of their members and the Pacific Coast Metal Trades Council, fought on. In April employers finally agreed to introduce the forty-four-hour week and, by increments, the Saturday half-holiday.[53]

These unauthorized strikes dramatized serious splits within the Bay Area labor movement. Divisions between labor conservatives supporting government policies and militants intent on seizing new opportunities were common enough during the war. Nor is this surprising, given labor's enhanced power and the government's efforts to circumscribe its use. Two factors distinguish the Bay Area from most other metal trades centers, however. First, conservative leaders were bound by trade agreements with employers as well as by government regulations. In the eyes of impatient metalworkers, these leaders were not merely unresponsive; they were doing the dirty work of the California Metal Trades Association. Second, the split in the local labor movement took a peculiar form. The key conflicts did not pit locals against national executives (as in Bridgeport) or shop stewards and rank-and-file committees against union officialdom (as in British engineering). The main line of antagonism in the Bay Area lay instead between new lodges and older labor institutions, a legacy of the East Bay's prewar labor relations and the resulting uneven impact of war conditions. East Bay craftsmen in 1917 had not secured the job controls enforced by their San Francisco counterparts. The license to evade trade standards that the SLAB and the McGuire agreement gave to employers thus imposed a special hardship on Oakland metalworkers, eager as they were to introduce union conditions already enjoyed across the bay. The fact that an agreement discriminating against East Bay workers had been reached without their involvement only heightened frictions between Lodge 233 and San Francisco organizations.[54] On issues of union security, too, the burden of government intervention fell mostly on the East Bay. Government policies barring demands for union recognition or the closed shop made little difference to San Francisco tradesmen, for they had achieved these goals before the war. East Bay craftsmen and laborers were not so fortunate, and their struggles to gain similar rights both unified them across skill lines and aligned them with radical leaders against moderates in the ITC and San Francisco lodges.

Conflicts over unauthorized demands and strikes eventually escalated into battles over labor leadership and organization in the Bay Area, as San Francisco officials purged insurgents and the latter devised alternative organizations. In the wake of the July 1918 East Bay strikes over upgraded workers' wages, officials of San Francisco Boilermakers' Lodge 6 prompted an investigation of Lodge 233's secretary Wolfe on charges that he had once been a scab and a Pinkerton agent. East Bay boilermakers continued to support Wolfe and returned him and his allies to union posts in August elections.[55] Having failed to drive Wolfe from office, the ITC finally made good on repeated threats and expelled the entire lodge in December for violating ITC authority and local agreements. ITC leaders went on to banish the Oakland Shipyard Laborers' Union and the Oakland, San Francisco, and San Jose machinists' locals in retribution for their roles in the February 1919 strikes. The International Brotherhood of Boilermakers, meanwhile, launched its own offensive against Lodge 233. President Weyand authorized McGuire to take control of dissident Lodge 233, but its members thwarted the takeover by voting renegade leaders back into office in March. After another round of elections in May reaffirmed support for Wolfe and his allies, national officials could only denounce "the radical element" for "monopolizing the floor and boosting industrial unionism."[56]

Repudiated by San Francisco and national labor leaders, Bay Area insurgents developed other institutional alliances. The Pacific Coast Metal Trades Council frequently defended the local autonomy of West Coast labor against both national union authority and the SLAB. In response to the February 1918 Macy award, for example, the council proclaimed that "insofar as the Pacific Coast is concerned, no organizations have agreed to abide by the decisions of their internationals or the Wage Adjustment Board."[57] By early 1919 the Pacific Coast Metal Trades Council was a leading voice for West Coast radicals in Seattle and the Bay Area, voting at its January convention to have no further dealings with the SLAB. Convention delegates further resolved that local and regional metal trades councils should be "gradually industrialized and their representatives will in time supersede international union representatives in the American Federation of Labor." The ubiquitous Wolfe joined this organization in 1918, and when the Boilermakers' executive dispatched McGuire to clean up Lodge 233, the Pacific Coast Metal Trades Council called for McGuire's removal and affirmed that recent strike decisions had been made by the rank and file, not by so-called irresponsible lead-

ers. Wolfe also found time to help organize a Pacific Coast district council
of the Boilermakers in April 1918. Like the Metal Trades Council, the district
council agitated for higher wages and the forty-four-hour week in defiance
of local trade agreements, the ITC, and the SLAB. The Pacific Coast district
council (again like the Metal Trades Council) also attacked Boilermakers'
president Weyand for his attempts in 1919 to purge Lodge 233.[58]

The Pacific Coast Metal Trades Council and Boilermakers' district council gave East Bay insurgents moral support and offered a base for radical
leadership that preempted national union authority. They had little influence
on day-to-day labor relations in the East Bay, however. Much more disturb-
ing to moderate union officials and the government was the move by East
Bay workers to withdraw entirely from the ITC and establish their own independent metal trades council. Efforts to do so reflected the usual dissatisfactions with San Francisco labor leaders—their adherence to unfavorable
agreements and their opposition to the July and September strikes—and a
sense that East Bay metalworking should no longer be a colony of the San
Francisco–based ITC. SLAB officials viewed the movement with alarm. "A
separate iron trades council in Oakland," fretted Brotherton, "will complicate the control of labor organizations here" by limiting the reach of ITC
authority.[59] The AFL's MTD had similar reservations, refusing to grant a
charter for an East Bay metal trades council. Following their expulsion from
the ITC for participating in the February 1919 strikes, East Bay machinists
and boilermakers went ahead and formed the Alameda and Contra Costa
County Metal Trades Council without AFL approval; the Shipyard Laborers' Union joined the new group a month later, bringing the Alameda council up to seventeen affiliates with 30,000 members.[60]

Thus by the end of the war a powerful insurgent movement had developed in the East Bay. The demands pressed by insurgents—enforcing SLAB
minimum rates, a forty-four-hour week, and improved wages and conditions
at outside shops—were hardly revolutionary ones. The movement nonetheless deserved its reputation for radicalism. In matters of trade union politics, East Bay labor leaders challenged AFL unionism by mobilizing an effective alliance of craftsmen and semiskilled labor and, particularly in early
1919, by centering organizational authority not in separate craft unions but
in local, industrywide institutions such as the Alameda Metal Trades Council.[61] The East Bay movement was profoundly destabilizing. In its penchant
for strikes, its "irresponsible" leadership, and its growing organizational
independence, the movement involved coordinated, broadly based defiance
of union and government authority. For local industrial relations in particular, the East Bay insurgency meant that employers could no longer rely on
the traditional bargaining partners and agreements that had provided sta-

bility before the war. As Brotherton recognized at the beginning of 1919, "old time conservative leaders who have the confidence more or less of the employers have been displaced in office by the more radical element who are now in control of the majority of local unions."[62] Brotherton and the EFC shared employers' frustrations. The refusal of East Bay metalworkers (with the support of San Francisco machinists and laborers) to follow SLAB procedures, obey SLAB awards, or even accept SLAB authority thwarted the government's overriding interest in speedy, uninterrupted ship production.

Reconstructing Union Control

The government's antidote to Bay Area shipyard militancy was to bolster the power of conservative union leaders, a strategy with clear roots in local industrial relations history. SLAB representatives pursued this goal on two fronts. First, they strengthened national union executives' control over their lodges; second, they lent their authority to San Francisco's ITC in its efforts to discipline insurgent locals.

The revision of the SLAB agreement in December 1917 was itself designed to curb the influence of uncooperative locals on the Pacific Coast. EFC vice president Charles Piez emphasized that settling the West Coast strikes had been complicated by the fact that "Mr. Gompers, who was most anxious to force an adherence to the Wage Adjustment Board's decision, did not have control over the twenty-nine International Presidents and these Presidents did not have effective control over the local union officers to carry out the purpose and intent of the memorandum creating the . . . Board. There was . . . very firm intent on the part of the Seattle and San Francisco representatives of local unions to drive a harsh bargain, no matter what the outcome."[63] To cope with this disruptive independence, the revised agreement gave union presidents control over labor representation. They alone could initiate SLAB proceedings, they approved (or disapproved) local complaints before the SLAB would heed them, and they decided whether local representatives would be invited to SLAB hearings. Government administrators stood ready to remind union leaders of their role as gatekeepers. When Lodge 233 sought to send its own delegation to a hearing in Philadelphia on August 5, 1918, San Francisco's EFC officer wired Piez that "only confusion will result if authority 233 recognized. Think you should take this matter up with National President of Boilermakers so that there may be no conflict."[64] Normal procedures had limited value during crises, of course. Strikes stopped production, and thus the SLAB dealt directly with local unionists to get workers back on the job. The government continued to reinforce national union authority in its battle against strikes, however. EFC administrators' usual first response to Bay

Area disputes was to have officials in Washington contact the appropriate union executive and urge him to rein in rebellious locals. The combination of government and union pressure often convinced strikers to return to work and follow authorized grievance procedures. East Bay workers' recalcitrance led Brotherton to urge sterner measures: "I believe it will require the personal attention of an International official of the Organization who has sufficient authority to remove local officers to come here and perfect the organization and discipline of the Boilermakers' Local."[65]

The EFC applied much the same strategy on a second front, supporting the ITC against "irresponsible" affiliates. Once again, standard procedures for handling disputes favored ITC power over its challengers. Shipbuilding employees who wanted their grievances addressed by the government had to submit the case through the ITC, because the SLAB generally intervened only when disputes could not be resolved in the "normal" manner. For much of the Bay Area, that meant the manner laid down in agreements between the ITC and the California Metal Trades Association. In one lively case, Lodge 233's Wolfe protested the firing of a Moore Shipbuilding employee (and Lodge 233 official) for union activities. Shipyard management countered that he had used his torch to engrave a boilerplate with the letters *IWW*. The Metal Trades Association secretary and the EFC Industrial Relations Division agreed to bypass Wolfe and have the ITC handle the case. Government and ITC officials favored procedures that reinforced their authority over insurgents even where trade agreements did not require them. Soon after the armistice Examiner Brotherton advised his superiors that he would strictly enforce the SLAB policy of not hearing grievances while men remained on strike. "The conservative and more responsible labor leaders," he added, "heartily endorse my action."[66]

Government officials did not confine themselves to these procedural steps in their support for ITC moderates. With some misgivings, they meddled in union affairs as well. In November 1918 Brotherton discreetly suggested to Macy that Boilermakers' president Weyand might sway an upcoming Lodge 233 election in favor of moderate candidates. Brotherton took a more direct role in local union politics by attempting to discredit leaders of the February strikes, arguing that "the best means of offsetting the work of the radical element in the unions . . . was to give wide publicity to the situation and to the probably [sic] results of cancellation of contracts. . . . I initiated a campaign of publicity, both thru the public press and thru personal conferences with public officials and influential citizens."[67] EFC officials also worked to prevent the formation of an East Bay metal trades council. San Francisco representative Herbert Fleishhacker urged the EFC's William Blackman to "communicate with J. O'Connell President Metal Trades [Department] and endeavor to discourage this movement."[68] Brotherton echoed Fleishhacker's view that an East Bay council would "complicate the control of labor organizations here" and warned that if the ITC expelled Lodge 233, the latter would surely go ahead and set up a rival body.[69] When it became clear that an East Bay council would be formed, the former head of the EFC's Industrial Relations Division urged MTD president O'Connell and SLAB member (and MTD secretary) Berres to "look most carefully into situation before granting any charter to proposed Oakland Iron Trades Council which would be under control of Wolff [*sic*] and Powers."[70]

This strategy of strengthening union authority was well suited to Bay Area conditions. It made sense in part because wartime labor unrest assumed the specific form of rebellion by East Bay lodges against San Francisco and national union institutions. The strategy also seemed reasonable because "responsible" union officials had the confidence of most employers and retained influence, however tarnished, among most workers. In both respects local industrial relations history was decisive in guiding SLAB intervention. That history determined the lines along which orderly labor relations would fracture under the pressures of war, and it bequeathed the tools for restoring stability. If the origins of government policies are clear, however, their success in reconstructing industrial relations stability is less certain. A reunification of the Bay Area labor movement under its traditional leadership did occur during the summer of 1919. ITC president Burton began efforts in March to bring IAM lodges and Lodge 233 back into the fold; in June the Oakland Shipyard Laborers' Union rejoined the council.[71] But the most important step toward reunification was to merge the San Francisco and Alameda metal trades councils. Both the AFL's MTD and the Pacific Coast Metal Trades Council encouraged compromise, and in early August the San Francisco ITC opted to rename itself the Bay District Metal Trades Council and to meet alternately in Oakland and San Francisco. Discussions aimed at formally amalgamating the new body and its Alameda rival began about the same time. Joint meetings followed in December. By this time the two organizations had become, "to all intents and purposes, one organization."[72]

This rapprochement cannot be attributed solely to government policies. The strikes begun in February had been sobering for Bay Area labor. Outside shops eventually conceded union demands, but East Bay shipyards refused to budge. Moreover, when workers finally heeded national orders and returned to their jobs, they discovered that shipyards had no work for many Lodge 233 shop stewards (and SLAB examiners showed some lack of enthusiasm for investigating cases of victimization).[73] The harder line taken by major employers was especially ominous because negotiations to replace the SLAB agreement (lapsing April 1) on a regional basis and to renew the

California Metal Trades Association–ITC contract (ending October 1) were not going well. In short, deteriorating relations with employers helped to reunify the local labor movement. The threat posed to Bay Area unions by organized employers did not make government policies irrelevant; rather, it made them all the more potent. Shipbuilding employees recognized that with the war over, the EFC was under no pressure to tolerate violations of agreements. In addition, it could now confront recalcitrant workers with threats to suspend ship production. An undercover agent of the United States Shipping Board's Investigation Department reported in July a "consensus of opinion" that "the only prospect the Coast has of receiving new contracts, and of preventing the cancelling of the present ones, is in the conservative action of labor."[74] The agent exaggerated the consensus, but the potential costs of flouting EFC authority and local trade agreements were indeed far greater by the summer of 1919. These new risks probably made government sanctions on behalf of moderate union leaders more effective.

    Where government strategies clearly failed was in sponsoring a new pact to take the place of the SLAB agreement when the latter expired in April 1919. Officials of the EFC's Industrial Relations Division helped to arrange a March conference of Pacific Coast unions, shipbuilders, and Metal Trades Department executives in Washington. Representatives reached a tentative agreement that continued SLAB wages and working conditions, gave employees the Saturday half-holiday, and established a conciliation board of shipbuilder and union delegates with final authority to settle disputes. West Coast union members unanimously rejected the agreement (as recommended by the Pacific Coast Metal Trades Council), however, because it failed to mandate closed shops, craft classifications, or higher wages. Negotiations resumed in San Francisco in July, but Los Angeles and Portland yard owners balked at any formal recognition of unions. Despite the growing movement to reassert open shops along the West Coast, most San Francisco and Seattle employers proceeded with the conferences. A settlement emerged by the end of August, "modeled on the lines of previous agreements with the San Francisco Iron Trades Council." Disputes would be handled by union stewards, business agents, and (finally) ITC officials; the workers would get an eight-cent per hour raise and the Saturday half-holiday; and there would be no discrimination against union members. Local unions ratified the agreement early in September.[75]

    If the EFC's plan for a West Coast replacement for the SLAB failed, it appeared in September that San Francisco and Seattle employers, at least, would organize postwar industrial relations with the same centralized controls advocated by EFC officials involved in San Francisco's wartime labor administration. At the end of September, however, shipbuilders withdrew from the agreement on the grounds that the United States Shipping Board had nullified the proposed wage increase. Nonshipbuilding employers belonging to the California Metal Trades Association in turn announced that they would not follow the agreement without the shipyards. Fifty thousand Bay Area metalworkers—virtually every employee of every craft and skill level—struck in response, with the full support of the Bay District Metal Trades Council and national union executives. Many of the outside shops backed down and signed the agreement. But shipyard employers, with few orders on their books, were able to resume operations without an agreement on November 24, and many of the larger plants affiliated with the California Metal Trades Association followed suit. The strike lasted, with diminishing effectiveness, until June, 1920, when the Metal Trades Council and its constituent unions formally gave up the battle.[76]

Acknowledging union invitations to renew negotiations in January, 1920, California Metal Trades Association secretary Fred Metcalf replied that his affiliates had 18,000 employees at work under a new regime. "We feel that direct dealing with our own men, and frank, open consideration and discussion of our mutual problems, with representatives selected from among their own number through the medium of secret balloting . . . was the only fair and just means of dealing with them. Our policy is the American plan."[77] The association's newspaper celebrated the new order as a triumph over the un-American (and inefficient) closed shop. Works councils elected by the entire yard formed the centerpiece of the new order. These would "perform—it was hoped with greater mutual satisfaction and harmony among employers and workers—those functions which had for so many years previously been virtually delegated to the labor unions."[78] Many of the outside shops continued to recognize unions, which retained considerable informal influence through the 1920s. For most of the Bay Area metal trades, however, including shipbuilding, the war era ended with union defeat, the demise of trade agreements, and the American Plan for employee representation.

What accounts for this sharp break with local industrial relations traditions? The two immediate precipitants of the October strike were probably not decisive. Unions and employers had deadlocked over the closed shop, and the tentative agreement did not grant this union goal. International presidents and the Pacific Coast Metal Trades Council accordingly issued a statement on September 19 that labor would continue to defend union conditions, if necessary by refusing to work with nonunion men. Shipyard management viewed the statement as a sign of bad faith but did not withdraw from the agreement at this time.[79] Employers had tolerated much the same situation before. The strike's second spark was the United States Shipping Board's decision not to approve the eight-cent per hour wage hike set by unions and employers. Shipbuilders claimed that this decision nullified the agreement. In fact, it did nothing of the sort. The EFC refused to compensate the yards for wage hikes over the Macy scale, but it did not prohibit them from paying out of their own pockets. Because most shipbuilders in the Bay Area worked under lump-sum rather than cost-plus contracts,[80] it may have been difficult to do so. Still, yard owners' efforts to persuade the EFC to take a hard line in public suggest that they found the wage issue a convenient excuse for a break they had other reasons to make.[81]

Greater tact by unions on the closed shop or by the EFC on wages might well have averted the October strike, but two more basic developments made it unlikely that prewar and wartime accommodations between employers and unions would continue into the 1920s. First, by October 1919 both employers and key EFC officials had lost confidence that *any* labor group could be a responsible partner in Bay Area industrial relations. Second, political conditions in the Bay Area made the open shop a much more plausible alternative than it had been during or before the war.

Employers' attitudes toward organized labor shifted over the course of 1919. For much of the war shipyard management had viewed the ITC as a bulwark against East Bay rebels, and this attitude clearly persisted during the February strike. The major shipyards protested to Berres (SLAB member and MTD secretary) that they had dealt with organized labor for eleven years and were willing to continue doing so. The East Bay rebels were another matter, however: "As we see the matter the present Oakland leaders disregard and violate their agreements and the wishes of their international officers."[82] The same yards repeated the argument for the benefit of their employees in a March 5 appeal to support a new local agreement: "This is a good time to remind you of the helpful part the Iron Trades Council has played in bringing about better working conditions in the metal industries of the San Francisco bay district."[83] Yet by the end of the summer, employers openly questioned the reliability of local union leadership. The official paper of the California Metal Trades Association looked back fondly on "the industrial harmony which with few exceptions [had] existed in this district for the last eleven years," a golden age that the association attributed to "a series of collective bargaining agreements made locally between representatives of the industries and the iron trades council, local representatives of the employees." The golden age ended during the war, however, with the development of "a new type of labor leader . . . who favored the one big union idea for the Pacific Coast"; San Francisco employers found it much more difficult to do business with such individuals.[84]

With ITC leadership challenged by radicals in Oakland and in coastwide organizations such as the Pacific Coast Metal Trades Council, employers thus became more skeptical about the prospects for restoring industrial peace on the basis of strengthened local union authority. Had the reunification of the Bay Area labor movement occurred earlier in 1919, employers might not have considered it necessary to give up on trade agreements in September. As it was, their own misgivings were confirmed by the unions' September pledge to enforce closed shops in violation of the new agreement. J.C. Jenkins and J. L. Ackerson of the EFC reinforced this view, arguing that the government had to draw the line against West Coast labor militants to safeguard the EFC's own contracts. Jenkins added that AFL leaders might even welcome a setback for western labor to solidify their control over unions there.[85] Doubtful about the ITC's ability to discipline Bay Area labor and encouraged by government signals, shipyard owners withdrew from their agreement with local unions.

The second major influence on industrial relations outcomes in Bay Area shipbuilding had more to do with local politics than with the shipbuilding industry itself. The metal trades strike at the end of 1919 anticipated similar confrontations in other local industries, including that traditional bastion of trade union power, the building trades. This citywide offensive coincided with a growing national enthusiasm for the American Plan. San Francisco had been an exception to open shop drives in the past, however, and the victory of employers in 1920 had local roots. As Michael Kazin shows, the political positions of labor and business elites were quite different after the war. Labor's economic clout before World War I rested in part on political power. Following the defeat of the Union Labor Party by anticorruption Progressives in 1911, however, San Francisco labor gradually abandoned independent political organization in favor of an electoral coalition with reform-minded middle-class constituencies. Labor's dependence on Progressive allies in municipal politics turned out to be its Achilles heel. It made no difference during the war, when economic conditions gave unions ample leverage. But in 1919 Progressive politics faltered, and labor could no longer fall back on independent political resources. Employers had not only lost confidence in unions, they also had the power to repudiate them, because the allegiance of city government now lay more with employers than with labor.[86]

Simple "American" antiunionism does not explain the Bay Area outcome. It was the combination of changing relations within the labor movement and new political class relations that gave San Francisco employers both the rationale and the resources to abandon trade agreements. Bay Area shipbuilding thus shows in particularly dramatic ways some of the changes in political alignments and industrial relations that appear on a national scale, with similar consequences for postwar restabilization. In contrast to their Bay Area counterparts, Great Lakes shipbuilders needed no such change in political fortunes to embrace the American Plan. The more typical heritage of open shop labor relations in the Great Lakes led to government and employer policies similar to those in munitions production, and the union-free employee representation scheme introduced by local SLAB administrators during the war proved to be more enduring than San Francisco labor's power.

CHAPTER 5

Freeing Shop Committees from
"Partisan Prejudices" in Great Lakes Shipyards

Prewar Great Lakes shipyards could be counted a rare success story in a foundering industry. In most regions of the United States, shipbuilding languished at a time when British yards could build merchant ships more cheaply and when navy orders were few and capricious. Great Lakes builders, by contrast, enjoyed the blessings of both geology and geography. Rich mineral deposits assured them a steady market for ore-carrying vessels, and the narrow passage to the Atlantic protected them from outside competition. As the nation mobilized for war, Emergency Fleet Corporation (EFC) and U.S. Navy officials took full advantage of the region's well-equipped facilities, giving Great Lakes firms enough orders to justify further expansion. The area also provided publicists with one of the best examples of the nation's ingenuity in waging war. Local yards turned out a number of larger transports that were then cut in half for passage through the canal and reassembled for Atlantic service.[1]

Shipyards throughout the Great Lakes grew rapidly in employment and output during the war years, with familiar consequences for labor relations. Job turnover soared, conflicts erupted over construction methods and working conditions, and employees joined unions and went on strike in record numbers. The setting for war production and government intervention was very different from that of the Bay Area, however. Great Lakes shipbuilders had already made significant progress in rationalizing ship fabrication, and they had long insisted on open shops; shipyard workers were generally new to unions, without the habits or institutions of solidarity common in the Bay

Area. From this starting point the development of industrial unrest during
the war would be very different from that seen in the Bay Area, as would be
the reforms promoted by the Shipbuilding Labor Adjustment Board (SLAB)
to stabilize labor relations.

Most major Great Lakes cities had at least one shipyard, but a center of
activity was in Cleveland and Lorain (a city just west of Cleveland on the
Lake Erie shore). The American Shipbuilding Company, by far the largest
builder around the Great Lakes, had its headquarters in Cleveland and yards
in both Cleveland and Lorain.[2] With several smaller yards also located in
Cleveland, these cities offer a contrast to the Bay Area that is both sharply
defined and typical of most Great Lakes shipbuilding.

THE INDUSTRIAL SETTING

Compared to San Francisco, prewar Cleveland typified American standards in its dramatic industrial growth and its largely nonunion, immigrant
work force. The city served as a hub for railroad and lake shipping, and
the Civil War had stimulated local oil refining, iron and steel production,
and varied machinery manufacturing. The pace of development transformed Cleveland from a modest midwestern town to one of the nation's
largest industrial cities within a few decades. Manufacturing employment
soared tenfold between 1870 and 1910, to 103,700, including 18,000 in
foundries and machine shops, 10,000 in steel mills, and 9,000 in automobile plants.[3] A center for steel production and second only to Detroit in auto
output, Cleveland boasted a metalworking industry with advanced manufacturing techniques and a relatively deskilled labor force. A survey in
1916 found that most of the city's 18,000 machinists were specialists who
could pick up required skills within six months. Almost half of the local
auto industry's employees learned their jobs in less than a month.[4] Ships,
of course, could not be produced on assembly lines by semiskilled hands,
yet Great Lakes shipbuilders led the move toward fabricated ship production before World War I. Ore carriers could be standardized, and this made
it possible to do some of the preliminary work (punching plates, assem-
bling components, and manufacturing fittings) in larger volumes with
more specialized equipment. Great Lakes shipbuilding still called for
skilled tradesmen, but management found a growing number of operations
where work could be subdivided and mechanized.[5]

Competing in national markets and not heavily reliant on skilled labor,
Cleveland employers enforced open shops.[6] Many of the city's metalwork-
ing firms belonged to a branch of the National Metal Trades Association
(NMTA), and they followed its standard regimen: no negotiations with

unions, mutual aid to break strikes. Great Lakes shipbuilders, including the American Shipbuilding Company, took the same line. When boilermakers organized a district lodge and walked out for the nine-hour day and union work rules in 1907, the yards cooperated to defeat the strike and blacklist unionists.[7] Leading Cleveland employers offered welfare programs as an alternative to collective bargaining, viewing such philanthropy as appropriate for an immigrant work force, consistent with local traditions of civic responsibility, and likely to yield both "social harmony and efficiency."[8] Employer policies may not have purchased social harmony, but they did help to limit unionization. At the outset of the 1907 Great Lakes shipbuilding strike, Boilermakers' lodges around the lakes claimed 2,000 skilled shipyard men. Defeat cost many unionists their jobs, and as late as 1915 Boilermakers' locals could claim only thirty-nine members from *all* Cleveland industries. In the middle of that year, when nearly 18,000 machinists worked in Cleveland and the war boom was already underway, International Association of Machinists (IAM) locals boasted 500 members. Lorain entered the war with no Boilermakers' lodge at all and a reputation—earned in part by steelworkers' refusal to join widespread strikes against U.S. Steel in 1909 and 1910—as barren soil for unions.[9] Obdurate employers were not the only problem. The city's rapid industrialization coincided with a wave of immigration from southern and eastern Europe, and 37 percent of Cleveland's 1890 population had been born abroad. The 1916 survey of local industry designated machinists as members of an "American" trade because the foreign born filled only 40 percent of vacancies; the figure for molders was 80 percent. Residential segregation by ethnicity rather than by occupation may have further undercut the social base for union loyalties. Some union organizers simply wrote off Cleveland workers as "asleep" and "taking no interest in the organization."[10]

Cleveland's metal trades unions developed neither the political clout nor the institutions of mutual support that might have compensated for inhospitable production practices, hostile employers, and cross-cutting ethnic ties. Shortly before the outbreak of World War I, for example, officers from a number of Cleveland's unions launched a new campaign for a metal trades council.[11] The effort failed, as had many before. Individual unions could not be convinced to supply funds or send delegates, and they would allow the council virtually no authority over trade affairs. Electoral politics offered little more promise as a base for union power. Labor leaders were themselves divided between AFL loyalists and a substantial socialist contingent. The latter had significant influence in the local labor movement, and their party polled well in municipal elections. More conservative labor leaders lost few opportunities to denigrate socialists as disruptive and utopian, but they, too, made periodic forays into electoral politics, organizing Labor's Political League in 1908 to reward friends and punish enemies.[12] Yet neither faction gave labor the political resources to redress the balance of power in local industrial relations. Around the turn of the century, reform-minded middle-class citizens seemed ready to ally with moderate socialists in opposition to business interests and political corruption, much as they did in a number of "socialist cities."[13] Instead, progressivism triumphed. A movement for municipal reform and clean government swept city elections in 1901, and Mayor Tom Johnson's administration (1901–9) cemented an electoral coalition of enlightened business leaders and professionals with substantial numbers of working-class voters. Workers earned real benefits from this alliance, including more equitable tax burdens and lower streetcar fares. The cross-class coalition and Progressive reform themes that dominated city elections, however, left little room for Cleveland workers to develop the independent power and distinct political identity shown by their San Francisco counterparts. Furthermore, Cleveland employees could not expect their city government to support union standards or give strikers equal protection in disputes.[14]

These features of Cleveland's industry and labor movement appear throughout the Great Lakes shipbuilding industry. Most local yards producing steel ships specialized in relatively standardized vessels and adopted some of the techniques of fabricated ship production. The open shop policies of the American Shipbuilding Company applied in all its yards, and the second-largest builder (Great Lakes Engineering Works, with yards in Ecorse and Ashtabula) was if anything more adamant in opposing unions.[15] Other Great Lakes shipbuilding centers displayed the same bleak picture of labor organization: few shipyard craftsmen belonged to unions, and metal trades councils, if they existed at all, commanded no respect from employers or loyalty from workers. Then came the war.

THE IMPACT OF WAR

The war boom brought Cleveland metal trades firms full order books by mid-1915, and American Shipbuilding Company executives reported yards working at full capacity the following year.[16] United States orders placed still greater demands on local plants and yards, and competition for labor led to widespread "poaching" of employees by rival firms by the middle of 1917. The American Shipbuilding Company was probably one of the culprits. Its work force doubled, to 12,000 employees, between early 1917 and April 1918.[17] Tight labor markets gave metalworkers a new security to organize, with unionization coming first to Cleveland's auto and machinery plants. Local IAM lodges claimed only 500 members as late as August 1915, and in early September the city's leading labor newspaper scolded machinists for their indifference: "The machinery workers of this city [must] show to the International Association that they are sincerely desirous of helping themselves in the matter of wages and reducing their hours of toil. [Then] they will find the union ready to back them up."[18] A month later employees finally began to heed this advice. Five hundred machinists at the Cleveland Automatic Machine Company declared a strike in October for the eight-hour day, overtime pay, and the reinstatement of fifteen men discharged for union activities. Employees at other firms soon took up the same demands, and by the end of the month over 5,000 machine trades workers had downed tools. They did so in most cases without benefit of IAM membership or guidance. Despite this lack of formal organization among the strikers, most firms granted the eight-hour day, raised wages, and made other concessions, but they refused to have any direct dealings with the union.

At first IAM lodges won little more recognition from strikers. Having "helped themselves," few machinists actually took out union cards. They simply accepted company offers and returned to work.[19] Enrollments picked up by early 1916, with new applications coming in at the rate of 200 per week. Only a small minority of the city's machinists signed up, but this represented a major gain over prewar years and enabled IAM officials to back demands for union conditions with credible threats to disrupt war production.[20] Organization among shipyard boilermakers, too, began late but spread rapidly. Boilermakers' vice president Ryan, on an organizing tour of the area in mid-1916, could still label the city "one of the weakest spots in the country." A full year into the shipbuilding boom, Boilermakers' Lodge 5 had fewer than 50 members. By early 1917, however, lodge membership reached 200, and it climbed steadily to 1,200 by August 1918.[21] A similar trajectory can be seen elsewhere around the Great Lakes.[22]

Mobilization among Great Lakes shipyard workers lagged well behind that of Bay Area workers in other respects, too. Less-skilled men remained almost entirely unorganized, and in 1917 (a year that saw industrywide stoppages in Seattle, Portland, San Francisco, Delaware River, and New York yards), most Great Lakes craftsmen eschewed strikes. Labor disputes occurred more frequently after 1917, but they remained fragmented. At no point in the war did metalworkers throughout Cleveland's shipyards (much less across the entire metal trades, as in San Francisco) strike together. Elsewhere around the Great Lakes, similarly, labor unrest rarely involved more than a single trade at a single plant or yard before 1918.[23] The narrow scope of these disputes points to local metalworkers' inability to overcome their organizational divisions. The Cleveland Metal Trades Council, resuscitated in 1915, continued to receive only lukewarm support from its affiliates. For example, several unions (including the IAM) refused to support an increase in dues for the council, a decision the council secretary derided as typical of "their desire to see the Metal Trades Council shot to pieces. . . . They have been persistent in their efforts to point out the insignificance of the Council." Three months later the council met to consider asking national union executives to order their local lodges to send representatives to the council.[24] This absence of effective institutions to coordinate metalworkers of different crafts, yards, or cities stands in sharp contrast with the situation in the Bay Area.

Over the course of 1918, however, Great Lakes shipbuilding workers began to make up lost ground. Local union officials gained influence, unionists made some progress toward organizational unity, and official labor institutions forged stronger ties to the workers in the yards. These developments owed a great deal to government controls and boom conditions. They also posed a challenge to shipyard industrial relations very different from that mounted in the Bay Area. The problem raised by labor mobilization was not that it would break down union authority but rather that union controls might invade open shops.

CONFRONTING THE OPEN SHOP ORDER

In laying siege to the open shop order, Great Lakes shipbuilding craftsmen benefited from both the war boom and certain government labor policies. Some aspects of government intervention fueled unrest. Cleveland shipyard employees voiced familiar complaints over delays in issuing and enforcing awards, and they resented federal regulations that denied them full use of their wartime bargaining power. In other respects, however, the SLAB introduced work rules that approached union standards, gave union officials new influence over industrial relations, and expanded opportunities for more effective labor organization.

Consider union standards. Great Lakes craftsmen complained that the government left management too much leeway in employing "second-class" mechanics. For all the grumbling about two-tier classifications, however, SLAB rulings improved conditions for skilled shipbuilders because most Great Lakes yards had many *more* than two tiers before the war. According to a Boilermakers' organizer reporting at the beginning of 1918, "Conditions under which shipyard men work and the wages paid are [the] most deplorable in [the country]," with "many classifications, and on top of that . . . the different classes [are] graded, [with] as many as four rates for riveters and so on."[25] The new framework for handling disputes established by the EFC also amplified union officials' voice in local labor relations. The government never recognized union agents as the legitimate representatives of shipyard employees, but when employers' hard line against unions endangered output, the EFC's overriding interest in ship production forced compromises on recalcitrant managers. Furthermore, when unions raised grievances or levied demands, they could sometimes bypass unresponsive employers and appeal directly to EFC and SLAB officials in the district. Where major decisions had to be made, the SLAB examiner might call employers and union delegates to hearings, and these could turn into de facto negotiating sessions. Examiner Walter Fisher brought shipyard employers' and local Boilermakers' representatives together, for example, in the middle of 1918 to discuss possible changes in SLAB awards and to examine piece rates for a number of jobs. The two sides eventually agreed on new wage rates, which the SLAB then ratified in its next award.[26] SLAB officials, finally, made indirect contributions to labor organization. The SLAB refused to impose closed shops, but like the National War Labor Board, it curtailed victimization, protected workers' right to organize, and checked some of the employers' customary anti-union tactics. Together with a tight labor market, these policies helped Great Lakes shipbuilding craftsmen to strengthen their organization.

One way in which they did so in 1918 was to develop more effective instruments for cooperative action. Cleveland Boilermakers' Lodge 5 and the Cleveland Metal Trades Council initiated meetings for all shipyard crafts around the city in March. As delegates' interest in the meetings grew, the council gained stature as a forum for discussing shipyard labor relations, grievances regarding classification, and shop committees.[27] Outside Cleveland, Boilermakers' officials sought to establish tighter links among Great Lakes shipbuilding centers, reorganizing the Great Lakes District Lodge (moribund since the defeat of the 1907 strike) in August. A year later the district lodge meeting attracted fifty-five delegates from around the lakes. Most ambitious of all were efforts to establish a regional council of metal trades unions comparable to San Francisco's Iron Trades Council (ITC) but on a much larger scale geographically. Shipbuilding craft union representatives launched the Great Lakes District Allied Shipbuilders' Council in August 1919 to coordinate demands for wage hikes, standardize conditions throughout the region, and defend gains made under the (now defunct) SLAB.[28] The EFC lent some indirect support to these initiatives, giving the Cleveland Metal Trades Council representation at hearings and consulting informally with council officials in complaints over the enforcement of SLAB awards.[29] None of these new organizations developed the influence wielded by the ITC, however. The EFC rarely treated them as responsible intermediaries for managing labor relations, and employers regarded them as they did other union institutions—as enemies to be avoided rather than as bargaining partners. These councils also won only limited allegiance from their own constituents. Cleveland Boilermakers' and Machinists unionists, in particular, regularly denounced the Metal Trades Council for its ineffectiveness and conservatism, and the Machinists bolted the council altogether at the end of 1918.[30]

More important than the formation of new joint councils was the development of workplace unionism in local yards and plants. Neither the EFC nor shipyard management had to take union officials seriously if the latter lacked strong ties to workshop organizations. After all, machinists' willingness in 1915 to strike for union conditions without forming any lasting ties to the IAM showed how employers could alleviate unrest without abandoning open shops or compromising management authority. A more substantial base for union power in shipbuilding emerged by the beginning of 1918. IAM business agent William Jack encouraged members to hold shop meetings and appoint committees in 1917, and shipyard shop stewards were soon presenting union demands and recruiting new members for both the IAM and the Boilermakers' union. The link between workplace and union was further strengthened where the shop steward also served as a local union officer and when unions brought stewards from multiple firms together for regular meetings. The IAM began doing so in March 1918.[31]

By sinking deeper roots in the yards and forging stronger links among workplaces, Great Lakes unions contested the open shop status quo in two ways. First, they focused conflict on the fractious issue of union rights. Local union leaders generally accepted the principle that they could not force union recognition or win the closed shop during the war. Precisely because this principle had to be observed, more circuitous forms of union involvement in disputes became all the more contentious markers of union-management relations. Union officials demanded the right to be consulted by the EFC in labor disputes and SLAB decisions, and employers opposed even this much recognition of "outside" representatives. SLAB awards that made any concessions to union work rules also touched a raw nerve among managers. American Shipbuilding Company president M. E. Farr charged that the April 1918 SLAB award would "impose labor union methods and exactions not only on shipbuilders but thousands of loyal workmen who are not affiliated."[32] Shop committees, too, acted as surrogates for larger battles over the open shop. Management often rejected yard committees' requests for conferences because they believed (sometimes rightly) that these were thinly disguised union delegations.[33] Provisions in the award for grievance procedures involving elected shop committees, Farr charged, were "unwarranted unnecessary and artificial and . . . not desired by the rank and file of workmen in Lake Shipyards."[34]

In the past Great Lakes employers had always been able to win struggles over union recognition. Their ability to do so came in part from their own resources and collective organization and in part from the fragmented and sporadic nature of worker protest. The balkanization of union struggles was both an achievement and a guarantee of open shop industrial relations, and wartime labor organization confronted the old regime in this second sense as well. The growing numbers of shipyard employees carrying union cards was not in itself decisive. More important, the strategic balance began to shift against employers as union leaders forged links to rank-and-file organizations and across hitherto isolated workplaces. Some of the smaller firms capitulated and signed union agreements. The two dominant shipbuilding companies and most of the smaller ones, however, remained adamant in opposition to unions. The American Shipbuilding Company went beyond belligerence to offer a more generous mixture of concessions and welfare measures, but the goal was still to insulate employee loyalties from unions and craft mates in other firms. Managers at the Lorain yards, for example, did their utmost to foster "a general spirit of good will among workers, foremen and management" through "weekly entertainment, usually music by the shipyard band, and some outside talent."[35]

SLAB administrators for the Great Lakes were thus caught between intransigent yard owners and labor unions with an increasing capacity to challenge employers and disrupt production. On the critical issue of formal recognition of unions, moreover, the EFC was committed to "existing standards," and local representatives refused to intervene in strikes for new union rights.[36] But this approach was unlikely to secure industrial peace. Worse, it risked discrediting the EFC in the eyes of union activists, thus making government management of labor relations still more difficult. State measures to handle the crisis centered on an employee representation plan intended to rationalize open shop practices while appeasing organized labor. In the eyes of the most enthusiastic local SLAB officials, their plan realized an ideal of industrial democracy unsullied by shortsighted and self-interested unions.

RESTABILIZATION: SHOP COMMITTEES
AND INDUSTRIAL DEMOCRACY

Enlightened employee management had a long history in Cleveland. The city's chamber of commerce urged members to include welfare work in their open shop program as early as 1898, and local employers embraced employee representation as an important part of up-to-date company welfare plans. Several Cleveland employer associations, for example, conducted a study of

Rockefeller's Colorado plan for "industrial democracy" in 1916 to determine its applicability to local conditions.[37] By this time the White Motor Company had a well-publicized system to "secure the more frequent cooperation of the men . . . and give them a voice in factory management." White Motor did not recognize unions, but even the socialist *Cleveland Citizen* commended the firm's elected employee committee and regular labor-management meetings for producing "as satisfied a lot of men . . . as there is in any shop in Cleveland."[38] The federal government adapted employee representation to war conditions and introduced it more widely in the shipbuilding industry.

The first SLAB award for the Great Lakes, in April 1918, included provisions for shop committee elections. The decision was one of the first government awards to provide for shop committees, and it tailored this form of representation to the workings of shipyards. Employees of a given trade had the right to choose a three-person craft committee, and the chairs of those committees formed a joint shop committee for the whole yard. Unsettled grievances moved from craft to joint committee and finally to the SLAB. The award also allowed joint committees to "call into conference a representative chosen by the committee" if initial meetings with company officials proved to be unsuccessful. Similar guidelines appear in awards for the North Atlantic, South Atlantic, and Gulf districts and for Portland shipyards. SLAB shop committees were most actively promoted and most widely adopted in the Great Lakes, however, and it was here that labor administrators worked out the details of the plan.[39] How would committee elections be conducted? At what point could "outside" representatives gain entry to conferences? What role, independent of the shop committee scheme, should unions play in handling grievances? Different parties supported very different answers to these questions, but the answers given by local SLAB officials and employers ultimately prevailed.

Disagreements over electoral procedures developed almost immediately, as rival factions contested whether shop committees properly represented the employees of a company or the members of a union. The award stipulated that workers of each "craft or calling" should elect committee members by secret ballot and "in such manner as the employees shall direct." Voting by craft (rather than by department, as in National War Labor Board plans) made it easier for trade unions to control election outcomes *if* they had organized a majority of the employees within their occupational jurisdiction. If they had not, the precise arrangements for choosing delegates became especially important. SLAB officials insisted that elections be held on neutral ground, preferably in the shipyard itself, so that both union and nonunion employees could participate. L. H. Bathurst, secretary of the new Boilermakers' district lodge, and Martin Krieps, a Boilermakers' organizer for the upper Great Lakes, strongly disagreed. Bathurst reminded SLAB examiner Walter Fisher that the award ordered elections held "in such manner as the employees may direct" and claimed that "the men have a perfect right to select their committees in the [union] Hall."[40] It had long been customary for unions to deputize members employed in a particular establishment to serve as a shop committee, charged with monitoring working conditions and looking after union interests. Unionists resented the SLAB's decision to hold elections in the shops and to make those delegates, rather than bona fide union committees, the official agents for handling grievances. Fisher replied that voting in union halls disfranchised nonunion men. "Only by holding [elections] in the yard can non-union employees have any fair opportunity for participation. . . . The rule works no injustice whatever on the union men who will certainly elect the committeemen if they are in the majority."[41]

Beyond demonstrating their solicitude for minority rights, Fisher and his successor, William Pitt, recognized that most shipyard employers would not deal with formal union committees. They saw their plan as a way to create shipyard institutions for handling disputes that would be independent of unions and thus agreeable to management. The key SLAB national administrators (Willard Hotchkiss and Henry Seager) both backed Fisher and Pitt, and in some cases they called on national union executives to force lodge officials to accept shop elections. As expected, unions did in fact control election outcomes in well-organized yards. But where unionists lacked a majority, as in some Lorain and Cleveland crafts, they lost control of the only employee bodies recognized by the SLAB as legitimate representatives for handling grievances.[42]

Equally contentious was the question of what role union officials outside the yards should play in labor relations. Shop committees would be of little value as a compromise between union recognition and open shop principles if union officials brought grievances directly to the examiner, bypassing shipyard conferences between committees and management. Fisher complained that union officials sought to "cut across lots and get directly to the Examiner or the Board,"[43] and he and Pitt demanded compliance with official procedure. For Fisher, this rule affirmed the government's policy of respecting prewar open shops. He declared himself willing to meet with labor union officials and listen to their concerns, as somewhat worried national SLAB officials urged him to do. In handling grievances, however, he insisted that "the principle of the open shop [is] to be maintained and . . . complaints [are] to come to me as Examiner, through the shop committees, and after a real opportunity had been afforded for the adjustment of grievances by conference between employee and employers."[44] Examiner Pitt took the same position when he replaced Fisher at the end of September 1918.

Shipyard managers had long dealt with disputes on an ad hoc basis and without union involvement. The SLAB shop committee scheme introduced formal procedures and workplace institutions for handling grievances, but it continued to exclude unions from the initial stages of appeal. When the business agent for the Cleveland Boilermakers' local asked the examiner to reconsider a decision, for example, Fisher's assistant replied that "if the case is to be re-opened, it will have to be re-opened through the regular channel, and come to the Examiner by way of the Shop Committee. Until you are called into the case at the final stage of the proceedings, as you may be, the Examiner will have to be excused from recognizing your authority in the matter."[45] Boilermakers' officials from around the Great Lakes, feeling that they had been "deliberately snubbed by the Examiner and that the Shop Committee machinery had been put forward not as a means of settling grievances but as a means of postponing" them, resolved early in September to have no further dealings with the examiner.[46]

At the behest of SLAB secretary Seager, Boilermakers' president Weyand persuaded district officials to cooperate with the examiner's office.[47] The problem of union involvement in "open shops" soon took a new form, however. At what stage in the grievance procedure could "outside representatives" enter into conferences with employers and the examiner? Boilermakers' district organizer Martin Krieps originally urged Fisher to have grievances handled jointly by business agents and shop committees, but Fisher insisted on the letter of the April award: union officials could be involved only after they were called in by shop committees.[48] The matter did not rest there, for the SLAB employee representative scheme created two kinds of committees, one for each craft and a joint shop committee for the yard as a whole. Could craft committees call outside agents into conference with yard management? The answer was of considerable importance. Craft committees were much more likely to be under union control than were joint shop committees, because the latter combined delegates from all crafts and occupations, including laborers. For employers, too, this question involved not merely union access to the examiner's office but also the unions' role in shipyard labor relations.

The April award assigned the right to call in outside representation to joint shop committees, and Fisher and Pitt interpreted this to mean that *only* joint shop committees could do so. A seemingly minor change in procedure appeared in October's revised award, which was meant to cover the entire East Coast. If a grievance concerned only a single craft, the appropriate committee was to handle the matter up through discussions with top management and could choose an outside agent to meet with yard managers. Union-controlled craft committees promptly invoked this clause and demanded to bring union officials into shipyard conferences. Once again, however, national SLAB administrators yielded to local conditions. Examiner Pitt argued forcefully that joint shop committees, with representatives from each craft, were in a better position to evaluate disputes objectively. By allowing craft unionists to bypass the joint committee, the October award would lead to "every grievance [being] presented in a partisan spirit by the men whose selfish interests are at stake."[49] SLAB officials in Washington responded on November 1 with a special document entitled "Statement in Reference to Shop Committees": "Where joint shop committees are established and operate under the guidance and supervision of the examiner, a craft committee should not call in an outside representative until after the joint shop committee fails to effect a satisfactory settlement."[50]

These rules governing elections and grievance procedures aimed to establish shipyard committees independent of unions for the day-to-day management of labor relations. Other examiner policies served the same end. Following the November 1 SLAB statement, Pitt proceeded to distribute cards for committeemen and prepare standard forms for filing grievances. The cards, conspicuously identifying the SLAB as the issuing authority, "would serve to impress [on] the committeeman that he is acting in the interests of the government . . . and free him to some extent at least from his partisan prejudices." The grievance forms emphasized the proper chain of appeal from aggrieved worker to joint shop committee and on to the examiner. They also omitted any reference to the joint committees' right to call in outside representatives. The form had an additional virtue for Pitt. "A great number of grievances," Pitt predicted, "will not be presented by the complainer when he finds it necessary to present the complaint in written form and appear to substantiate his charges before it will receive consideration."[51] As the expiration of SLAB authority approached, local EFC officials intensified their efforts to have shop committees learn to resolve disputes without appealing to any outside agency, union or governmental. EFC district representative George Gephart argued that committees were by this time "pretty well educated" to consider "grievances in an impartial manner so that they would gain the confidence of the management."[52] Statistics on the handling of grievances bear out Gephart's optimism. Out of 298 Great Lakes grievances recorded by the EFC, craft or joint committees settled 227 within the yards and resolved another 49, following appeals, in a second round of joint shop committee conferences.[53] District procedure thus made union officials formally eligible to participate in only 22 of these 298 disputes.

Shortly after the April 1918 award introducing shop committees, Great Lakes shipyard employers protested the scheme as a violation of open shop principles. As implemented by Fisher, Pitt, and Gephart, however, employ-

ee representation proved to be a successful compromise between unreconstructed employers and union leaders intent on using wartime power to win
a formal place in local industrial relations. Employers' objections vanished
by the August SLAB hearings on the Great Lakes, and fifteen of twenty-two
shipbuilding firms had committees in place at the end of the year. Most companies expected to continue these arrangements after the SLAB lapsed.[54]
Energetic and imaginative local examiners deserve some of the credit for this
success in reforming open shops amid growing union mobilization, but the
Great Lakes shop committee plan was not primarily the personal triumph
of Fisher or Pitt. The policies they adopted buttressed the authority of the
examiner's office as well as the independence of shop committees. In his
insistence that grievances go through shop committees, Fisher also sought
to prevent unions from bypassing his own office and appealing directly to
SLAB officials in Washington. In one such case Hotchkiss noted Fisher's
charge that Krieps was "deliberately setting out to break the authority of the
examiner's office," adding, "Fisher is very much aroused on this subject."[55]
Fisher himself emphasized the link between his own authority and that of
his shop committees. Short-circuiting the procedure for handling disputes,
he reminded Seager, would "inevitably [break] down the position of these
committees in the yards and the influence of the Examiner's office."[56] The
link between the examiner's authority and shop committee independence
is also suggested in Fisher's and Pitt's successful efforts to have the EFC pay
joint shop committee members for attending meetings (a policy not observed
in other districts). Such payments, issued directly by Pitt, further distanced
committees from unions and made them, in Pitt's words, more like a "judi-
cial body" acting on behalf of the examiner's office.[57] This preoccupation with
the institutional standing of the SLAB examiner was one important mechanism that filtered general national guidelines into particular local policies for
employee representation.

     In their determination to free shop committees and grievance procedures
from "partisan" unions, Great Lakes examiners sometimes clashed with
national SLAB officials. Fisher resigned at the end of September and Pitt did
so in December; issues surrounding employee representation played a role
in each case.[58] Everit Macy, Albert Berres, Hotchkiss, and Seager were all less
dogmatic than Fisher in refusing union officials a hearing before grievance
procedures had run their course. They accepted the rule as sound, but they
also urged Fisher not to antagonize union leaders needlessly.[59] Similar frictions developed between Pitt and his Washington superiors. Having won the
statement that craft committees could not call in outside representatives, Pitt
vehemently opposed Seager's recommendation that he not force the point.
Doing so, Seager argued, might actually "crystallize the local opposition to

shop committees" on the part of unions.[60] But here, too, local conditions proved to be decisive in shaping policy. Seager and Macy accepted Pitt's plan as the standard for handling Great Lakes shipbuilding conflicts. The recommendation that the local examiner occasionally make diplomatic concessions to union leaders, Seager and Macy reassured Pitt, was intended only to preserve the essentials of his plan.[61] George Gephart, succeeding Pitt as the key EFC labor relations representative in the Great Lakes area, continued the same approach to employee representation.[62] Its persistence across three examiners and in the face of occasional skepticism on the part of national officials clearly demonstrates the weight of local industrial relations conditions (rather than local personalities) on government policy.

Before the SLAB shut down on March 31, 1919, EFC officials urged shipbuilders throughout the country to develop some alternative arbitration procedures in consultation with unions. The model recommended by the EFC and first adopted by the Bethlehem Shipbuilding Company replaced the board with an adjustment committee composed of five union officials appointed by the AFL Metal Trades Department (MTD) and five company representatives. The Bethlehem agreement continued existing wages and working conditions unless union-company conferences agreed on changes, and it maintained shipyard committees "in the same manner as provided for" in the SLAB awards.[63] EFC investigators found the Great Lakes Engineering Works and several smaller concerns in the area to be adamantly opposed to any such agreement with unions. EFC director Charles Piez was more successful in persuading American Shipbuilding Company president Farr to meet with MTD officials, and conferences yielded an agreement on April 8. The agreement closely resembled the Bethlehem model in establishing a joint committee of MTD and company appointees who would be the final arbiters of disputes.[64] Having insisted on an open shop even during the war, the company thus appeared to embrace unions in 1919—the year San Francisco employers began moving toward a break with the ITC.

Great Lakes union lodges found no reason to celebrate the agreement, however. Local IAM officials complained that their members at the American Shipbuilding Company's Cleveland yard "were ridiculed by the non-union men," adding that "it is next to impossible to organize the men at that plant." Boilermakers' representatives voiced similar criticisms and "claimed that the agreement was . . . not at all a union agreement."[65] From the standpoint of Great Lakes union organizers, these were valid objections. In most respects the agreement maintained the same restrictions on local unionism that examiners had imposed, merely substituting for the SLAB a committee of national AFL and company officials. Local unionists had been largely excluded from negotiation of the agreement from the start. When Bathurst invited shipyard owners to meet in March to discuss some new framework for settling disputes, Gephart advised him that employers would not do so and that, in any case, the proposal was mooted by negotiations between the MTD and the American Shipbuilding Company.[66] The formation of the company-union arbitration board also took place above the heads of local unionists. The MTD merely notified district officials and requested their "cooperation."[67] In the particulars of the agreement, finally, local lodges faced the same obstacles as they had under Fisher and Pitt. Shop committee elections still had to take place within the plant, and they still had to be open to union and nonunion voters alike. The agreement also continued to make joint shop committees the key agency within the yards for handling disputes, with unresolved grievances bypassing local lodges in favor of conferences between company and MTD delegates.[68]

The American Shipbuilding Company's agreement with the MTD, then, hardly represented an unqualified endorsement of unions, a point President Farr emphasized when he briefed company directors on negotiations with the AFL.[69] This accommodation with national union officials at the expense of local ones was in any case both opportunistic and short-lived. The EFC's recommendation that shipbuilders come to terms with the MTD carried considerable weight, coming as it did from the only buyer of steel ships. Unlike most Bay Area builders, moreover, the American Shipbuilding Company did government work on a cost-plus basis, and the company made sure that EFC auditors approved its arrangements with the MTD.[70] Once these incentives disappeared, so did the American Shipbuilding Company's interest in dealing with national unions. "On March 11, 1920," President Farr informed company directors, "at approximately the same time the last ship under contract for the Emergency Fleet Corporation was ready for dock trial, the agreement with the Metal Trades Department . . . [was] terminated." By contrast, the firm's enthusiasm for SLAB shop committees remained keen. After reporting his break with the MTD, Farr went on to announce that "a shop committee plan . . . similar to the plan provided for in the agreement . . . was being installed in the several plants."[71] The companies that had refused to deal with the MTD shared this commitment to the SLAB employee representation plan. The largest of these, the Great Lakes Engineering Works, assured Gephart that they "had great faith in their ability to control the situation through the Committees."[72]

The SLAB's reorganization of employee representation helped to turn back the key challenges to employers' unilateral control of shipyard labor relations. Those challenges came above all from developments in the labor movement that wartime economic conditions and government protections made possible: closer cooperation among metal trades unions, greater leverage for craft union officials, and the spread of workplace organization. The effect of government policies was not just to limit these developments but also to dislocate them. The EFC kept more encompassing labor institutions (citywide lodges, industrywide councils, regional bodies) and workplace organization relatively independent of one another.

This was easily done in the case of organizations such as the Cleveland and Great Lakes metal trades councils. The potential impact of such institutions was enormous. They could have provided Cleveland workers with substantial resources, including mutual support in disputes, coordinated leadership, and finances pooled over a larger membership and a wider area. With these resources workers might have made better use of their wartime bargaining power and resisted employers' postwar counterattacks more effectively. Although the SLAB reinforced the powers of San Francisco's ITC, it almost entirely excluded comparable Great Lakes organizations from deciding and administering awards. These policies helped to keep the various joint councils anemic throughout the war. The most ambitious of them, the Great Lakes District Allied Shipbuilders' Council, got too late a start to make any real contribution to labor relations or worker protest. Cleveland's Metal Trades Council had a longer life, but it remained more a meeting ground for a handful of trade union leaders than a vital center of Cleveland's labor movement.[73] Lack of interest in the council reflected not only its limited functions (limits the government reinforced by largely ignoring the body) but also its remoteness from workers in the plants and yards. Metal Trades Council officials seem never to have contested SLAB procedures in which shop committees and the examiner handled grievances. When the IAM representative lobbied council colleagues about the dismissal of a prominent member by the American Shipbuilding Company, council members could reply only "that this was a matter for the joint shop committee to discuss." In another case J. P. McWeeny, the Cleveland business agent for the Boilermakers' union, criticized the council for being remiss in establishing machinery to handle shipyard grievances.[74] EFC policies, then, helped to ensure that the Cleveland Metal Trades Council would remain relatively isolated and powerless. A more effective council would not have guaranteed militant leadership; San Francisco's ITC was powerful but conservative. However, the weakness of new union institutions in Cleveland did mean that more aggressive activists had no institutional base of the kind provided by East Bay unions and the Alameda Metal Trades Council.

Individual craft unions fared better. These made far greater progress than metal trades councils and won considerably more influence with the EFC. National SLAB administrators in particular proved to be willing to accommodate local union officials on an ad hoc basis if this would avert conflict.

Nonetheless, Great Lakes SLAB policies limited union involvement in plant-level industrial relations and kept workplace organization as far as possible under examiner rather than union control. In the best-organized cities (Chicago, Superior, and Duluth) Boilermakers' unionists succeeded in controlling craft committee elections, in some cases even ignoring the requirement that voting take place away from union halls. The frequent protests of union officials, however, testify to their tenuous influence with committees elsewhere. Furthermore, if they resorted to elections at union meetings to ensure union representation, local EFC representatives stood ready to order new elections or refuse to meet with improperly constituted committees.[75]

The joint shop committees that anchored shipyard labor relations were still more insulated from union control, combining representatives of nonunion as well as unionized occupations. Even in strongly organized Chicago, unionists gave up on the Chicago Shipbuilding Company's joint shop committee. Boilermakers' officials ordered their members off the committee, and a nonunionist who remained reported that workers belonging to "this organization were no longer taking an interest in the Joint Shop Committee and were planning to take up all of their cases with the Examiner through the Business Agent of the Union."[76] Fisher frustrated their efforts to do so, however, refusing to discuss grievances with union delegates until they had been invited into conferences by the joint shop committee itself. Looking forward to the end of the SLAB, unionists could see that even this small opening for union involvement might be closed. As Pitt recognized, they had good reason to fear that "the operation of the joint shop committee . . . [would] prove detrimental to their interests" when the SLAB disbanded.[77] Certainly Pitt's successor, George Gephart, applied his energies in this direction. In the one case (the Toledo Shipbuilding Company) where a joint shop committee clearly pursued union interests, he criticized their "partisan action" and willingness "to give favorable consideration to every grievance coming before it": "They seem to conceive their function to be that of upholding the rights of the men exclusively. . . . Our problem until April 1st is to rid them of this feeling."[78] Gephart accordingly applauded the action of another joint shop committee in electing to work on Saturday afternoons despite Bathurst's efforts to enforce the half-holiday.[79] Local union officials had the same frustrations with the committees and procedures established by the American Shipbuilding Company and the AFL's MTD.

Great Lakes SLAB examiners thus organized representation strictly on the basis of workers' roles as company employees, not as members of unions. Shop committees similarly served as instruments for adjudicating disputes between employees and management rather than articulating and defending "selfish" class interests. In these ways the SLAB's shop committee scheme provided a bridge to postwar stability. In terms of industrial relations, district policies made union officials' influence dependent on SLAB administrators, and the examiners' rigid insistence on procedure limited union involvement in labor relations within the yards. With the end of the SLAB in March 1919 and of the MTD agreement a year later, local unions' limited influence and tenuous roots became obvious. The same system for separating union leaders from shipyard labor relations also contained labor protest by isolating shipbuilding workers from outside support. As Fisher and Pitt intended, routine procedures for handling grievances eliminated union intermediaries from employee-management conferences.[80] There is no clear evidence that these arrangements actively attached worker loyalties to their employers. But the distance created between employees and unifying labor institutions outside the yards meant that where grievances went unsettled, protest would be fragmented, if it developed at all. The SLAB shop committee scheme thus put employers' traditional methods of fighting unions, including paternalistic concessions to isolated employee groups, on more solid ground.

Labor unions and worker militancy were in retreat all around the country by late 1919, and the collapse of Cleveland's labor movement in particular cannot be traced to specific SLAB policies. Nonetheless, the success of government policies in isolating local union leadership may help to explain the remarkable speed with which union gains disappeared. IAM lodge officials began fretting over membership losses as early as January 1919. They also linked their declining fortunes to the atrophy of union influence in the workplace, offering bounties to shop stewards who brought in new members and establishing a committee in October 1920 "to try and revive the shop steward movement."[81] The exclusion of unions from workplace industrial relations and the isolation of rank-and-file organization from city- or industrywide union institutions also shaped patterns of labor protest. Shipbuilding workers repeatedly struck en masse in the Bay Area. In many cases all employees of a given firm went out as one; on several occasions strikes paralyzed the entire shipbuilding industry, most "outside" shops, or both sectors together. Labor disputes in Great Lakes shipbuilding centers such as Cleveland were much more fragmented. Of twenty-one known Great Lakes shipbuilding strikes between 1916 and 1920, eleven were confined to single departments (e.g., a boiler shop) or trades (e.g., riveters) at individual shipyards. Out of the remaining ten disputes, only two involved more than a single shipyard. One of these two brought out only riveters at the nearby Cleveland and Lorain yards; the other took place at shipyards in Chicago, Duluth, and Superior—strong union towns by Great Lakes standards—and occurred before the SLAB assumed control.[82]

For obvious geographic reasons, it was harder to mobilize general strikes in the Great Lakes than it was in the Bay Area, but several Great Lakes cities, including Cleveland, had two or more yards in close proximity. Moreover, facilities separated by distance were often linked by common ownership (eight yards belonged to American Shipbuilding and three to Great Lakes Engineering). The limited coordination of labor unrest across workplaces and occupations had less to do with geography than with industrial relations institutions. Joint shop committees sometimes played a direct role in preventing disputes from erupting into strikes or spreading to other yards. During a walkout in July 1919, the committee at Great Lakes Engineering's Ecorse shipyard joined management in posting a notice reading, "We, the members of the Shop Committee, wish the men to live up to the agreement," and most workers complied.[83] McDougall-Duluth's committee made a similar appeal to striking ship painters in April 1920, urging them to take up their grievances "in the regular manner with management."[84] Even in the absence of such specific appeals, the institutionalization of union-free labor relations at individual shipyards closed off opportunities for union militants to mobilize support. The contrast to the Bay Area, where rebellious union leaders defied national authority on the basis of broad and cohesive popular support, could hardly be more striking. In February 1920 members of the Cleveland Metal Trades Council launched yet another campaign, hoping that by organizing workers they could improve and standardize working conditions and "prevent sporadic and unauthorized strikes and the scandalous labor 'turnover' that is so prevalent in some shops."[85] Here, as in the Great Lakes generally, the attempt was no more successful than past efforts had been.

SUMMARY: LABOR PROTEST AND LABOR POLICY IN SHIPBUILDING

Comparing Bay Area and Great Lakes shipbuilding serves two major purposes. The first is to show how wartime labor militancy shaped government strategies for industrial relations reform. The second, pushing this analysis one step back, is to demonstrate how the structure of prewar class relations in local industry influenced both labor mobilization and state policy. This second goal makes the shipbuilding case studies especially useful, for here were two centers of the same industry, under the same federal regulatory agency, but entering the war with very different backgrounds.

Shipbuilding depended on skilled labor from many trades, but yards in a position to concentrate on a few standard vessels could adopt specialized equipment and make use of less-experienced workers on some of the more routine operations. Great Lakes shipbuilders moved further in this direction before World War I than did those in the Bay Area. Metal trades firms outside the shipyards mirrored this contrast in production methods. Cleveland's automobile plants and high volume manufacturers of auto parts employed a less-skilled labor force than did the small machine shops and heavy equipment producers that dominated Bay Area metal trades.

The power of skilled workers extended from the workplace into the labor movement, industrial relations, and politics.[86] The sheer density of union organization in San Francisco far surpassed that in Cleveland. No less important, San Francisco workers had developed effective organizations for coordinating action across occupations and workplaces. The ITC linked workers and union officials in different crafts and varied sectors of the metal trades, while less-skilled metal workers joined the organized labor movement through membership in the Shipyard Laborers' Union and the ITC in the year before the United States entered World War I. Cleveland machine trades workers, by contrast, began 1917 with neither common organization nor traditions of joint action. The city's Metal Trades Council had few members and little influence; workers of distinct shipbuilding crafts, if they unionized or struck at all, did so apart from other shipbuilding crafts or metal tradesmen from outside the yards. Municipal politics and ethnic relations reinforced these differences in the character of city labor movements. San Francisco's electoral politics and binary racial divisions mobilized white working-class voters as a unified block. Greater ethnic diversity, together with the early arrival of Progressive politics in Cleveland, had the opposite effects: electoral coalitions cut across class lines, and the language of municipal reform further neutralized labor's independent political influence. Contrasting patterns of union organization and political mobilization, finally, went hand in hand with different employer strategies. Metal trades employers in both Cleveland and the Bay Area were well organized, and the Cleveland Chamber of Commerce and the California Metal Trades Association standardized labor policies among their respective members. Cleveland employers stood together in defending open shops and unilateral management control of plant labor relations. Their San Francisco counterparts, unable to defeat unions, regulated labor relations through industrywide collective bargaining and trade agreements.

Shipbuilding workers in Cleveland and the Bay Area thus entered World War I bearing different resources and facing different obstacles. Bay Area workers could build on their strengths—powerful unions, joint organization, and conciliatory employers—to take advantage of war conditions. Their very strength, however, created a large and visible gap between what seemed to be within their reach and what the government and national union executives would concede. In Cleveland the war instead gave workers opportunities to begin constructing institutions that their San Francisco counterparts took for granted. Government intervention also introduced conditions, such as job classifications and protections against discrimination, that the men could not have won unaided. Their main obstacle at first was neither their government nor their union leaders but instead employers' continuing refusal to recognize or bargain with unions.

Patterns of wartime labor mobilization developed out of this mix of prewar precedents and initial government policies. Craft and even skill boundaries had been bridged in San Francisco by early 1917, and Bay Area workers sustained remarkable solidarity throughout the war—as demonstrated in the September and December 1917 strikes. Institutions that united workers across craft and geographic lines, notably the ITC, the Alameda Metal Trades Council, and the Boilermakers' Pacific Coast District, played the leading roles in wartime labor mobilization. Comparable institutions in Cleveland and Great Lakes shipbuilding were either impotent or nonexistent. Instead labor organization there proceeded (slowly) along the sectional lines laid down before the war. This organizational setting, rather than any clear differences in ideological commitment to working-class solidarity, accounts for the atomistic character of Great Lakes labor protest. By the middle of 1918, however, labor mobilization in *both* cases threatened industrial relations stability. In the Bay Area the hitherto less-organized East Bay emerged as a hotbed for new unions and locals. East Bay workers were especially hostile to the government's insistence on "existing conditions." Their newly minted organizations (Boilermakers' Lodge 233, the Shipyard Laborers' Union, and the Alameda Metal Trades Council) provided the base for militant leaders and undermined trade agreements between the California Metal Trades Association and responsible union leadership—the keys both to prewar industrial relations stability and to the SLAB's initial efforts to keep the peace. The limited development of institutional alternatives to craft unions in Cleveland kept the labor left much more isolated. Still, trade union growth and workplace organization in Great Lakes shipyards challenged the open shop by making it more difficult for employers to insulate plant labor relations and labor unrest from "outside" control and coordination.

Both the character of these crises and the opportunities that industrial relations traditions made available to government administrators structured their efforts to restore order. EFC officials in each case relied on national union executives to discipline uncooperative locals or members. The SLAB had been established by agreement with these executives, and the government insisted that they live up to their obligations. SLAB strategies for securing industrial peace went well beyond these expedients, however. The SLAB also revamped labor relations practices to achieve more lasting stability, and here government policies sharply diverged. The approach to Bay Area unrest involved reinforcing the ability of responsible local unions to counter insurgent movements. New procedures for handling grievances empowered the ITC as well as national union leaders while disfranchising East Bay militants. SLAB administrators in the Great Lakes took the opposite tack, decentralizing bargaining and decision making. They established employee committees unaffiliated with unions and made them (rather than union officials) the responsible agencies for handling disputes. Doing so blocked union control of rank-and-file organization and unrest (rather than strengthening it, as in San Francisco) and fortified management hegemony at work.

Government reforms in employee representation, then, corresponded to local industrial conditions and conflicts. They also proved to be effective, at least in the short run. By the fall of 1919 San Francisco's central labor organizations had reintegrated rebellious locals, and negotiations with employers promised a new local agreement. Government support for the central labor bodies and for orderly collective bargaining assisted these developments. In the Great Lakes area joint organization among shipyard workers in 1919 was little more developed and had little more influence over yard labor relations than it did before the war. Craft unions had many more members, but their ties to workplace organization remained tenuous, particularly in the case of the new joint shop committees. Local SLAB policies deserve much of the credit for these outcomes. The system of employee representation and procedures for handling unrest, introduced by SLAB and EFC officials over the initial opposition of employers, prevented metal trades councils and craft lodges from establishing roots in the yards or control over plant labor relations. When war conditions passed, union organization quickly withered.

Government policies thus looked to enhance union-management control of workplace labor relations as the basis for restabilization in the Bay Area, whereas Great Lakes administrators sought to give open shops a more secure foundation by elaborating nonunion mechanisms for employee representation. In neither case were these patterns of restabilization fully realized. Organized Bay Area employers, including the large shipbuilders, repudiated their agreement with the ITC and declared for open shops. The biggest Great Lakes shipbuilder broke ranks with other metal trades employers and agreed to work with the AFL's MTD in setting working conditions and handling disputes. The break with wartime strategies for containing labor unrest in the Great Lakes area was more apparent than real, however. American Shipbuilding Company directors, acting to accommodate their only buyer, did so only until they had fulfilled their contracts, and it had the MTD play the same role as the SLAB in keeping local unions out of workplace industrial relations. The final outcome was not a reversal of roles by Bay Area and Great Lakes shipbuilders so much as a movement by San Francisco yards toward the "American" norm.

Changing political conditions both locally and nationally were decisive in Bay Area shipyards' turn from trade agreements to open shops. Employers had ample reason to doubt the value of trade agreements at a time when the centralized union controls needed to make those agreements work had broken down. They also had an alternative model of labor relations—open shops tempered with welfare capitalism—urged on them by a growing national movement for the American Plan. It was the new political setting, however, that made a *successful* open shop drive possible. Locally labor's political clout had waned since before the war, a fact obscured by unions' extraordinary wartime economic leverage. Having abandoned independent labor politics for an alliance with middle-class Progressives, unions became vulnerable when Progressive allies deserted them politically and employers attacked them at work. A similar dynamic at the national level may have contributed to the EFC's turn against unions in late 1919. In federal as in San Francisco politics, the coalition of Progressives and moderate unions lost coherence and influence after the 1918 election. As prolabor voices in the Wilson administration weakened, it may have been easier for EFC officials such as Charles Piez to take a hard line against the strongest union shipbuilding centers (Seattle in January and San Francisco in September 1919). By refusing concessions on wages, the EFC precipitated the Bay Area strike; by their rhetoric and their complicity with employer claims that no wage hikes would be permitted, EFC officials encouraged employers to make their break with unions.

The move by Bay Area owners toward their Great Lake counterparts in excluding unions from shipyard labor relations thus mirrors national changes in state policy and political alignments. Wartime labor insurgency, by heightening class tensions, helped break up the Progressive-labor alliance that had supported relatively pro-union policies. And in San Francisco, even more than at the federal level, the shift in the political center of gravity away from labor led to visible and dramatic reversals of fortune in industrial relations. The development of labor insurgency and government policy in San Francisco and the Great Lakes may highlight distinctive local class relations, but the final outcomes bring national political dynamics back to center stage.

Conclusion: Employee Representation and Restabilization

Nine months after the American declaration of war, *Iron Age* alerted its readers to the growing power of "the radical, the mercenary, and the unpatriotic elements of labor."[1] The problem, W. H. Barr reminded National Metal Trades Association delegates in April 1918, was not merely the "drift among labor unionists towards socialism." "Socialists are so thick in Washington," too, "that you cannot help but stumble over them."[2] In fact, many government officials shared Barr's anxiety. An investigator for the United States Shipping Board was not unusual in reporting efforts by "agitators" in Portland, Oregon, to organize "Soldiers [*sic*] and Workmen's Organizations . . . a sort of Bolsheviki movement."[3] Amid rampant strikes and demands for far-reaching changes in industrial governance, elites in the United States, like those abroad, feared the worst. Their fears proved to be greatly exaggerated for several reasons. Among them was the emergence of a new industrial relations order by the early 1920s that helped to secure management authority and discipline labor conflict. A major tributary of that new order, I have argued, flowed from government efforts to resolve the wartime labor crisis. And reforms in the structure of employee representation were a key element in both state strategies and postwar stability.

America's distinctive resolution of wartime upheavals emerges most clearly against the contrasting experiences of Germany and Britain. Postwar industrial relations in the latter cases made unions a bulwark against excessive worker demands and unconstitutional strikes, with union authority backed by the state in Germany and by voluntary agreements in Britain. American employers organized labor relations on the assumption that unions, not their own workers, were the paramount threat. Employee representation reforms followed these different agendas. In all three cases progressive employers and reform-minded politicians endorsed shop committees as solutions for labor strife and economic inefficiency, but the organization of workplace harmony took sharply divergent forms. Germany's government required works councils in most establishments and subordinated them to unions, whereas in Britain collective bargaining agreements placed shop stewards and works committees under joint union-management control. Employers in the United States took care that employee representation excluded "outside agitators," whether federal bureaucrats or union officials. All three schemes countered wartime challenges by upholding basic management prerogatives and limiting opportunities for "irresponsible" action.

Using these cases as a comparative backdrop, I highlight the role of America's wartime government in reforming employee representation and, by that means, fostering postwar stability. I do so in part 1 with reference to Germany and Britain. In response to wartime labor unrest, legislation and military decrees in Germany imposed union-controlled councils on recalcitrant employers; the revolutionary government then made works councils the centerpiece of Weimar industrial relations. The British Ministries of Munitions and Labour worked toward similar ends through the medium of collective bargaining. The government actively (and in major industries successfully) pressed employers and unions themselves to systematize and jointly regulate employee representation. As for the United States, there is little in wartime labor policy to support Barr's charge that socialists ruled Washington. The National War Labor Board promoted shop committees as a means to represent employees and handle grievances on a nonunion basis, and its elaboration of a rule of law in open shops proved to be highly influential after the armistice. Closer examination of federal intervention, however, shows that other agencies met worker insurgency in different ways. For railroad shops and some major shipbuilding centers, the government followed a more "European" strategy of bolstering union authority over shop floor worker organization and labor relations.

Two themes run through my account of government strategies. First, I stress the legacies of prewar class relations. There were in each case distinctive tensions between the industrial or political status quo and the demands of total war, tensions expressed both in the nature of wartime labor upheavals and the opportunities available for restabilization. Second, I combine national and industry comparisons to identify a particular configuration of political and industrial relations forces driving U.S. policy.

The first national comparison pairs the United States with Germany and focuses attention on political dynamics. If we view the war crisis "from be-low," we see that wartime labor insurgency in the United States posed nei-ther the political demands nor the threat to government stability seen in Germany, with its statist traditions and class-based constitutional regime. Taking the view "from above," the collapse of Wilson's Progressive-labor alliance and the sharp rightward shift in the political center of gravity late in 1918 contrast with the rise of a liberal–Social Democratic Party (Sozial-demokratische Partei Deutschlands, or SPD) coalition in 1916 and its dom-inant position after the revolution. Only the latter balance of political pow-er supported a corporatist resolution of the crisis in employee representation. Comparing these cases also calls attention to the political position of employ-ers. U.S. business leaders not only confronted a lesser threat from below; particularly after the 1918 election, they could also rely on a sympathetic Congress and judiciary, which heavy industry in revolutionary Germany could not do. U.S. employers enjoyed a strategic position that allowed them the luxury of sloppy thinking: they could lump together the American Fed-eration of Labor, Industrial Workers of the World, and socialists of all kinds as an undifferentiated Bolshevik menace rather than distinguish between "responsible" union allies and enemies to the left. By late 1918 the needs of many German employers and dominant political actors (especially the mil-itary and the SPD) converged in support of union control over employee representation as an antidote to the council movement. The United States saw neither the autonomous rank-and-file movement nor the coincidence of in-terests between employers and political elites that elsewhere favored corpo-ratist reform of employee representation.

These conclusions mirror those in comparative studies of worker control movements and restabilization in Europe.[4] The larger part of this study, by contrast, argues for the independent influence of prior labor relations on wartime government policy. Juxtaposing the cases of Britain and the Unit-ed States highlights two different dynamics of labor mobilization and gov-ernment response. Britain entered the war with craft unions firmly en-trenched in manufacturing practices and collective bargaining agreements, leaving the government little choice but to enlist union officials in efforts to speed production and curb strikes. All too often union members would have none of it. Particularly in engineering, they repudiated their executives and relied on "unofficial" organization and leaders to defend their interests. American employers before the war generally organized the labor process and industrial relations without regard for union work rules or representa-tives. Government administrators in turn were under much less pressure to intervene in work practices or to assign to union leaders responsibility for carrying out wartime labor policy. In this setting unions retained much of their legitimacy and freedom of action. Labor mobilization could proceed under "official" auspices, particularly at the local level, and high on workers' agenda were employer recognition of union work rules and collective bargaining rights—a pattern reinforced by America's late entry into the war. With different labor relations histories went differences in the wartime crisis. British trade agreements and U.S. open shops were well-established solutions for the common problems of defending management prerogatives and containing strikes.[5] Wartime insurgency undermined both solutions. In Britain unofficial movements jeopardized the union authority and formal agreements on which the government, like prewar employers, relied to manage labor relations. Workplace labor organization under local union control put America's open shop order at risk. Craft unions gained leverage over work practices, employees acquired the institutional resources for broader collective action, and "irresponsible" leaders won new opportunities for popular influence.

These contrasting industrial relations crises, rather than political alignments or state stability, best account for British and U.S. measures to restore order. The argument is strengthened by comparisons among U.S. industries. Differences in prewar labor relations between railroad shop crafts and munitions production or between San Francisco and Great Lakes shipbuilding parallel those between Britain and the United States more generally. Government policies followed suit, as legacies from before the war defined the nature of the problems, the dispositions of employers, and the opportunities for reform. For the Ministry of Munitions and for labor administrators in American railroads and Bay Area shipbuilding, the problem appeared to be one of local defiance of union authority; in the munitions industry and around the Great Lakes, the challenge was to curb unrest while honoring the open shop. And much as Germany's political situation led industrialists to make common cause with unions against revolution, so British and San Francisco employers relied on unions in defense against more rebellious bodies. Labor militancy at odds with local union organization was more the exception than the rule in the United States, however, and few managers regarded unions as allies against disorder. Having raised the alarm over "the radical, the mercenary, and the unpatriotic elements of labor," Walter Drew went on to emphasize that unions offered neither "control [nor] responsibility."[6] They were, instead, the heart of the problem.

Prewar industrial relations bequeathed potential solutions as well as distinctive problems. Government reforms of employee representation built on and rationalized strategies already employed prior to 1914. In key British industries, in U.S. railroads, and in San Francisco shipbuilding, this meant strengthening union control over workplace labor organizations, bargaining,

and grievance procedures—shoring up a regime of trade agreements threatened by unofficial movements. The NWLB and Great Lakes administrators,
by contrast, elaborated shop committee plans that curbed some of the worst
abuses of existing open shops, putting nonunion workplace representation
and labor relations on firmer ground.[7]

These political and industrial relations influences on state policy, separated by juxtaposing the U.S. first with Germany and then with Britain, come
back together as the focus shifts from cross-sectional comparisons to dia-
chronic analysis of the United States alone. The Wilsonian electoral coalition,
even more than America's characteristic lack of administrative coherence,
opened up an unusually broad range of policy options. Until the end of 1918
intervention on behalf of labor became a realistic political possibility. As
Melvyn Dubofsky and others point out, wartime measures such as setting
minimum wages, defending workers' right to join unions, and disciplining
rogue employers demonstrated labor's new influence in government.[8] Over
the brief time that political alignments expanded possibilities, however, it
was labor relations conditions in specific war industries that determined
which possibility would be realized. And the outcomes were not as generally supportive of unions as some historians have argued,[9] particularly in
the role that state administrators assigned to unions in representing employees. The United States Railroad Administration gave shop craft unions (and
especially their national leaders) a virtual monopoly on the tasks of handling
disputes, negotiating national and local agreements, and implementing
awards. The Shipbuilding Labor Adjustment Board (SLAB) did much the
same in San Francisco. NWLB decisions and SLAB examiners for Great Lakes
shipbuilding, by contrast, followed a different tack. They certainly improved
basic standards and curbed autocratic and abusive employer behavior, but
they also ratified and fortified the open shop. Unions won no formal role in
procedures for dealing with grievances, bargaining with employers, or administering decisions. The government assigned these tasks instead to committees of employees that excluded "outside" representatives and had no
right of appeal to union officers.

Ultimately this proved to be the "typical" direction of industrial relations
reform in the United States. Within a year of the armistice, many Bay Area
shipbuilders turned to the open shop with the tacit support of Emergency
Fleet Corporation executives. Among the shop crafts, the postwar Railroad
Labor Board sanctioned a retreat from industrywide bargaining and allowed
half the industry to repudiate organized labor altogether, often in favor of
company unions. The government's refusal to parry open shop drives even
in industries where it once actively supported union authority demonstrated a return to political normalcy after 1918. Political alignments once again

marginalized organized labor and left business influence in the federal government uncontested, as shown most clearly in the staffing and partisanship of the Railroad Labor Board.

The causal weights of political coalitions and labor relations legacies vary too much over time to sustain generalizations about the origins of state policy. At least for the war period, however, my account sides with "class-centered" theories, discounting the independent role of the state in two ways. First, electoral alignments and administrative fragmentation can account for the fact that wartime policies varied; they cannot explain why specific policies took effect in particular industries.[10] Second, the varied and at times chaotic character of war labor policy evidently had less to do with the American state's administrative underdevelopment—a major focus of state-centered theories[11]—than with the electoral balance of power. When the latter shifted back to the right, minimizing labor's national political influence, variations in employee representation policies largely disappeared. To give my historical account a theoretical gloss, one can say that features of the state permitted alternative policies, but class relations in particular settings selected specific outcomes from among these alternatives. The government had consistent interests of its own, to be sure, above all in speeding war production and curbing strikes. As the government entered particular industrial settings, however, each with its distinctive balance of power embedded in work practices and labor relations, different policies proved to be best suited to meeting government interests.

Two other views of the state and labor, more historiographical than theoretical in character, require rethinking in the light of this case study. Wartime states are commonly thought to act with an energy and autonomy far surpassing peacetime norms. In this they seem to conform to familiar arguments in state theory. Fred Block, for example, argues that the independent power of the state is greatest during crises such as depressions and wars, when working-class pressure waxes and capitalist veto power wanes. Engels, too, made state neutrality an exception associated with periods of more or less evenly matched class struggle.[12] It is certainly true that World War I augmented the power of governments. In the arena of industrial relations policy, however, U.S. state autonomy diminished during the war. Political alignments, administrative arrangements, and an ad hoc, fire-fighting approach to labor unrest all made the government *more* responsive to existing balances of power between labor and capital.[13] The heightened responsiveness of state policy to the pulling and hauling of workers and employers is in turn a useful reminder that distinctions between "rank and filism" and state- (or employer-) centered accounts are unprofitable.[14] What best explains the varying state reforms of wartime work relations is neither the state itself nor rank-and-file protest. It is instead the character and organization of struggles between workers and employers.

Long-standing inequalities of power embedded in labor relations, combined with the sharp rightward shift in national politics, ensured that non-union employee representation would be the most lasting of wartime reforms. Although my focus is more on the origins of government policy than on its impact, the case studies warrant some more speculative conclusions about restabilization after the upheavals of war. Employee representation reforms helped to stabilize industrial relations by rationalizing management control and balkanizing labor protest. In both respects government policies showed the way.

Late in 1917 a report on the rapid progress of employment managers' associations extolled the movement as "a good deal more broad minded and democratic than getting together chiefly to condemn and combat unions." The author argued that more systematic personnel management, by "enlightening selfishness," would "undoubtedly serve to improve the . . . conditions of employment" and thus make unions less attractive to employees.[15] This was a hope widely shared from World War I through the 1920s.[16] The movement to put the "handling of men" on a more scientific basis included, among much else, efforts to replace arbitrary supervision with more rule-bound exercise of authority. It also endorsed formal procedures for airing and adjudicating grievances, thus "making the employee really feel that he is getting a square deal."[17] Enlightened selfishness, finally, often dictated that employees be given regular opportunities and institutions for raising concerns and discussing conditions ("collective bargaining" is too strong a term) with management. Such arrangements for in-house consultation were probably the least-common component in plans to rationalize workplace authority. Even so, company unions—the most elaborate version of these schemes—would account for one-third of "organized" American workers by the mid-1920s.[18] Prewar open shop employers often proclaimed a similar commitment to "the square deal." Wartime experience with labor and government intervention, however, led many more firms to adopt enlightened management techniques, and the momentum continued well into the 1920s. Where implemented with some consistency and a semblance of good faith, these reforms seem to have assuaged workers' resentments of "unfair" (i.e., arbitrary or inequitable) and "un-American" (i.e., abusive or autocratic) management practices.[19] In addition, more rule-bound employer authority rendered industry safer for the kinds of "industrial democracy" practiced by progressive businesses in the 1920s.

Wartime government intervention in employee representation fostered this accommodation in two ways. First, shop committee plans introduced by the NWLB typically called not only for in-plant bargaining but also for other components of a workplace rule of law, notably grievance procedures, checks on capricious supervision, and rights of appeal over foremen. In this they served as models for more enlightened open shop management. In chapter 2 I note that employers were not always willing pupils. Their initial responses to wartime demands for union recognition and union shop committees commonly involved sanctimonious announcements that they were "always willing to meet with aggrieved employers," and nothing more. Herein lies the government's second contribution. Federally sponsored shop committees forced recalcitrant employers to go beyond noblesse oblige (and the minimum concessions required to fulfill war contracts), but they also spared open shop managers the obligation to include unions in the workplace rule of law, and this compromise proved to be acceptable to most employers under siege from organized labor. What began as a grudging compromise was often retained after the war, when management, not federal administrators, became the last court of appeal for industrial jurisprudence.

The organization of workplace authority, grievance procedures, and representation without "external" union involvement also contributed to a balkanization of labor conflict and thus to a wider industrial relations stability in the 1920s, making industry safer for democracy in a second sense. Nonunion employee representation clearly did not prevent disputes, but it did help to isolate protest from outside support, leadership, and coordination. Strike patterns after the war bear the imprint of different employee representation arrangements. In Britain union responsibility for workplace representation curbed "unofficial" movements but also increased the "average" scope of conflicts that did break out. The proportion of disputes engaging entire industries was greater in the 1920s than in the prewar years. Similar responsibilities assigned to San Francisco's Iron Trades Council and to national unions in railroads led to disputes on a corresponding scale—citywide in San Francisco in 1919 and industrywide among the shop crafts in 1919 and, more impressively, in 1922. In the munitions industry and Great Lakes shipbuilding, by contrast, labor conflict was much more often confined to individual plants. This was a pattern typical of the United States as a whole during the 1920s.[20] David Montgomery notes that workers' efforts to regulate production continued after the epic battles of 1917–19, but most often through acts of sabotage rather than the corporate demands of craft unionists.[21] Whatever the continuities in impulse, there is a world of difference in worker identities, organization, and action between such furtive resistance to management by small groups of employees and collective movements for workers' control.

Here, too, government-sponsored reforms played a formative role. Wartime labor struggles threatened to undermine the open shop order both by strengthening unions' workplace roots and by coordinating worker demands and activism on a citywide basis. Government shop committee plans made these tasks more difficult. These enactments of industrial democracy organized representation around the individual citizen of the firm and made federal administrators, not union officials, the only recognized source of redress outside the plant.[22] As with enlightened personnel management, moreover, the government's approach won its most enthusiastic support from employers after the armistice, when even this limited recourse to external authority disappeared. The argument can be recast in the language of social movement theory. Wartime state intervention shaped the labor movement less through a calculus of political opportunities than through the creation of particular mechanisms for mobilizing workers. Arrangements for employee representation institutionalized certain alliances and allegiances rather than others. NWLB (and Great Lakes) shop committees made individual plants or departments the normal basis for organizing employees, choosing delegates, and conducting disputes. More encompassing units of labor organization and union activists claiming broader constituencies were given at best secondary and ad hoc recognition, and none at all once government oversight ceased. These cases also affirm the importance of industrial relations institutions for those studying labor as a social movement. The inner constitution of workplace labor relations helps to account for the outward pattern of solidarity and leadership in worker mobilization.

By rationalizing workplace authority and quarantining labor conflict, employee representation schemes in the 1920s accomplished by different means some of the same ends as did David Brody's "workplace contractualism" in the New Deal or the "internal state" of Michael Burawoy's post–World War II machine shops.[23] The workplace rule of law implemented under the New Deal, Brody argues, offered workers a highly prized square deal. The organization of workplace supervision and grievance procedures in the "Allied" machine shop also fostered cleavages among work groups or departments rather than conflicts between management and workers as a whole. In both periods, however, these mechanisms for industrial relations stability were constructed through agreements between unions and management. Employee representation arrangements in the 1920s produced similar results without the inconveniences of unions.

This regime proved to be no more durable than its counterparts in Germany and Britain. Much as particular configurations of political and industrial relations conditions supported distinct resolutions of wartime insurgency, so changes in those conditions would render old solutions obsolete.

State-mandated union authority over employee representation served Germany well in the face of revolution. The system survived thereafter in part because for a time it helped employers and unions alike to cope with hyperinflation and in part because the SPD retained political clout. By the late 1920s neither the economic nor political anchors for state-mandated union power remained. Recession made state protections for labor unacceptable even to relatively enlightened employers. When the SPD-liberal center of gravity lost its hold, the Weimar industrial relations system—and Weimar democracy—collapsed.[24] In Britain trade agreements that tightened union control over workplace organization curbed rank-and-file movements and, by the early 1920s, allowed the state to withdraw from industrial relations. But the system worked as well as it did in part because of high unemployment through the 1920s. With economic recovery in the run up to World War II, unofficial action in defiance of joint agreements and executive authority would once again challenge the efficiency, if no longer the legitimacy, of the industrial relations order.[25] Reformed open shops in the United States helped to consolidate management control of production and quarantine industrial unrest in the 1920s. And as in Britain, "private" solutions ensured that industrial conflict would not be politically charged or disruptive—a third means by which employee representation reforms made industry safer for democracy.[26] A decade later, however, these private virtues became public vices. Most dramatically they drew the fire of a new wave of labor militancy. But they also appeared increasingly at odds with the Keynesian demand for macroeconomic regulation.[27] In political terms employee representation on a nonunion basis was a viable strategy at a time when skilled workers dominated the labor movement and manufacturing workers were not a cohesive force in electoral politics.[28] Amid a mass movement of industrial unionism and an electoral realignment that gave labor more political clout, older forms of employee representation no longer secured stability.

Much as the character of pre–World War I labor relations shaped both the wartime crisis and government measures to restore stability, so did employee representation in the 1920s have legacies for the New Deal system. Particularly as the depression took hold, violations of the "rule of law" promised by the 1920s' industrial relations regime both fueled unrest and built popular support for new forms of workplace constitutionalism. Reforms undertaken after World War I to secure open shops, involving more elaborate mechanisms for regulating labor relations within each firm, also equipped and disposed management to negotiate employment conditions with unions on a plant or company basis rather than through industrywide bargaining. Furthermore, the National Labor Relations Board followed NWLB precedents in organizing representation elections around the assumptions of individual choice by employees of a single firm. The decisive difference, of course, is that the NWLB arranged representation on an open shop basis; the NLRB required union recognition and collective bargaining with "outside" officials.[29]

The New Deal system in turn has given way to new strategies for managing work and conflict.[30] Because the "new industrial relations" relies more on union-free human relations management than on collective bargaining,[31] the 1920s might appear to offer instructive precedents.[32] Certain prerequisites of open shop industrial relations are clear in both periods. Trade unions now, as then, have few footholds in the most important and expansive economic sectors; they have diminished political influence; and their New Deal role in providing macroeconomic stability, unknown in the 1920s, became unworkable by the 1980s. Yet the historical parallels are also misleading. Much as business in the World War I era reformed prewar management in response to new challenges, so more recent business strategies should be seen as reconstructing American exceptionalism under new conditions.[33] Two central arguments of this book underline the very different histories of these open shop regimes. Employee representation in the 1920s developed out of the breakdown of prewar open shops and the growth of wartime insurgency, and wartime government responses to that crisis both constructed and popularized employee representation reforms. Industrial relations innovations since the 1970s, by contrast, have been undertaken amid general labor quiescence and without direct government guidance. One parallel between the two epochs will surely be sustained, however: the new industrial relations is unlikely to provide any more enduring foundation for American exceptionalism than did its predecessor.

Notes

INTRODUCTION

1. Wilson, "An Address in Buffalo," 15.

2. By the early 1920s *employee representation* in the United States had become a euphemism for company unionism. I will use the term more broadly and neutrally to refer to workplace labor relations institutions and procedures by which workers can articulate interests and seek redress. The mechanisms for employee representation varied tremendously in their constituencies, jurisdictions, and power, and they could be accountable primarily to unions, employers, rank-and-file workers, a political party, or the state. These abstract variables were subjects of real contention among interested parties. Much of this book asks which forms of employee representation won the backing of national governments and why.

3. Surveys include articles in Haimson and Tilly, eds., *Strikes, Wars, and Revolutions,* and in Cronin and Sirianni, eds., *Work, Community, and Power;* Horne, *Labour at War;* Lindemann, *The "Red Years";* J. Williams, *The Home Fronts;* Carsten, *Revolution in Central Europe.*

4. Montgomery is the historian who has made the greatest efforts to recover the radicalism of wartime labor unrest (*House of Labor*). See also Fraser, "Dress Rehearsal," 212–55; Haydu, *Between Craft and Class,* ch. 7; McCartin, "Labor's 'Great War.'"

5. Muray, *Red Scare;* Preston, *Aliens and Dissenters;* McClymer, *War and Welfare,* ch. 7.

6. Wilson, "An Address in Buffalo," 15.

7. I use the term *craftsmen* throughout this book because skilled occupations in the metal trades were dominated by males and heavily invested with the ethos and rituals of masculinity. It would be both misleading and anachronistic to substitute a gender-neutral term. Similarly I allow *men* or *workmen* where this is

both historically accurate (women rarely did railroad repair work, for example) and consistent with common usage of the time (as in "ordering the men back to work").

8. Report from Newark by International Association of Machinists' business agent H. W. Brown, *Machinists' Monthly Journal*, July 1918, p. 640.

9. American Federation of Labor, Reconstruction Program, 1918, reprinted in Commons, ed., *Trade Unionism*, 562–78.

10. Comparative surveys of World War I era council or rank-and-file movements include essays in Cronin and Sirianni, eds., *Work, Community, and Power*; G. Williams, *Proletarian Order*; Sirianni, *Workers' Control*; and Gluckstein, *The Western Soviets*.

11. Hopes and plans for reconstruction and labor reform in the United States are discussed in Dawley, *Struggles for Justice*, ch. 6; Murphy, "John Andrews"; Kennedy, *Over Here*; Shapiro, "The Great War and Reform"; and Kaplan, "Social Engineers as Saviors." British parallels are covered in Cline, "Winding Down the War Economy"; Hurwitz, *State Intervention in Great Britain*; and Marwick, *The Deluge*. For such themes in Germany, see Maier, *Recasting Bourgeois Europe*; and Kocka, *Facing Total War*.

12. These accounts are fleshed out in chapter 1.

13. The leading example is the work of Hawley, including *The Great War*. See also Best, *The Politics of American Individualism*; Cuff, *The War Industries Board*; Wiebe, *The Search for Order*; and, for similar issues in the period up to 1916, Sklar, *Corporate Reconstruction of American Capitalism*. Where scholars do consider the postwar impact of wartime labor policies, they tend to focus either on the repression of the left during and immediately after the war or on the long-term legacies for the New Deal. The contributions to industrial relations stability during the 1920s are largely neglected. See, for example, Laslett, "State Policy toward Labour"; Brody, *Labor in Crisis*; Fraser, "Dress Rehearsal" and *Labor Will Rule*; and Harris, "The Snares of Liberalism."

14. Standard works include Brody, "Rise and Decline of Welfare Capitalism"; Nelson, "The Company Union Movement"; Jacoby, "Union-Management Cooperation"; and Gitelman, *Legacy of the Ludlow Massacre*. In contrast to studies of the 1920s, literature on the New Deal routinely integrates analysis of national politics, industrial relations, and employee representation. See, for example, the essays in Fraser and Gerstle, eds., *The Rise and Fall of the New Deal*. Dawley is unusual in suggesting the political functions of 1920s managerial reforms (to preempt a hostile progressive political alliance) (*Struggles for Justice*, 157–58, 165).

15. For an overview and competing views of American labor in the 1920s, see Bernstein, *The Lean Years*; Montgomery, "Thinking about American Workers"; and the reply to Montgomery by Maier, "The 1920s." On management reform, productivity, and labor control, see Lazonick, "Technological Change"; and Jacoby, *Employing Bureaucracy*. Cohen offers a balanced assessment for the case of Chicago in *Making a New Deal*.

16. This has been an enduring theme in Montgomery's work, from *Workers' Control in America*, through "New Tendencies" and *House of Labor* (esp. ch. 9), to "Industrial Democracy." See also two other essays in Lichtenstein and Harris, eds., *Industrial Democracy in America*: McCartin, "'An American Feeling'"; and

Harris, "Industrial Democracy and Liberal Capitalism." Focusing more on management and political elites than on workers, Gerber examines the appeal of corporatist and cooperative ideology in the United States and Britain in "Corporatism"; Shapiro takes up similar themes for various species of liberals and mainstream labor in "Hand and Brain" and "The Twilight of Reform."

17. Together, the metal trades and shipbuilding accounted for nearly half (44.5 percent) of employees on strike during the first six months of the war. Railroads, at 3.8 percent, ran a somewhat distant fourth behind coal (at 11.3 percent) (National Industrial Conference Board, *Strikes*, 4–5).

18. I emphasize the distinctiveness of America here not because it alone is distinctive but because that country is the focus of my book. The same rationale for comparison would apply if the study were centered instead on Britain or Germany.

19. Early versions of these basic points appear in the work of Tilly (*As Sociology Meets History*), Abrams (*Historical Sociology*), and Abbott ("Sequences of Social Events"). More recent elaborations include Sewell, "Three Temporalities"; Griffin, "Temporality, Events, and Explanation"; and Aminzade, "Historical Sociology."

20. Contributions to this literature include Lipset, "Why No Socialism?"; Katznelson, *City Trenches*; Wilentz, "Against Exceptionalism"; Hattam, *Labor Visions and State Power*; Voss, *American Exceptionalism*; and Kirk, *Labour and Society*.

21. For unions, see Lipset, "North American Labor Movements"; and Shalev and Korpi, "Working Class Mobilization." On employers, see Friedman, "The State and the Working Class"; and Jacoby, "American Exceptionalism Revisited." These all-purpose explanatory factors also appear in comparative accounts of other U.S. institutions. See the essays in Shafer, ed., *Is America Different?*

22. Two examples are Kimeldorf, *Reds or Rackets*; and Marks, *Unions in Politics*. For the 1920s, see also Laslett, "State Policy toward Labour," 533.

23. Three useful collections highlighting the contributions of the state and employers are Tolliday and Zeitlin, eds., *Shop Floor Bargaining*; Jacoby, ed., *Masters to Managers*; and Tolliday and Zeitlin, eds., *The Power to Manage?* The fast-growing literature on the ways in which American constitutional and labor law shaped working-class politics has also served to "bring the state back in" to labor history. See, for example, Tomlins, *The State and the Unions*; Orren, *Belated Feudalism*; and the surveys by Wythe Holt ("The New American Labor Law History") and Raymond Hogler ("Labor History and Critical Labor Law").

24. See, for example, Derber, "The Idea of Industrial Democracy"; Connor, *The National War Labor Board*, 181–83; and Dubofsky, *The State and Labor*, 108–10.

25. J. Smith, "Organized Labor"; Dubofsky, "Abortive Reform"; and McCartin, "'An American Feeling.'"

26. The most strident formulation of this view is Zeitlin, "Rank and Filism." See also the more judicious (and varied) recommendations of Victoria Hattam in "Economic Visions and Political Strategies," 83–84, 129; Dubofsky, *The State and Labor*, xi–xviii; and Lyddon, "Industrial-Relations Theory."

27. Montgomery, "New Tendencies"; Jacoby, "American Exceptionalism Revisited," 209–12. Roy Adams makes a similar claim in *Industrial Relations*, x, 34–62.

28. Dawley (*Struggles for Justice*, 236–37), in a comparative aside, highlights American employers' labor relations policies rather than political variables in explaining why a corporatist class compromise of the kind seen in Germany and Britain did not follow the war. This is a sensible conclusion. Because he glosses over differences between Germany and Britain, however, Dawley cannot make better use of the comparison to distinguish political and industrial relations influences on wartime and postwar government policies. For another valuable contribution of Dawley's, see his "Workers, Capital, and the State." Here he emphasizes how the political weakness of American labor allowed employers to consolidate control after the war without corporatist concessions.

29. "Class-centered" accounts vary greatly in the class factions deemed most influential, the mechanisms of influence, and the degree of autonomy conceded to the state. Classic formulations include Poulantzas, *Political Power and Social Classes*; and an early work by Block, "The Ruling Class." Jessop surveys other examples in *The Capitalist State*. A good illustration of the class-centered approach to welfare policy is in Stephens, *The Transition from Capitalism*.

30. General formulations of state-centered theory appear in Evans, Rueschmeyer, and Skocpol, eds., *Bringing the State Back In*; and Skocpol, "Political Responses to Capitalist Crisis." Applications to welfare policy include essays in Weir, Orloff, and Skocpol, eds., *The Politics of Social Policy*; and Skocpol, *Protecting Soldiers and Mothers*. Similar political variables have been invoked to explain America's working-class politics in Katznelson, "Working-class Formation and the State"; Shefter, "Trade Unions and Political Machines"; and Hattam, *Labor Visions and State Power*.

31. Two exemplars of the corporate liberal interpretation of progressive politics are Kolko, *The Triumph of Conservatism*; and Weinstein, *The Corporate Ideal*. Interpretations of New Deal policy that also emphasize the guiding role of capital include those by Quadagno (for whom business elites acted on the state; see "Welfare Capitalism") and Levine (for whom the interests of capital were internalized within the state; see *Class Struggle*). For perspectives on the New Deal that give pride of place to working-class pressure, see Jenkins and Brents, "Social Protest"; Piven and Cloward, *Poor People's Movements*; and Goldfield, "Worker Insurgency."

32. Block argues that state managers pursue their own interests but that "the exercise of state power occurs within particular class contexts." He applies this logic to whole societies rather than sectors within a country, however; see his *Revising State Theory*, 84. For a somewhat similar line of argument applied to welfare reform, see Valocchi, "The Class Basis of the State."

33. Political opportunities include resources made available as well as obstacles imposed by the state. Theoretical formulations include Tilly, *From Mobilization to Revolution*; and McAdam, *Political Process*. Studies that apply this logic to labor politics and organization include Marks, *Unions in Politics*; Hattam, *Labor Visions and State Power*; and Dubofsky, *The State and Labor*.

34. Good examples from labor history include Wilentz, *Chants Democratic*, and essays in Frisch and Walkowitz, eds., *Working-Class America*. Contemporary ethnographies include Halle, *America's Working Man*; and Fantasia, *Cultures of Solidarity*.

35. G. Jones, "The Language of Chartism"; and, with the goal of building rather than burning bridges, Sewell, *Work and Revolution;* Fantasia, *Cultures of Solidarity.*

36. Katznelson offers a sophisticated version of this view in "Working-Class Formation."

37. Examples include Rancière, "The Myth of the Artisan"; Reddy, *The Rise of Market Culture;* and several essays in Berlanstein, ed., *Rethinking Labor History.*

38. A recent collection with an unusually lucid review of the literature is Laraña, Johnston, and Gusfield, eds., *New Social Movements.*

39. This approach is more common in historical case studies than in theoretical reflections on social movements. Moore applies it to peasant mobilization, and Skocpol follows his good example; see Moore, *Social Origins;* Skocpol, *States and Social Revolutions.* Voss deploys a similar logic in her work on the Knights of Labor (*American Exceptionalism*), and Aminzade does so for French working-class politics (*Ballots and Barricades*). Gould elaborates the argument for the Parisian upheavals of 1848 and 1871 (*Insurgent Identities*), emphasizing how formal organization expands the scope and heightens the salience of identities developed through quotidian social networks.

40. Examples include Traugott's study of the Parisian Mobile Guard and National Workshops in 1848 and Foster's analysis of Clyde workers' committees after World War I. See Traugott, *Armies of the Poor;* and Foster, "Working-Class Mobilisation on the Clyde."

41. This is a central theme in Voss, *American Exceptionalism.* Goldthorpe makes a similar argument, to the effect that organization to achieve political leverage in corporatist regimes tends to highlight more encompassing class interests; see Goldthorpe, "The End of Convergence." And in *Between Craft and Class,* I attribute changes in the goals of industrial protest to different forms of workplace organization.

42. Kimeldorf, "Bringing Unions Back In"; Cornfield, "The U.S. Labor Movement"; Kimeldorf and Stepan-Norris, "Historical Studies"; Katznelson, "The 'Bourgeois' Dimension."

43. To take an extreme pairing, why did a small, militant wildcat strike over the 1975 firing of a New Jersey foundry worker quickly peter out, whereas five years later a fairly small, militant wildcat strike against the firing of a Polish shipyard worker snowballed into a mass movement of three-quarters of a million workers within two weeks (and ten million within three months)? Compare Fantasia, *Cultures of Solidarity,* ch. 3; and Goodwyn, *Breaking the Barrier.*

44. On the links between industrial relations and political change in the collapse of Weimar democracy, see Weisbrod, "Economic Power and Political Stability"; and Abraham, *The Collapse of the Weimar Republic.* For the electoral erosion of the SPD's political influence, see especially L. Jones, *German Liberalism.*

45. By the same token, important features of the postwar American Plan would reappear in New Deal industrial relations, despite dramatic changes in the political fortunes of labor. The individual employee remained the basic unit of industrial citizenship, the rule of law continued to be a guiding principle of workplace labor relations, and the plant or firm remained the upper limit for representation rights and collective bargaining. Treatments of these themes include Sisson, *The*

Management of Collective Bargaining; Brown, *The Origins of Trade Union Power*; Brody, "Workplace Contractualism"; Tomlins, *The State and the Unions*.

46. This view of employee representation in the 1920s as both an innovative solution to old problems and contingent on a temporary balance of class relations in industry and politics shares a similar logic with recent interpretations of the origins of national industrial relations systems. These interpretations combine institutional analysis with "history from below" to trace industrial relations arrangements in different countries back to the outcomes of past struggles. Sisson's account of national patterns of collective bargaining offers one example (*The Management of Collective Bargaining*). Raising issues closer to the themes of this book, Brody ("Workplace Contractualism") asks why the union-management relations that congealed in the United States during the 1930s took the form of "workplace contractualism" rather than of Britain's more informal approach to shop floor control. His answer emphasizes how production practices and supervisory techniques developed earlier in the century narrowed the possibilities for worker autonomy and encouraged employees to embrace the rule of law.

47. Kimeldorf demonstrates this point for two centers of longshoring in *Reds or Rackets*.

48. Zolberg, "How Many Exceptionalisms?"

INTRODUCTION TO PART 1

1. *The Survey*, Dec. 14, 1918, pp. 335–38.

2. Metalworkers (and, to a lesser extent, coal miners) entered the war endowed with long traditions of organization and militancy, and they were the primary targets of wartime government intervention and workplace rationalization.

CHAPTER 1: POLITICAL STABILITY AND INDUSTRIAL RELATIONS REFORM IN GERMANY AND BRITAIN

1. Selections from the August 11, 1919, Weimar constitution appear in Kahn-Freund, *Labour Law and Politics*, app. 3.

2. Spencer, *Management and Labor*; H. Mommsen, "The Free Trade Unions."

3. Summaries include Feldman, *Army, Industry, and Labor*; and Kocka, *Facing Total War*.

4. Moses, *Trade Unionism in Germany*, 1:204–5; Feldman, *Army, Industry, and Labor*, 28; Schorske, *German Social Democracy*.

5. Feldman, *Army, Industry, and Labor*, e.g., 73–93; Armeson, *Total Warfare*; Kocka, *Facing Total War*, 69–72. Employers outside heavy industry were more likely to bow to wartime pressures voluntarily (Schneider, *German Trade Unions*, 116).

6. Kocka, *Facing Total War*, 91–92.

7. Feldman, *Army, Industry, and Labor*, ch. 3 and, esp., pp. 204–48, 317–21, 473–76, 520; Armeson, *Total War*, p. 102 and chs. 5–6; Kocka, *Facing Total War*, 91–92, 134–40. Although the provisions for works committees followed prewar precedents in factory codes and mining laws, the Auxiliary Service Law made these committees mandatory on a far wider scale.

8. E. H. Tobin, "War and the Working Class," 270–75; Feldman, *Army, Industry, and Labor*, 117, 333, 459; Schorske, *German Social Democracy*, 308–12.

9. Feldman, *Army, Industry, and Labor*, 373–79.

10. Schorske, *German Social Democracy*, 35, 261, 318–23; Schonhoven, "Localism," 225; Muller, "Syndicalism and Localism."

11. Feldman, *Army, Industry, and Labor*, 352–56; Gluckstein, *The Western Soviets*, 99–101.

12. Ryder, *The German Revolution*, 121; Feldman, *Army, Industry, and Labor*, 337–39.

13. Kocka, *Facing Total War*, 155–59, particularly emphasizes how every petty theft of food or black market transaction made to meet basic needs corroded government legitimacy. On the links between material hardships and antigovernment feeling, see also Tobin, "War and the Working Class," 295–97; Rosenberg, *Imperial Germany*, 94; and Bessel, *Germany after the First World War*, 41–42.

14. D. Morgan, *The Socialist Left*, 82–84; Ryder, *The German Revolution*, 117, 121. As if to underscore the lesson, General Groener directed local military authorities to "make a sharp distinction between the Majority Social Democrats, on the one hand, and the Independent Socialists and Sparticists, on the other. It was necessary to collaborate with the former and permit them to hold meetings but, at the same time, to make sure that they 'fulfill their promises and try to enlighten and pacify their people.' Every effort was to be made to isolate the Independent Socialists and to act ruthlessly against those caught inciting strikes" (Feldman, *Army, Industry, and Labor*, 344).

15. The relative prominence of different radical factions varied from one city to another. David Morgan provides a brief inventory (*The Socialist Left*, 56–58), and Nolan notes cases where insurgency was channeled through militant DMV locals (*Social Democracy and Society*, 257).

16. Feldman, *Army, Industry, and Labor*, 449–54; Schneider, *German Trade Unions*, 125; Gluckstein, *The Western Soviets*, 105; D. Morgan, *The Socialist Left*, 104–5.

17. Useful general accounts of the revolution include Rosenberg, *Imperial Germany* and *The German Republic*; Burdick and Lutz, *Institutions of the German Revolution*; Ryder, *The German Revolution*; W. Mommsen, "The German Revolution," 21–54; and Bessel, *Germany after the First World War*. Not surprisingly, interpretations differ. Among the debates are whether the revolution is best described as constitutionalist or socialist (most now favor the former) and whether the councils, had they not been stamped out by the SPD and the army, would have given Weimar Germany a more secure democratic foundation.

18. This characterization of the councils as initially the crucial channels for liberal and antiwar demands is valid even if (as W. Mommsen, "The German Revolution," 28–37, argues) they had little long-term potential as pillars of a more democratic order.

19. Rosenberg, *Imperial Germany*, 217.

20. Bessel, "State and Society," 202–3; D. Morgan, *The Socialist Left*.

21. D. Morgan, *The Socialist Left*, 223, 271; Gluckstein, *The Western Soviets*, 128–30.

22. Friedlander, "Conflict of Revolutionary Authority"; Carsten, *Revolution in Central Europe*, 127–40; Schorske, *German Social Democracy*, 318–23; Burdick and Lutz, *Institutions of the German Revolution*.

23. Tampke, *The Ruhr and Revolution*, 113, 120–32, 161; Geary, "The Ruhr"; Carsten, *Revolution in Central Europe*, 154–55; and D. Morgan, *The Socialist Left*, 148, 223–28.

24. Local variations on these themes appear in D. Morgan, *The Socialist Left*, 68, 73, 164–74; W. Mommsen, "The German Revolution," 28–37; Nolan, *Social Democracy and Society*, 244, 283; Ryder, *The German Revolution*, 200–203, 268; and Tampke, *The Ruhr and Revolution*, 162.

25. W. Mommsen, in "The German Revolution," emphasizes how far workers' attitudes fell short of revolutionary socialism, as does the ex-Sparticist Toller in his *I Was a German*, 139. The pragmatic origins of support for left-wing leaders and programs is suggested by Bessel, "State and Society," 202; and Rosenberg, *The German Republic*, 28. Maier also emphasizes the council movement's challenge to management authority along with its more familiar political radicalism (*Recasting Bourgeois Europe*, 139).

26. Quoted in Burdick and Lutz, *Institutions of the German Revolution*, 56.

27. Ibid., 73. The quotation is from notes taken at the meeting rather than from a verbatim transcript.

28. Friedlander, "Revolutionary Authority"; Carsten, *Revolution in Central Europe*, 127–132.

29. Of the congress's 489 delegates, 288 belonged to the SPD. Burdick and Lutz, *Institutions of the German Revolution*, 13–14, 54–55, 229; Carsten, *Revolution in Central Europe*; and Herwig, "Congress of Workers' and Soldiers' Councils."

30. Burdick and Lutz, *Institutions of the German Revolution*, 206, quoting from minutes of a joint meeting of the cabinet and the Central Committee of the Congress of Workers' and Soldiers' Councils, Jan. 28, 1919.

31. D. Morgan, *The Socialist Left*, 125, 220–21, 230–40; Carsten, *Revolution in Central Europe*, 145–51, 173–77, 214–18; Nolan, *Social Democracy and Society*, 269; Tampke, *The Ruhr and Revolution*, pp. 113–32 and ch. 10; Lindemann, *The "Red Years*," 44–45.

32. Hugo Stinnes was a coal magnate and a leader of the more conservative employer bloc; Carl Legien headed the ADGB. Moses, *Trade Unionism in Germany*, reprints the agreement (2:455–57).

33. Quoted in Peukert, *The Weimar Republic*, 108.

34. On the background and motivations behind the Stinnes-Legien agreement, see especially Feldman, "German Business"; Moses, *Trade Unionism in Germany*, 1:216–26; Kocka, *Facing Total War*, 70, 139–40; and Bessel, *Germany after the First World War*, 142–44.

35. Burdick and Lutz, *Institutions of the German Revolution*, 268 (Koeth quotation); "Decree Regulating Collective Agreements, Workers and Employer Committees, and Arbitration of Labor Disputes," reprinted in *Monthly Labor Review*, Apr. 1919, pp. 160–67; International Labour Office, *Works Councils in Germany*, 5; Moses, *Trade Unionism in Germany*, 2:295–96.

36. D. Morgan, *The Socialist Left*, 267–68; Reich, *Labour Relations in Republican Germany*, 156. Further to the left, Sparticists would have had the council system take the place of republican political institutions, but their view seems to have had limited support by the summer of 1919.

37. Walter Rathenau headed the electrical industry giant Allgemeine Elektriz-

itäts Gesellschaft; Wichard von Moellendorff was one of the firm's engineers. Both were involved in wartime and postwar economic planning.

38. Maier, *Recasting Bourgeois Europe*, 11–12, 141–42; Hardach, *The First World War*, 251–52.

39. On the political and legislative background to the Works Council Act, see Reich, *Labour Relations in Republican Germany*, 41–43, 163–167; D. Morgan, *The Socialist Left*, 267–69; Moses, *Trade Unionism in Germany*, 2:309–11; Maier, *Recasting Bourgeois Europe*, 160–63; Berthelot, *Works Councils in Germany*, 23; L. Jones, *German Liberalism*, 58.

40. *Vorwärts* (newspaper of the SPD), Aug. 10, 1919, quoted in Berthelot, *Works Councils in Germany*, 19.

41. By 1922, 75 percent of works councilors belonged to socialist trade unions, well above the unions' overall share of the labor force (Kahn-Freund, *Labour Law and Politics*, 27).

42. Reich, *Labour Relations in Republican Germany*, 166–67, 219–22; Guillebaud, *The Works Council*, 20–22, 93, 154–57, 207–9, 216; Stern, *Works Council Movement in Germany*, 28.

43. International Labour Office, *Works Councils in Germany*, 18. See also D. Morgan, *The Socialist Left*, 314–19.

44. D. Morgan, *The Socialist Left*, 346; Moses, *Trade Unionism in Germany*, 2:314–19; Reich, *Labour Relations in Republican Germany*, 167–68; Guillebaud, *The Works Council*, 43–46.

45. Wunderlich, *Labor under German Democracy*, 4–7, 180–81; Reich, *Labour Relations in Republican Germany*, 123–24. In 1919 alone government arbitration authorities were involved in about 85,000 disputes (Reich, *Labour Relations in Republican Germany*, 125). Within the plants the government's factory inspectors also worked to mediate disputes and to ensure "responsible" works council leadership (Guillebaud, *The Works Council*, 22). David Morgan notes the threat of force behind the government's reforms (*The Socialist Left*, 319).

46. "Factory Inspectors Report on Operation of German Works Councils," *Monthly Labor Review*, Feb. 1922, p. 3 and passim. See also Reich, *Labour Relations in Republican Germany*, 190–91.

47. Berthelot, *Works Councils in Germany*, 67–68, 81; Stern, *Works Council Movement in Germany*, 38; "Factory Inspectors Report on Operation of German Works Councils," *Monthly Labor Review*, Feb. 1922; Wunderlich, *Labor under German Democracy*, 23–24, 68. Even among those most conservative of German employers—mine owners—employers recognized the value of collective bargaining and arbitration as weapons against rank-and-file radicalism. See Weisbrod, "Entrepreneurial Politics," 161. On German corporatism during the period see Maier, *Recasting Bourgeois Europe*; and Nocken, "Corporatism and Pluralism."

48. Guillebaud, *The Works Council*, 57–58, 114; Wunderlich, *Labor under German Democracy*, 25–26, 29–31; Moses, *Trade Unionism in Germany*, 2:345, 355

49. After 1920 the SPD had effective veto power over centrist government coalitions. SPD and union influence survived in part because of divisions between conservative and progressive employer blocs. See Abraham, "Corporatist Compromise," 61; idem, *Collapse of the Weimar Republic*, 116–17, 144; Kahn-Freund, *Labor Law and Politics*, 13; and L. Jones, *German Liberalism*. This account

of industrial relations is consistent with interpretations of Weimar welfare policy as a precocious social democratic experiment built on what was still too narrow a social and political base. See Weisbrod, "Economic Power and Political
Stability," and especially Peukert, *The Weimar Republic.*

50. Lloyd George's telegram from Paris is quoted in K. Morgan, *Consensus and
Disunity,* 49.

51. The best survey is in Great Britain, Commission of Enquiry into Industrial Unrest, *Reports of the Commission,* and the commission's more detailed reports
for specific regions. See also Wrigley, *Lloyd George and Labour,* 291–93.

52. General summaries include Cole, *Trade Unionism and Munitions* and *Workshop Organization;* Hurwitz, *State Intervention in Great Britain;* Hinton, *The First
Shop Stewards' Movement,* pt. 1; Wrigley, "The Ministry of Munitions," 32–56;
idem, "State Intervention in Industrial Relations"; and Burgess, "Political Economy of Engineering Workers."

53. On early conflicts and agreements concerning dilution, see Great Britain,
Ministry of Munitions, *History of the Ministry of Munitions,* 5, pt. 1:128, 138–39,
150–52; Cole, *Trade Unionism and Munitions;* Jefferys, *Story of the Engineers,* 125–
26, 135, 174–75; and Horne, *Labour at War,* 81. Clegg, Fox, and Thompson note
that dilution was less common in shipbuilding, mainly on account of opposition
from the admiralty (*History of British Trade Unions,* 139–40). Reid confirms the
point for the case of Clyde shipbuilding and on the specific issue of substituting
women for skilled men ("Dilution, Unionism and the State").

54. Great Britain, Ministry of Munitions, *History of the Ministry of Munitions,*
4, pt. 1, sect. 5. The most thorough treatment is Rubin, *War, Law, and Labour.*

55. Wrigley, *Lloyd George and British Labour,* 158; Feldman, *Army, Industry, and
Labor,* 207.

56. Cole, *Trade Unionism and Munitions,* 123–25, 157–62; Hinton, *First Shop Stewards' Movement,* 52–54; Clegg, Fox, and Thompson, *History of British Trade Unions,*
161–67, 209.

57. Less-skilled British workers, like industrial unionists in Germany, had
fewer objections to industrial policy—at least in the area of dilution. Workers'
Union leader John Beard strongly supported the Munitions of War Act because
it provided union recognition, legally binding agreements, and guaranteed access to conciliation procedures. As for provisions promising the restoration of
trade union practices after the war, these had "very little concern for the members of the Workers' Union" (*Workers' Union Record,* Aug. 1915, pp. 1–2).

58. *Amalgamated Engineers' Monthly Journal,* June 1914, pp. 35–36. On prewar
shop steward organization and its uneasy relations with official union procedures
and authority, see Jefferys, *Story of the Engineers,* ch. 7; Croucher, "Amalgamated Society of Engineers"; Holton, *British Syndicalism,* 30–33, 66–68, 140–43; and
Wigham, *The Power to Manage,* 63–84.

59. For general surveys of the Shop Stewards' Movement, see Cole, *Workshop
Organization;* Pribicevic, *The Shop Stewards' Movement;* and Hinton, *First Shop
Stewards' Movement.* Reid ("Dilution, Unionism, and the State") and Rubin (*War,
Law, and Labour*) argue that the split between rank and file and *local* union offi-
cials has been overstated. In Glasgow, Reid suggests, district committee mem-
bers at least cheered members on even if they did not issue the orders to strike.

In comparative perspective, however, British engineering workers were clearly more divided between shop floor and "official" leadership and organization than were their counterparts in Germany or the United States. For the purposes of the present argument, it is also important to remember that union officials and government labor administrators themselves regarded rank-and-file militancy led by shop stewards as a major problem requiring strong countermeasures. The reports of the Commission of Enquiry into Industrial Unrest and the *History of the Ministry of Munitions* are useful guides to officials' thinking.

60. Hinton, *First Shop Stewards' Movement*, chs. 3–4.

61. Cole, *Trade Unionism and Munitions*, 130–33; Hinton, *First Shop Stewards' Movement*, ch. 5.

62. Great Britain, Ministry of Munitions, *History of the Ministry of Munitions*, 6, pt. 1:101; Jefferys, *Story of the Engineers*, 183–85; Cole, *Trade Unionism and Munitions*, 134–40.

63. By these criteria, Reid ("Dilution, Unionism, and the State," 68) and McLean (*Legend of Red Clydeside*) are certainly right to distinguish between the industrial militancy of Clydeside engineers and the political radicalism of a much smaller group of socialists during and after the war.

64. Foster's interpretation of Clydeside politics is especially concerned (as his critics are not) with the ways in which radical vanguards can gain genuine support from—and shape collective action among—rank-and-file workers of quite varied political orientations. See Foster, "Strike Action and Working-Class Politics"; and idem, "Working-Class Mobilisation on the Clyde."

65. Haydu, "Employers, Unions, and American Exceptionalism."

66. Price, *Labour in British Society*, 148; Hinton, *Labour and Socialism*, 106–8. Wartime insurgency developed most fully in engineering, but similar tensions appeared among miners, railroad workers, and dockers. For these other industries, see Cole, *Trade Unionism and Munitions*, 176–86; Kendall, *Revolutionary Movement in Britain*, 161–66; Church, "Employers, Unions and the State," 41–43; Clegg, Fox, and Thompson, *History of British Trade Unions*, 177, 192, 429; and Schneer, "War, the State and the Workplace," 101–7.

67. General discussions of the postwar crisis include Kendall, *Revolutionary Movement in Britain*, 188–194; Cronin, "Coping with Labour"; Nottingham, "Recasting Bourgeois Britain"; Wrigley, "The State and Labour," 263–71.

68. Kendall, *Revolutionary Movement in Britain*, 138–39; McLean, *Legend of Red Clydeside*; and Foster, "Working-Class Mobilisation on the Clyde," 169–70.

69. Quoted by Middlemas, *Politics in Industrial Society*, 143. This summary of the immediate postwar period largely agrees with Cronin, *Labour and Society in Britain*, 34–37, in highlighting a blurring of industrial and political challenges, particularly in mining. It agrees, too, with half of Middlemas: there was a crisis of industrial authority that had crucial political implications, but there was never a threat of "political breakdown" (p. 14 and ch. 3).

70. Great Britain, Ministry of Munitions, *History of the Ministry of Munitions*, 6, pt. 1:115; Hinton, *First Shop Stewards' Movement*, ch. 4; Hardach, *The First World War*, 194.

71. Some of these larger goals of government planners are reviewed by Cline in "Winding down the War Economy," 159; Church, "Employers, Unions and the

State," 41–43; and, for the postwar period, K. Morgan, *Consensus and Disunity,* ch. 3. On the government's own reliance on unions before the war, see Fox, *History and Heritage,* 246–50; Fulcher, *Labour, Employers, and the State,* 101–5; and Powell, *British Politics and the Labour Question,* 37–38.

72. The most important example is the 1917 Shop Stewards Agreement. Other examples of a continuing reliance on bilateral agreements and procedures for handling disputes are noted by Rubin, *War, Law, and Labour,* 246; Cole, *Trade Unionism and Munitions,* 157; and Hurwitz, *State Intervention in Great Britain,* 151–62. This reading strikes a middle course between Middlemas and his critics. Middlemas is right to emphasize how state policies—including in the area of employee representation—reinforced union authority. But as Rubin (*War, Law, and Labour,* 19) and others argue, these policies were not part of a larger corporatist compact in which organized labor and capital became quasi-public governing institutions. Instead the state encouraged—but did not impose—an industrial rule of law established by unions and employers themselves, avoiding where possible direct controls (more successfully after the war than during it, of course). This mixed outcome has been described with such hybrid terms as "bipartite corporatism" (Robert Currie, *Industrial Politics*), "collective laissez-faire" (Otto Kahn-Freund), and "liberal collectivism" (Richard Price).

73. On the Whitley plan see Seymour, *The Whitley Councils Scheme;* Halevy, *The Era of Tyrannies,* 159–208; and Charles, *Industrial Relations in Britain.*

74. Great Britain, Commission of Enquiry into Industrial Unrest, *Reports of the Commission.*

75. Seymour, *The Whitley Councils Scheme,* 229.

76. Interim (First) Report, reprinted in Bureau of Industrial Research, *Industrial Council Plan in Great Britain,* 16. See also Seymour, *The Whitley Councils Scheme,* 230; Clegg, *Industrial Relations in Britain,* 186. The publication of the Whitley Report was itself delayed by the government until its recommendations won general approval from trade unions (Wrigley, *Lloyd George and British Labour,* 201).

77. Letter of Oct. 20, 1916, reprinted in Bureau of Industrial Research, *Industrial Council Plan in Great Britain,* 5–6.

78. Second Whitley Report, reprinted in Bureau of Industrial Research, *Industrial Council Plan in Great Britain,* 48; Wolfe, *Works Committees and Industrial Councils,* 43–50.

79. *Monthly Labor Review,* Aug. 1919, p. 131. The department responsible for encouraging Whitleyism was eliminated altogether by 1924. See Lowe, *Adjusting to Democracy,* 77, 92–95; Clegg, Fox, and Thompson, *History of British Trade Unions,* 248–50, 441–44.

80. Out of sixty joint industrial councils listed by Seymour (*The Whitley Councils Scheme,* 220–21), twenty-eight had no subordinate works councils. See also Charles, *Industrial Relations in Britain,* 205–10; and Sheldrake, *Industrial Relations and Politics,* 37.

81. Seymour, *The Whitley Councils Scheme,* 37–38, 86, 185; Horne, *Labour at War,* 248; Lowe, *Adjusting to Democracy,* 93–94.

82. Great Britain, Ministry of Munitions, *History of the Ministry of Munitions,* 6, pt. 2:32–33. See also Hinton, *First Shop Stewards' Movement,* 213–15, 233–34.

83. Haydu, *Between Craft and Class,* 148–57.

84. "Memorandum of Conference between the Engineering Employers' Federation and Thirteen Trade Unions." The ASE, largest of all engineering unions, remained wary and refused to sign on until 1919. In practice, however, local ASE officials followed its terms (Cole, *Trade Unionism and Munitions*, 153).

85. May 9 minutes, quoted by Wrigley, *Lloyd George and British Labour*, 194.

86. Wrigley, *Lloyd George and Labour*, 109–12. After the strike, the Scottish engineering employers' federation "insisted that member firms formalise factory bargaining by recognising union representatives" (Foster, "Working-Class Mobilisation on the Clyde," 172).

87. Wrigley, *Lloyd George and Labour*, 88. See also Rubin, "Law as a Bargaining Weapon."

88. On the 1922 lockout see Great Britain, Parliament, *Report concerning the Engineering Trades Dispute;* Wigham, *The Power to Manage*, 117–24; and Labour Research Department, *Labour and Capital in Engineering*.

89. Despite major strikes in December 1918 and the following year, unions and employers in cotton showed a similar willingness to strengthen centralized collective bargaining. Here too, this approach won Ministry of Labour backing. See K. Morgan, *Consensus and Disunity*, 65–66; Wrigley, *Lloyd George and Labour*, 97, 163–64; Armitage, *Politics of Decontrol of Industry*, 63–72, 83–92; Charles, *Industrial Relations in Britain*, 145; and, more generally, Price, *Labour in British Society*, 161–64.

90. Lowe, *Adjusting to Democracy*, 78–79, 126–27; idem, "The Government and Industrial Relations"; and Sheldrake, *Industrial Relations and Politics*, 56.

91. Conference Report on Conciliation and Arbitration, quoted by Wrigley in *British Industrial Relations*, 5. See also Turner, *British Politics and the Great War*, 386–87; K. Morgan, *Consensus and Disunity*, 57–59; and Wrigley, *Lloyd George and Labour*, 131–41.

92. Quoted by Wrigley, *Lloyd George and Labour*, 176.

93. Lowe, *Adjusting to Democracy*, ch. 2; Cronin, "Coping with Labour," 126–27; Fulcher, *Labour, Employers, and the State*, 114–15. The policy implications of broader political realignments are discussed in Wrigley, *Lloyd George and Labour*, 100–101, 202–6, 311–14; Tanner, *Political Change and the Labour Party*, 433–36; Powell, *British Politics and the Labour Question*, 64–73; and Cronin, "Coping with Labour," 132–36.

94. United States Department of Labor, Information and Education Service, *Report of the Employers' Industrial Commission*, 9. See also Turner, *British Politics and the Great War*, 389, 446–47; Gospel, "Employers and Managers," 167–69; McIvor, *Organised Capital*, 273–75.

95. Scholars who disagree on many other points still see government initiatives as having promoted stability. Concurring opinions include Fox, *History and Heritage*, 303–5; K. Morgan, *Consensus and Disunity*, 67–76; Lowe, "The Government and Industrial Relations," 203; Middlemas, *Politics in Industrial Society*, 128, 147–51; and Hinton, *Labour and Socialism*, 115–16.

96. Clegg, Fox, and Thompson, *History of British Trade Unions*, 449–50, 545, 549–50; Gospel, "Employers and Managers," 171–73. Where the balance of power strongly favored employers, trade agreements typically survived, but provisions for employee representation under union auspices could be little more than for-

malities—available for use by management when needed and otherwise ignored. This was the case in much of the auto industry during the 1920s, with its relatively deskilled work force and more fragile workplace unionism. See Haydu, *Between Craft and Class*, 171–72; Zeitlin, "Internal Politics of Employer Organization: The Engineering Employers' Federation 1896–1939," 71–72.

97. By the same token, as Clegg, Fox, and Thompson note (*History of British Trade Unions*, 550–51), strikes were more likely to affect entire industries.

98. This conclusion shares with works by Middlemas a strong emphasis on the larger significance of internal union authority and workplace control while rejecting (as many others do) his view that the state played an ongoing corporatist role in this new industrial relations regime. Quite apart from exaggerating the importance of consultation among union, business, and government leaders, Middlemas is pushed toward a corporatist interpretation partly because he overstates the "political" character of the crisis to begin with and partly because he underestimates employers' willingness to accommodate unions on their own (see, e.g., *Politics in Industrial Society*, p. 14, ch. 3, and p. 128). In effect he is imposing a German story on the British case.

CHAPTER 2: REFORMING OPEN SHOPS IN THE UNITED STATES

1. *The Survey*, Oct. 5, 1918, p. 19.

2. *Iron Age*, Sept. 26, 1918, p. 764. Midvale's plan is discussed in Wolfe, *Works Committees and Industrial Councils*, 207–12; and Brody, *Labor in Crisis*, 85.

3. General surveys of the spread of employee representation include National Industrial Conference Board, *Works Councils in the United States* and *Experience with Works Councils*; National Metal Trades Association, *Report of the Committee on Works Councils*; Bureau of Industrial Research, *American Company Shop Committee Plans*; and Nelson, "The Company Union Movement." On conflicting definitions of *industrial democracy*, see Montgomery, *Fall of the House of Labor*, ch. 9, which focuses more narrowly on the shop committees that figured in most programs; McCartin, "Labor's 'Great War,' " whose treatment includes a wide range of labor rights and standards; and essays in Lichtenstein and Harris, *Industrial Democracy in America*.

4. The metal trades, quite appropriately, figure prominently in scholarly work on the development of the "American" system of manufacture. See, for example, Habakkuk, *American and British Technology*; Piore and Sabel, *The Second Industrial Divide*; and Chandler, *Scale and Scope*.

5. Nelson, *Frederick Taylor* and *Managers and Workers*, esp. 48–57, 69–74; Clawson, *Bureaucracy and the Labor Process*; Calvert, *The Mechanical Engineer in America*.

6. Clark, *Manufactures in the United States*, 2:96, 358–60; Wagoner, *The U.S. Machine Tool Industry*; and Rogers, "Developments in Machine-Shop Practice."

7. Automobile production methods before World War I are examined in Meyer, *The Five Dollar Day*; Gartman, *Auto Slavery*; Peterson, *American Automobile Workers*; and, with a comparative view, Lewchuk, "Fordism." On small arms, see M. Smith, *Harpers Ferry Armory*. One sign of deskilling in small arms manufacture was the high proportion of women among employees—19.7 percent in 1914 (National Industrial Conference Board, *Women in the Metal Trades*, 2).

8. Montgomery, *Fall of the House of Labor*, 201, 321–23, 438–41, notes arrangements like these at Westinghouse and General Electric. For examples of arsenal practices, see Aitken, *Taylorism at Watertown Arsenal.*

9. The conflict between craft standards and modern management practice has been most thoroughly explored by Montgomery in *Workers' Control in America.* See also United States Congress, Committee on Labor, *Hearings to Investigate Shop Management;* Clawson, *Bureaucracy and the Labor Process;* and Haydu, *Between Craft and Class,* ch. 2.

10. Montgomery, *Fall of the House of Labor*, 275; Wolman, *Ebb and Flow in Unionism.* The figure of 11 percent overstates union density in those sectors that would be central to wartime munitions, including as it does relatively well-organized occupations such as railroad repair and hand tool manufacture. Bain and Price (*Profiles of Union Growth,* 50) put British union density for metals and engineering at 29.2 percent in 1911.

11. Ashworth, *The Helper;* Perlman, *The Machinists.*

12. For the social side of unions, see especially Rosenzweig, *Eight Hours.* On trade policy, see Perlman, *The Machinists,* 151–53; United States Bureau of Labor, *Regulation and Restriction of Output.*

13. For prewar metal trade councils, see Ramirez, *When Workers Fight,* 105–16; I review evidence on workshop organization before 1914 in Haydu, *Between Craft and Class,* 75–76, 105–7, 113–15.

14. Major contributions or reviews include J. Holt, "Trade Unionism in Steel Industries"; Shalev and Korpi, "Working Class Mobilization"; Brown, *Origins of Trade Union Power;* Friedman, "The State and the Working Class"; Laslett, "State Policy toward Labour."

15. Haydu, "Employers, Unions, and American Exceptionalism"; Jackson, *Formation of Craft Labor Markets.*

16. For the machine trades, see Haydu, "Employers, Unions, and American Exceptionalism"; and Montgomery, *Workers' Control in America,* 48–49, 56–58. Other industries are examined in Griffin, Wallace, and Rubin, "Capitalist Resistance to Labor"; Brody, *Steelworkers in America;* Yellowitz, "Skilled Workers and Mechanization"; and Ernst, *Lawyers against Labor.*

17. Public statement of the Manufacturers' Association of Bridgeport, *Bridgeport Herald,* Sept. 19, 1915. Similar statements appear in the principles of the National Metal Trades Association and many of its constituent associations.

18. For employers' associations and anti-union tactics, see Bonnett, *Employers' Associations;* Ramirez, *When Workers Fight,* 87–97; Harris, "Getting It Together"; and Fine, *"Without Blare of Trumpets."*

19. Lipset, "North American Labor Movements"; Fox, *History and Heritage;* Friedman, "The Decline of Paternalism"; Gitelman, "Being of Two Minds"; Harris, "Employers' Collective Action."

20. This argument is developed at greater length (and with more qualifications) in Haydu, "Employers, Unions, and American Exceptionalism." For similar accounts of how the timing of change in both technology and industrial structure affect employer strategies, see Dore, *British Factory—Japanese Factory;* Kimeldorf, *Reds or Rackets,* ch. 3; Sisson, "Employers and Collective Bargaining"; Gospel, *Markets, Firms, and Management.* Harris, in "Employers' Collective Action," notes

that even small employers producing in small batches with a skilled work force took the open shop line in Philadelphia after 1901. As Harris emphasizes, they were able to do so in part because of the labor market policies of big employers in the city. It may also be that the period *after* 1901 is not the best suited for explaining the origins of open shop strategies. For the present purposes, however, the important point is one with which Harris would agree: before World War I, most metal trades employers regarded unions as incompatible with management control of the workplace. For a survey of contrasting patterns of labor organization and employer policies in other industries, see Kirk, *Labour and Society.*

21. National Metal Trades Association (NMTA), *Proceedings of the Annual Convention,* Apr. 9–10, 1913, p. 15.

22. *Cleveland Citizen,* Apr. 1, 1916; Perlman and Taft, *Labor in the United States,* 410; *Machinists' Monthly Journal,* May, 1919, p. 454.

23. Minutes of the Manufacturers' Association of Bridgeport, May 4, 1916. The strike figures are from NMTA, *Proceedings of the Annual Convention,* Apr. 27–28, 1916, p. 22; Potter, "War-Boom Towns I," 240.

24. Other aspects of wartime economic mobilization are covered in Cuff, *The War Industries Board;* and Clarkson, *Industrial America in the World War.*

25. Wartime labor policy thus continued the voluntaristic tradition Sklar identified in prewar approaches to economic regulation; see Sklar, *Corporate Reconstruction of American Capitalism,* ch. 1. Conner makes a similar argument for National War Labor Board policies in *The National War Labor Board.*

26. United States War Department, *Report on Industrial Relations,* 27 (quotation); Lombardi, *Labor's Voice in the Cabinet,* 260 and passim.

27. Bing, *War-Time Strikes,* 54.

28. Baker's Nov. 21, 1917, letter is reprinted in United States War Department, *Report on Industrial Relations,* 83–84 (see also 28–31); Bing, *War-Time Strikes,* ch. 7.

29. Army agencies responsible for labor standards and disputes also consulted leaders of the Amalgamated Clothing Workers Association (ACWA). This remained an unofficial relationship, however, in deference to the AFL's antipathy toward the ACWA. See Fraser, *Labor Will Rule,* 118–20; Wolfe, *Works Committees and Industrial Councils,* 122–24.

30. "Recommendation of the National Industrial Conference Board of Means for Preventing Interruption by Labor Disputes of Necessary War Production," reprinted in United States Bureau of Labor Statistics, *National War Labor Board,* 28 (quotation); Johnson, *The Politics of Soft Coal,* 82–83; Bing, *War-Time Strikes,* 164–65, 170; Warne, *The Workers at War,* 120–22; and Wehle, "Adjustment of Labor Disputes," 124–26. Regarding shipbuilding, see chapter 4.

31. "Principles and Policies to Govern Relations between Workers and Employers in War Industries for the Duration of the War," reprinted in United States Bureau of Labor Statistics, *National War Labor Board,* 32–33.

32. Wehle, *Hidden Threads of History,* 23.

33. Johnson, *The Politics of Soft Coal,* 81–82; United States War Department, *Report on Industrial Relations,* 20, 31, 74; Bing, *War-Time Strikes,* 156 n. 1. In munitions production the War Department insisted that employees remain on the job pending a decision by its Industrial Service Section.

34. Testimony at National War Labor Board hearings in Bridgeport, July 18,

1918, NWLB Records, Case Files (entry 4), Docket 132; Bing, *War-Time Strikes*, 195–96. For craftsmen who had long associated their skills with their "manhood," the sudden growth of female employment in the machine trades added insult to injury. Female employment in the wartime metal trades reached about 12–13 percent of the work force. See National Industrial Conference Board, *Women in the Metal Trades*, 36; Wagoner, *The U.S. Machine Tool Industry*, 104, 113; *Iron Age*, July 18, 1918, pp. 146–47, and Oct. 24, 1918, p. 1018.

35. The cost of living increased 29 percent over August 1915 levels by June 1917; 58 percent by June 1918; and 74 percent by December 1918. Real wages in the metal trades dropped 13 percent between December 1915 and December 1917. Bing, *War-Time Strikes*, summarizes data on wage rates and notes differentials by region and industry (7–9, 190, 215–17).

36. Anderson, in *Machinists' Monthly Journal*, Sept. 1917, p. 756. See also IAM president William Johnston's report for 1918 in ibid, June 1919, p. 512.

37. *Machinists' Monthly Journal*, Sept. 1918, pp. 823–24.

38. Montgomery, *Workers' Control in America*, 95.

39. *Cleveland Press*, Oct. 2, 4, 16, 1915.

40. *Machinists' Monthly Journal*, Oct. 1917, p. 853; Bing, *War-Time Strikes*, 68, 172; McCartin, "Labor's 'Great War,'" chs. 4–7.

41. Watson, *Machines and Men*, 92–93, 97–98, 120–22; Jefferys, *Story of the Engineers*, 151–59; Wigham, *The Power to Manage*, 63–64, 68–71, 74–75.

42. Examiner's Report, NWLB Records, Case Files, Docket 720, p. 3; and "Brief for Respondents," ibid., p. 15.

43. "A. W. Reports" (typescript of reports from a spy planted in the Bridgeport IAM local by the Manufacturers' Association of Bridgeport, Bridgeport Public Library), Apr. 5, 7, 26, May 12, Aug. 9, 1916; *Bridgeport Herald*, Mar. 25, 1917; *Bridgeport Post*, July 14, 1917; letter, George Bowen (IAM Lodge 30 business agent) to Robert McWade, Apr. 30, 1917, Department of Labor, Conciliation Service, Conciliation Service Records, ser. 33, File 347; statement by John Hart, Remington tool room steward, July 2, 1918, hearings, NWLB Records, Case Files, Docket 132; *Labor Leader*, Apr. 18, 1918.

44. Letter, A. M. Jamieson to Harvey Brown, Nov. 3, 1918, NWLB Records, Case Files, Docket 720 (quotation); letter, Harvey Brown to members of lodges 340, 571, and 606, June 27, 1918, NWLB Records, Case Files, Docket 720, Exhibit 27.

45. Brief for Respondents, NWLB Records, Case Files, Docket 720, pp. 37–39, 70–72; "A. W. Reports," Apr. 5, 1916; Bing, *War-Time Strikes*, 201; *Machinists' Monthly Journal*, Aug. 1918, p. 764.

46. By establishment, 43.5 percent of strikes involved union rights; by employees idled, 54.5 percent did (National Industrial Conference Board, *Strikes*, 9).

47. Montgomery, *Workers' Control in America*, 124–27.

48. Testimony by Mr. McDonald, NWLB Records, Case Files, Docket 147, pp. 36, 41 (first quotation); and report by James Barrett, June 18, 1918, NWLB Records, Case Files, Docket 147 (second quotation).

49. *Iron Age*, Aug. 31, 1916, p. 463 (first quotation); transcript of hearing held May 18, 1918, NWLB Records, Case Files, Docket 19, p. 64 (second quotation). See also *Iron Age*, Sept. 7, 1916, p. 561; idem, Sept. 14, 1916, p. 620; idem, Oct. 5, 1916, p. 803; *Machinists' Monthly Journal*, Nov. 1916, pp. 1096, 1098–99.

50. Brief of the Pittsfield Metal Trades Council, NWLB Records, Case Files, Docket 19; letter, Chesney to the NWLB, May 14, 1918, NWLB Records, Case Files, Docket 19; and transcript of May 18, 1918, hearings, NWLB Records, Case Files, Docket 19 (testimony by Chesney, pp. 50–52, 64, and by Mr. "Sedderholm" [probably Cederholm, an IAM organizer], pp. 53–54).

51. Testimony by David Kerlin (secretary of Pittsfield Metal Trades Council), transcript of May 18, 1918, hearings, in NWLB Records, Case Files, Docket 19, p. 21; Leahey, "Skilled Labor," 44–50; Montgomery, *Fall of the House of Labor*, 442–47; McCartin, "Labor's 'Great War,'" 203, 217–18.

52. Brief for Respondents, NWLB Records, Case Files, Docket 720, pp. 37–39, 70–72; letter, Department of Labor Conciliator Reeves to Secretary of Labor Wilson, NWLB Records, Case Files, Docket 720, Exhibit 4; telegram, Major Hawkins (manager of the International Arms and Fuze Company) to IAM president Johnston, June 12, 1918, NWLB Records, Case Files, Docket 720, Exhibit 38. International Arms and Fuze was the only large firm in Newark to recognize unions.

53. Examiner's Report, NWLB Records, Case Files, Docket 720, p. 26. As usual, estimates of strike participation varied greatly, from the employers' 6,000 to union claims of up to 15,000 (ibid., 3). The figure used is from Ruth Pickering, "Newark and the War Labor Board," *The Nation*, Oct. 26, 1918, p. 3.

54. Memo (unsigned, but probably written by either Taft or Frank Walsh), May 4, 1918, NWLB Records, Case Files, Docket 132; *Bridgeport Post*, July 12, 1917; *Bridgeport Herald*, July 15, 1917; Department of Labor, Conciliation Service, Conciliation Service Records, ser 33, File 567.

55. NWLB Records, Minutes of Executive Sessions (entry 6), June 1, 1918, morning session, p. 35. Similar sentiments can be found among Bridgeport employers. See, for example, Manufacturers' Association of Bridgeport, Minutes of the Executive Board, August 30, 1917; Department of Labor, Conciliation Service, Conciliation Service Records, ser. 33, Files 819 (Locomobile) and 817 (Bryant).

56. *Iron Age*, Jan. 10, 1918, p. 142. Drew served as legal counsel for the National Erectors' Association. Fine, *"Without Blare of Trumpets,"* reviews the contributions of Drew and the NEA to the open shop movement.

57. Minutes of Executive Sessions, June 27, 1918, NWLB Records, pp. 22, 47–48.

58. This argument is a variation on the familiar point that a fusion of economic and political power and conflict tends to radicalize working-class protest. The focus here is on behavior, not beliefs. One can advance a structural explanation for the targets of labor protest without assuming that specific worker ideologies necessarily flow in these same institutional channels.

59. The figures include all industries. The metal trades (not including shipbuilding or railroads) accounted for roughly one-third of strikes and one-quarter of strikers during this period (National Industrial Conference Board, *Strikes*, 8–9).

60. Dubofsky, *State and Labor*, ch. 3. His view is shared by McCartin in "Labor's 'Great War.'"

61. The best treatment of the origins of the board is in Conner, *The National War Labor Board*, ch. 2. See also Lombardi, *Labor's Voice in the Cabinet*, 232–244; Bing, *War-Time Strikes*, ch. 10; and Cuff, "The Politics of Labor Administration."

62. Gitelman, "Being of Two Minds," 203–4. In the American context, "rela-

tively enlightened" meant maintaining open shops while proclaiming every employee's right to join a union.

63. "Report of War Labor Conference Board to the Secretary of Labor, March 29, 1918," reprinted in United States Bureau of Labor Satistics, *National War Labor Board*, 31–33.

64. Out of 1,251 controversies referred to the board, only 199 came as joint submissions (United States Bureau of Labor Statistics, *National War Labor Board*, 20). Even in these cases, awards could be enforced over the objections of either party only if President Wilson took executive action on the board's behalf. He did so in two cases: in the well-publicized refusal of Smith and Wesson to obey an NWLB award, Wilson commandeered the plant; when Bridgeport workers struck in defiance of an award, he threatened them with the draft and blacklisting from war work. In principle the president could also have the War Industries Board and the U.S. Employment Service starve a recalcitrant firm of materials and labor until it complied. I have found no examples this.

65. The NWLB made 490 awards in its short life, directly affecting 1,100 establishments and 711,500 employees; these awards also served as models for other firms in an industry or locality. See National War Labor Board, *Report*, 9–10; Perlman and Taft, *Labor in the United States*, 408–9; United States Bureau of Labor Statistics, *National War Labor Board*, 20–23.

66. NWLB Records, Minutes of Executive Sessions, Oct. 25, 1918, re: Saginaw, p. 46. The board made the same suggestion to Bridgeport workers in denying their request for classification.

67. The awards were for Worthington Pump (two separate cases, NWLB Records, Case Files, Dockets 14 and 163), Bethlehem Steel (ibid., Docket 22), and Midvale Steel (ibid., Docket 129). At the first company the board's awards allowed multiple grades; at Bethlehem and probably at Midvale, the companies never implemented the decision.

68. Thomas Savage's report on May 20, 1918, hearings with company representatives, NWLB Records, Case Files, Docket 22; "Conclusions submitted by the Secretary and Chief Examiner," July 9, 1918, ibid.; and memo to Walsh, probably from Savage, June 20, 1918, ibid.

69. The NICB itself embraced these principles in its recommendations to the Council of National Defense for wartime labor policy and again in negotiations with AFL representatives on the War Labor Conference Board (United States Bureau of Labor Statistics, *National War Labor Board*, 27–28).

70. Connor, *The National War Labor Board*, ch. 3 and 124–25.

71. Letter, Locomobile Company (Bridgeport, Conn.) to John Casey (commissioner of conciliation), quoted in *Machinists' Monthly Journal*, Feb. 1918, p. 101.

72. Bing, *War-Time Strikes*, 54; Gitelman, *Legacy of the Ludlow Massacre*, 224.

73. Wehle, *Hidden Threads of History*, 54; Gitelman, *Legacy of the Ludlow Massacre*, 224–25.

74. MacKenzie King, quoted in Montgomery, *Fall of the House of Labor*, 349–50. On clashing visions of shop committees, see ibid., 411–20; McCartin, "'An American Feeling.'" Montgomery places particular emphasis on radical visions; for a more nuanced discussion of employers' views, see Gitelman, "Being of Two Minds," 214–16.

75. Overviews of NWLB shop committee policies include Conner, *The National War Labor Board;* French, *The Shop Committee;* and Brandes, *American Welfare Capitalism,* 121–29.

76. NWLB Records, Minutes of Executive Sessions, October 23, 1918, pp. 43–44 (Osborne quotation), 45–46 (Taft quotation).

77. "Machinists' Memorandum" in response to Gitchell award, NWLB Records, Case Files, Docket 720, Exhibit 21.

78. Letter, Sam Lavit to the NWLB, reprinted in the *Labor Leader,* Sept. 26, 1918.

79. Bing, *War-Time Strikes,* 162.

80. Memo, F. H. Bird to Lauck, Sept. 5, 1918, NWLB Records, Case Files, Docket 22; letter, Examiner Henderson to Woods, Oct. 15, 1918, NWLB Records, Administrative Files, files of E. B. Woods; letter, Field Investigator Agnes Johnson to Elizabeth Christman, Nov. 10, 1918, NWLB Records, Case Files, Docket 22; McCartin, "Labor's 'Great War,'" 346–47, 351.

81. Report from William Stoddard to Taft and Walsh, July 9, 1918, NWLB Records, Case Files, Docket 19.

82. Note from Stoddard to Woods, Oct. 9, 1918, and Woods to Stoddard, Oct. 9, NWLB Records, Case Files, Docket 19. On board members' assumptions about the likely outcome of outside elections, see Minutes of Executive Sessions, Nov. 21, 1918, NWLB Records, p. 46.

83. NWLB Records, Minutes of Executive Sessions, Nov. 21, 1918, pp. 39–50, 65 (quotation on 43); Conner, *The National War Labor Board,* 135–36.

84. Conner, *The National War Labor Board,* 111–13; McCartin, "Labor's 'Great War,'" 316–23; undated, unsigned report on April and May strikes, NWLB Records, Case Files, Docket 22.

85. NWLB Records, Minutes of Executive Sessions, June 1, 1918, pp. 15 (Grace quotation), 25, 26 (Rice quotation); Gitelman, *Legacy of the Ludlow Massacre,* 225.

86. Letter, Woods to Gregg, Dec. 11, 1918, NWLB Records, Case Files, Docket 22.

87. Memo, F. H. Bird to Lucien Cheney, Sept. 5, 1918, NWLB Records, Case Files, Docket 22. See also Conner, *The National War Labor Board,* 123.

88. Bing, *War-Time Strikes,* 81.

89. Letter, Lavit to the NWLB, reprinted in *Labor Leader,* Sept. 26, 1918.

90. *Internal state* is shorthand for how authority is exercised and conflict managed at work—a more open-ended use of the term than that in Burawoy, *Manufacturing Consent,* ch. 7.

91. See Jacoby, *Employing Bureaucracy,* ch. 4; Murphy, "John Andrews."

92. NWLB Records, Minutes of Executive Sessions, June 1, 1918, morning session, p. 44. Walsh meant to say the "National Association of Manufacturers."

93. "Representation of Employees in Plants of the Bethlehem Steel Corporation," NWLB Records, Case Files, Docket 22; letters between Cheney and Lauck, Sept. 2, 3, 5, and 7, 1918, ibid.; transcript of proceedings, Jan. 15, 1919, pp. 8, 13, 28; report by Johnston and Sullivan, Apr. 11, 1919, ibid.

94. Statement by William Sink, former steward at Bullard Engineering Co., to NWLB field representative Isaac Russell, Aug. 20, 1918, quoted in *Labor Leader,* Aug. 22, 1918; NWLB Records, Minutes of Executive Sessions, June 1, 1918, morning session, p. 26.

95. Montgomery, *House of Labor*, 443, 446–47; and McCartin, "Labor's 'Great War,'" 223–26.

96. *Machinists' Monthly Journal*, Jan. 1919, p. 35; McCartin, "Labor's 'Great War,'" 228–30.

97. McCartin, "Labor's 'Great War,'" 234–36, 248 n. 104 (quotation).

98. Memo from Pittsfield administrator R. C. Dickey, Feb. 7, 1919, NWLB Records, Case Files, Docket 19; Montgomery, *Fall of the House of Labor*, 449.

99. *Bridgeport Post*, Aug. 30–Sept. 18, 1918; *Bridgeport Herald*, Sept. 1, 8, and 15, 1918; Bucki, "Dilution and Craft Traditions."

100. *Labor Leader*, Sept. 26, 1918.

101. Lavit's view is summarized in a letter from Russell to Lauck, Sept. 4, 1918, NWLB Records, Case Files, Docket 132. See also *Bridgeport Post*, Sept. 4, 1918; *Bridgeport Herald*, Sept. 8, 1918; and letter, Woods to Lauck, Sept. 6, 1918, NWLB Records, Case Files, Docket 132.

102. *Labor Leader*, Dec. 19, 1918.

103. *Bridgeport Herald*, Mar. 23, 1919 (quotation); Hawley, "Employers Report Shop Committees Successful"; and correspondence between Alpheus Winter and Bridgeport firms re: employee committees, from Willard Aborn (temporary chair, Local Board of Mediation) to W. D. Angelo (assistant chief administrator, NWLB), May 12, 1919, and from Lauck to Lavit, May 6, 1918, all in NWLB Records, Case Files, Docket 132.

104. Minutes of Local Board of Mediation and Conciliation meeting, Mar. 31, 1919, NWLB Records, Case Files, Docket 132; *Bridgeport Herald*, Mar. 23, 1919.

105. *Labor Leader*, Mar. 27, 1919.

106. "Machinists' Memorandum" from mid-August 1918, NWLB Records, Case Files, Docket 720, Exhibit 21; F. H. Bird, "Report on Shop Committee System, Bethlehem Steel Company, Lebanon Plant," Feb. 13, 1919, NWLB Records, Case Files, Docket 22.

107. Aborn and Shafer, "Representative Shop Committees," 30.

108. Montgomery, in *Fall of the House of Labor*, 420, raises the possibility that NWLB committees, because they disregarded craft boundaries, could have served as cells for industrial union movements. He properly emphasizes, however, that they could have done so only if they had been effectively coordinated by militant leadership outside the plants. McCartin is less guarded, claiming that the NWLB actually *did* reshape labor unrest in the direction of mass unionism ("Labor's 'Great War,'" 94–95; "'An American Feeling,'" 72–77). In most cases, however, insurgent movements developed before the implementation of NWLB awards, with local union leaders themselves often criticizing the board's subsequent interventions. And as McCartin himself notes, even if the board's shop committee plan had favored a more encompassing local labor movement, it could have done so only until the armistice. In the case of Bridgeport, this would have been approximately six weeks if shop committee elections had been held immediately following the board's decision. Most shop committee elections took place in November and December.

109. On the relationship between electoral politics and state labor policy, see Friedman, "Worker Militancy and Its Consequences"; and Dubofsky, *The State*

and Labor. Two important treatments of American courts and organized labor before the New Deal are Hattam, *Labor Visions and State Power;* and Orren, *Belated Feudalism.* Robertson adds that federalism heightened the bias against labor as states competed with one another to attract business; see Robertson, "The Bias of American Federalism."

110. *Railway Age,* Oct. 20, 1916, p. 679. The carriers were still fuming over the 1916 Adamson Act, pushed through by Wilson to avert a railroad strike by granting operating employees the eight-hour day. Other landmarks of the new relation between organized labor and the federal government include the 1913 appointment of William Wilson, formerly of the Mine Workers Union, as secretary of labor; the 1914 Clayton Act's declaration that labor is not a commodity (hailed by Gompers, mistakenly, as exempting unions from antitrust liability); and President Wilson's address to the AFL convention in 1917.

111. The federal government was willing and able to discipline munitions employers whose labor relations endangered war production. It was quite another thing to assert government control over the industry as a whole. In mid-1918 Felix Frankfurter attempted to establish a metal trades board similar in powers to the specialized labor boards in shipbuilding and construction. Frankfurter's plan would have enhanced the government's power to standardize conditions throughout the munitions industry, and it assigned to national union officials (together with employer representatives) a virtual monopoly in the handling of disputes. Employers balked, first insisting that Frankfurter water down the powers of the board, and then withdrawing their nominees (and cooperation) altogether. See the following items in War Labor Policies Board Records, Correspondence of the Chairman (entry 2): memorandum for discussion at July 16, 1918 meeting, in folder titled "National Metal Trades Board (May and July 1918)"; letter, Frankfurter to Wilson, Sept. 19, 1918, in "National Metal Trades Board (Sept. 1918)" folder; complaints registered by the NICB's prospective representatives to the board's designated chair, Henry Suzzalo, Nov. 4, 1918, in "National Metal Trades Board, Oct. 1918" and "National Metal Trades Board, Nov. 1918" folders; telegram from Frankfurter to Emery, Oct. 24, 1918, telegram from Alexander to Frankfurter, Oct. 29, 1918, minutes of Nov. 1, 1918, meeting, and NICB resolution of Nov. 21, 1918, in "National Metal Trades Board, Oct. 1918" and "National Metal Trades Board (Nov. 1918)" folders. See also the following in the War Labor Policies Board Records, Perkins Correspondence (entry 4): letter from Emery to Frankfurter, Oct. 23, 1918 (in "F. Frankfurter" folder); telegram from Perkins to Emery, Oct. 25, 1918, and memo of conference with Emery and Magnus Alexander of the NICB, Oct. 26, 1918 ("Metal and Building Trades" folder).

112. Quoted in *Monthly Labor Review,* Apr. 1919, p. 73.

113. Surveys include Perlman and Taft, *Labor in the United States;* Montgomery, *Fall of the House of Labor,* chs. 8–9; Kopald, *Rebellion in Labor Unions,* highlighting unofficial strikes; and Brody, *Labor in Crisis,* on steel. Aggregate statistics collected by Edwards in *Strikes in the United States* suggest that strikes were more likely to be connected with trade unions in 1919–22 than in 1916–18 (p. 33). The relative importance of wages and hours and of union rights as strike issues remained about the same in the two periods (p. 37).

114. National Metal Trades Association, *Report of the Committee on Works Councils*, 3, 4 (quotation), 6; National Industrial Conference Board, *Experience with Works Councils*, 185–91; United States Bureau of Labor Statistics, *Characteristics of Company Unions*, 51.

115. Of the twelve opponents of shop committees quoted by Wolfe, only one hinted that unionization was a cause of concern; see Wolfe, *Works Committees and Industrial Councils*, appendix.

116. National Industrial Conference Board, *Works Councils in the United States*, 3, 5–13, 116; ibid., *Experience with Works Councils*, 13–14. See also Wolfe, *Works Committees and Industrial Councils*; National Industrial Conference Board, *Experience with Works Councils*.

117. On company unionism and company union membership in the United States, see National Industrial Conference Board, *Experience with Works Councils*; Lescohier and Brandeis, *Labor in the United States*, 349–50; Wakstein, "The Open Shop Movement"; Nelson, "The Company Union Movement"; McQuaid, "Corporate Liberalism in American Business." Overall union membership and union density figures are in Bain and Price, *Profiles of Union Growth*; and Wolman, *Ebb and Flow in Unionism*; company union membership in Germany is reported in Moses, "The Concept of Economic Democracy." Machinists offer one important example of declining unionization: 11.1 percent belonged to unions in 1910. The war boom brought this figure to 33.9 percent, but by 1930 it had dropped back to 8.9 percent. See Wolman, *Ebb and Flow*, 222; and idem, *Growth of American Trade Unions*, 157, 159.

118. The range of support for employee representation plans included a large majority of members of the U.S. Chamber of Commerce, the small and medium-size firms that made up the extremely conservative NMTA, and such "corporate liberal" giants as General Electric and Standard Oil.

119. Bulletin of the Manufacturers' Association of Bridgeport, June 1, 1921, summarizing the conclusions of the New England Conference on Employee Representation, May 24, 1921. See also NMTA, *Report on Works Councils*, 5; and the reports on works committees reprinted in the appendix to Wolfe, *Works Committees and Industrial Councils*. On employee representation and industrial jurisprudence, see Jacoby, *Employing Bureaucracy*, ch. 4 and pp. 180–85; Nelson, "The Company Union Movement," 357; French, *The Shop Committee*, 95–99. Nelson also notes the importance of NWLB shop committees as a model for employee representation in the 1920s (*Managers and Workers*, 161).

120. *Iron Age*, July 31, 1919, p. 314, Dedford is quoted in Kennedy, *Over Here*, 276; see also the report on the NMTA annual convention of Apr. 23–24, 1919, in *Iron Age*, May 1, 1919, p. 1153.

121. On the industrial conference, see Conner, *The National War Labor Board*, 173–78; Brody, *Labor in Crisis*, 115–28; and Harvey, "Rockefeller, Hoover, and Wilson."

122. The British figure is from Clegg, Fox, and Thompson, *History of British Trade Unions*, 550; the U.S. statistics are calculated from the United States Bureau of Labor Statistics, *Strikes in the United States*, 38.

123. Ozanne, *Century of Labor-Management Relations*, 122–23. Bell Telephone was one exception, and it was one of the few cases where a company union

evolved into a bona fide union during the 1930s. See Schacht, "Toward Industrial Unionism."

124. Tipper, "How to Check the Radical," 737.

125. Walter Merritt in *Iron Age*, June 16, 1919, p. 1627, and June 26, 1919, p. 1706. See similar arguments, from the other side of the political spectrum, in Dunn, "The Industrial Welfare Offensive." Prothero, *Dollar Decade*, quotes one business leader's 1926 call for legislation to suppress all labor organization "involving the employees of more than one and the same employer" (152).

126. Quoted by Kennedy, *Over Here*, 272. See also Wolfe, *Works Committees and Industrial Councils*, 231, 235; Shepard, "Industrial Representation and the Fair Deal"; Brody, *Steelworkers in America*, 268–69.

127. Only seven of the plans found by the National Industrial Conference Board in 1922 had been established by the NWLB itself (National Industrial Conference Board, *Experience with Works Councils*, 185–91).

128. Undated bulletin on the NWLB by the American Anti-Boycott Association, NWLB Records, Administrative Files (entry 15). Employer representatives on the NWLB and their counterparts in other government labor bureaus often advised firms to resolve disputes with their employees without the case coming to the NWLB, precisely to avoid public scrutiny and "outside" interference. See Lombardi, *Labor's Voice in the Cabinet*, 256; Gitelman, "Being of Two Minds," 214–15.

129. Transcript of proceedings, Jan. 15, 1919, testimony by Mr. Currier, NWLB Records, Case Files, Docket 22, p. 13 (quotation); "Representation of Employees in Plants of the Bethlehem Steel Corporation," employee pamphlet, Oct. 1918, NWLB Records, Case Files, Docket 22; F. H. Bird, "Report on Shop Committee System, Bethlehem Steel Company," Feb. 13, 1919, ibid.

130. National Industrial Conference Board, *Experience with Works Councils*, 17; Manufacturers' Association of Bridgeport, Minutes, Apr. 2, 16, Sept. 13, 1918; Manufacturers' Association of Bridgeport, Bulletin, Sept. 21, 1918; National Industrial Conference Board, *Works Councils in the United States*, 10.

131. United States Bureau of Labor Statistics, *Characteristics of Company Unions*, 51.

132. Perlman and Taft, *Labor in the United States*, 409; Examiner Donahue to Lauck, Jan. 8, 1919, NWLB Records, Case Files, Docket 720. See also the case of International Harvester in Ozanne, *Century of Labor-Management Relations*, ch. 7.

133. Aborn and Shafer, "Representative Shop Committees."

134. To this extent, Kazin's argument for San Francisco applies to the nation as a whole; see Kazin, *Barons of Labor*. Judd, in *Socialist Cities*, makes a similar case that progressive alliances between working-class and middle-class reformers eventually undermined labor's political influence. See also Oestreicher, "Urban Working-Class Political Behavior."

135. This is roughly the configuration of forces to which scholars have attributed corporatist trends after World War II.

136. The best discussions of "Progressive" attitudes toward labor problems and the failure of a liberal-labor alliance are found in the work of Shapiro: "The Great War and Reform" and "Hand and Brain."

137. Conner, *The National War Labor Board*, ch. 11, covers the demise of the board. On employers' views, see also Urofsky, *Big Steel and the Wilson Administration*, 296–98, 315–17, 333.

138. In 1918, 1.1 million employees had wages and working conditions fixed by collective agreement; the figure rose to 6 million in 1919, 9.5 million in 1920, 13 million in 1921, and 14 million in 1922. Coverage remained at about this level for the rest of the decade. Guillebaud, *The Works Council,* 39; Reich, *Labour Relations in Republican Germany,* 108–12.

139. The figure of 7 percent (Wolman, *Ebb and Flow in Unionism,* 133) is for 1933 and may thus be a bit higher than those for the late 1920s. I have been unable to find data on collective bargaining coverage during the 1920s for the United States (or Britain).

140. This view was common among liberal academicians in the war labor administration, including Frankfurter at the War Labor Policies Board, Walter Lippman in the War Department, Leon Marshall and Henry Seager of the Shipbuilding Labor Adjustment Board, and NWLB secretary Jett Lauck. Although the postwar wave of labor unrest alienated many Progressives from organized labor, John Commons was not alone in mid-1920 in arguing that if employers "finally defeat the unions by an open shop movement, then there will be nothing for the American workman to do except to follow European workmen—Socialistic, Bolshevistic, I.W.W.-istic" (*The Survey,* July 17, 1920, p. 533).

141. *Iron Age,* Jan. 1, 1920, p. 1. By the same token, the National Association of Manufacturers labeled suggestions that the government retain responsibility for mediating disputes or protecting union rights after the war as "partisan, pro-labor union, socialistic propaganda" (quoted in J. Smith, "Organized Labor," 280). Gitelman notes that in 1919, amid widespread fears of revolution, a close adviser of John Rockefeller's (Mackenzie King) recommended something like a Stinnes-Legien agreement: Rockefeller should make concessions, including recognition, to "responsible" unions in his oil companies. Reassurance from Starr Murphy that the industrial and political situation was not so threatening after all helped to persuade Rockefeller to refuse those concessions (Gitelman, *Legacy of the Ludlow Massacre,* 302).

142. Gordon, in *New Deals,* argues that during the 1920s employers discovered the value of collective bargaining for economic stabilization. New Deal backing for this "regulatory unionism" in turn owed less to political realignments than to employers' inability to sustain economic controls on a voluntary basis. My view of the 1920s is rather different. I highlight management's reliance on reformed open shops for orderly labor relations, while Gordon emphasizes the perceived value of unions for economic stabilization. Even in the latter area, Gordon reads back into the 1920s union virtues that were widely appreciated only in the 1930s: most of the endorsements of regulatory unionism he cites come from the early 1930s, not the 1920s; and when Gordon turns from employers' preaching to their practices, he finds the uses of unions for economic regulation to be few and far between. (The only example offered from the metal trades—electrical engineering—showcases enlightened open shop management, not union recognition.) As for the economic versus political origins of state policy, the relative importance of each varied over time even during the World War 1 era. In the light of the German experience, however, it seems clear that the political alignments discounted by Gordon are crucial for explaining the limited role of unions in American industrial relations in the 1920s.

INTRODUCTION TO PART 2

1. Skowronek, *Building a New American State;* Skocpol, *Protecting Soldiers and Mothers.*

2. Cuff, *The War Industries Board,* 7–11, 69–73, 141–47; Cuff, "The Politics of Labor Administration," 562–65; Lombardi, *Labor's Voice in the Cabinet,* 260, 297. See also Howell Harris, "The Snares of Liberalism," 152.

3. See, for example, Conner, *The National War Labor Board,* on the board itself; Kennedy, *Over Here,* 141–43; Bustard, "The Human Factor" 4, 94–95; Beaver, *Newton D. Baker,* 5–6.

4. Beaver, *Newton Baker,* 6, 35–36; Statement of the Secretary of War to the Munitions Manufacturers of Connecticut, Nov. 21, 1917 (reproduced in United States War Department, *Report on Industrial Relations,* 83–84). On Wilson's political coalition and its effects on labor administration, see Dubofsky, *The State and Labor,* chs. 2–3.

CHAPTER 3: CORPORATISM, VOLUNTARISM, AND
COLLECTIVE BARGAINING IN RAILROAD SHOPS

1. *American Machinist,* Nov. 2, 1922, p. 704. See also Colvin, *60 Years with Men and Machines.*

2. Davis, "Bitter Storm," 16–20.

3. As Stromquist points out, general trends toward standardization, specialization, and dilution did not entirely bypass railroad shops (*A Generation of Boomers,* 115, 126). These processes were much less advanced in railroad shops than in other metal trades, however. A review of prewar work rules, for example, found craft practices to be far more common in railroad shops (United States Railroad Labor Board, *Presentation by Railway Employes' [sic] Department,* pt. 2). See also United States Railroad Labor Board, *Rules prior to National Agreement;* Hines, *War History of American Railroads,* 176; Calvert, *The Mechanical Engineer in America,* 72–75.

4. Wolf, *The Railroad Labor Board,* 59; Montgomery, *Workers' Control in America,* 63.

5. Licht, *Working for the Railroad,* 232; Stromquist, *A Generation of Boomers,* 192–93.

6. *The Car Worker,* Oct. 1907, p. 31.

7. The "Federation of Federations" was launched in 1912 as a rival to the AFL's ineffectual Railway Employees' Department; it served as the basis for a reorganized RED in 1914. See Davis, "Bitter Storm," 57–64; *Boilermakers' Journal,* Apr. 1915, pp. 271–72, and May 1915, pp. 352–53.

8. Testimony before the U.S. Senate Commission on Industrial Relations (1916), reprinted in United States Railroad Labor Board, *Industrial Relations on Railroads,* 33. On the system federations' period of insurgency, see Montgomery, *Workers' Control in America,* 81–82, 107, 124; Foner, *History of the Labor Movement,* 167–69.

9. Wood, *Union-Management Cooperation,* 50–55.

10. The Brotherhoods of Locomotive Enginemen, Railway Conductors, Locomotive Firemen, and Railroad Trainmen were the unions representing the four basic groups of operating employees.

11. Davis, "Bitter Storm," 80–82, 93–94; Hines, *War History of American Railroads*, 7.

12. Testimony before the United States Commission on Industrial Relations, reprinted in United States Railroad Labor Board, *Industrial Relations on Railroads*, 16; see also ibid., 15, 27.

13. United States Railroad Labor Board, *Rules prior to National Agreement;* idem, *Presentation by Railway Employes' Department*, pts. 2 and 3.

14. *Boilermakers' Journal*, Aug. 1916, p. 599. As of late 1917, shop craft unions held contracts covering 70 percent of Class 1 railroads (Lecht, *Railway Labor Legislation*, 31).

15. By 1917 there were sixty-one such agreements; separate craft agreements existed on only twenty-three lines (June 1, 1921, hearings, statement by Bert Jewell [RED president], United States Railroad Labor Board, National Mediation Board Records, Docketed Case Files (entry 56), Docket 380, pp. 38, 49). See also circular from George Pring (president of RED Division No. 1 [western lines]) to division members, June 24, 1916, RED Master File of Official Circulars, AFL RED Records, ser. 3; and United States Railroad Administration, *Annual Reports, 1918*, 3.

16. Davis, "Bitter Storm," 79; Wood, *Union-Management Cooperation*, 54–55.

17. Kerr, *American Railroad Politics*, 40.

18. Wolf, *The Railroad Labor Board*, 12; McAdoo, *Crowded Years*, 470; Wehle, *Hidden Threads of History*, 57.

19. For an overview of federal control of the railroads, see Dixon and Parmelee, *War Administration of the Railways*.

20. Hines, *War History*, 161–63.

21. Official Circular No. 30, May 4, 1917, RED Records, scr. 3; United States Railroad Labor Board, *Presentation by Railway Employes' Department*, pt. 1, pp. 23–24; Wood, *Union-Management Cooperation*, 49–50. Shop craft unions also limited the entry of women into skilled occupations (or, in Wharton's words, prevented "the debasement and demoralization of the standards and ideals of American womanhood" [letter, Wharton to Hon. A. Caminetti, Commission of Immigration, Aug. 31, 1917, reprinted in RED Official Circular No. 54 (Oct. 15, 1917), RED Records, ser. 3]). A 1918 survey found a much higher proportion of female employees (12.9 percent) in a sample of metal trades firms than existed in railroad shop crafts (5 percent). See National Industrial Conference Board, *Women in the Metal Trades*, 6; and Greenwald, "Women Workers and World War I," 156–57, 159.

22. Hines, *War History of American Railroads*, 167–68, 177.

23. Board No. 2 handled 1,276 cases between its establishment in May 1918 and its dissolution in April 1920. See Wolf, *The Railroad Labor Board*, 50–54; RED Official Circular No. 75 (July 2, 1918) and No. 79 (Aug. 20, 1918), RED Records, ser. 3; Kerr, *American Railroad Politics*, 91–92.

24. Kerr, *American Railroad Politics*, 74–75, 132–42. For the Progressives' vision of social efficiency see Haber, *Efficiency and Uplift*; and E. M. Tobin, *Organize or Perish*, 55–60.

25. These arrangements typically covered single lines, but the Southeastern Agreement established joint committees of management and union delegates from lines throughout the region.

26. Letter, Walker Hines to Bert Jewell, June 5, 1919, reprinted in RED Official Circular No. 98, RED Records, ser. 3; Wolf, *The Railroad Labor Board*, 40.

27. Hines, *War History of American Railroads*, 161–63; United States Railroad Administration, "Report on Labor," *Annual Reports, 1918*, 8; Davis, "Bitter Storm," 88–90.

28. United States Railroad Administration, *Reports for Fourteen Months*, 15. On railroad regulation and government centralization, see Kerr, *American Railroad Politics*, 80; Skowronek, *Building a New American State*, 278.

29. Official Circular No. 86 (December 30, 1918), AFL RED Records, ser. 3. See also circulars 79 (Aug. 20) and 80 (Sept. 6).

30. Memo, W. S. Carter to Director General Hines, June 3, 1919, in U.S. Railroad Administration Records, Subject Classified Files of the Division of Labor 1918–22 (entry 83), folder A-14-30; RED Official Circular No. 98 (June 6, 1919), copy in U.S. Railroad Administration Records, entry 83, folder A-14-30; Wolf, *The Railroad Labor Board*, 18–31.

31. Memo, Carter to Hines, June 3, 1919, U.S. Railroad Administration Records, entry 83, folder A-14-30.

32. RED Official Circular No. 98 (June 6, 1919), copy in U.S. Railroad Administration Records, entry 83, folder A-14-30.

33. Memo, Carter to Hines, July 21, 1919, U.S. Railroad Administration Records, entry 83, folder A-14-30.

34. Letter, Jewell to Hines, July 7, 1919, U.S. Railroad Administration Records, entry 83, folder A-14-30.

35. To put pressure on the Railroad Administration, RED officials began balloting members on a strike in July. Their subsequent refusal to put the ballot to use further discredited them in the eyes of shop craft workers. See Davis, "Bitter Storm," 103–5.

36. *Machinists' Monthly Journal*, Sept. 1919, p. 854.

37. *Railway Age*, Aug. 8, 1919, p. 237.

38. *Boilermakers' Journal*, Oct. 1919, p. 752.

39. *Iron Age*, Aug. 14, 1919, p. 446.

40. Decisions Rendered by Railway Boards of Adjustment, Board No. 2, U.S. Railroad Administration Records, entry 95, Dockets NV-114 (Hocking), AG-688 (St. Louis Southwestern), SE-814, 1376, 1637 (re: payment of committeemen), and 1119 (Wheeling and Lake Erie).

41. Letter, H. H. Reed (special assistant to the director of the Division of Labor) to W. G. Choate (assistant general manager, Gulf Coast Lines, Houston), Apr. 28, 1919, in Railroad Adminstration Records, entry 83, File A-14-107.

42. Circular No. 39, July 3, 1918, copy in Correspondence of Chairman and General Secretary (entry 2), War Labor Policies Board Records, "Railroad Administration" folder. See also Kerr, *American Railroad Politics*, 92.

43. The arrangement, one government adviser recalled, "greatly increased [unions'] membership and influence" (Wehle, "War Labor Policies," 335). See also RED Circular No. 79 (Aug. 20, 1918) and 80 (Sept. 6, 1918), in RED Records, ser. 3.

44. *Boilermakers' Journal*, Nov. 1919, p. 924.

45. Agreements between Railroads and Labor Organizations, 1917–1920, Railroad Administration Records, entry 118, folder marked "Interpretation of Rule 35."

46. Jewell to Hines, July 7, 1919, Railroad Administration Records, entry 83, File A-14-30. See also Troy, "Labor Representation in American Railways," 297–98.

47. *Railway Age*, Mar. 14, 1919, p. 571.

48. The basic proposal is described in Hines's letter to the regional railroad directors, Nov. 10, 1919, Subject Classified General File of the Director General, 1918–27, Railroad Administration Records, entry 1, File E38-18/4-6. See also Wood, *Union-Management Cooperation*, 83–84.

49. Memo, Franklin to Carter, Nov. 4, 1919; Jewell to Frank McManamy (assistant director, Division of Operations), Nov. 6, 1919. Both in Railroad Administration Records, entry 1, File E38-18/4-6.

50. Letter, Hines to regional directors, Nov. 10, 1919, in Railroad Administration Records, entry 1, File E38-18/4-6.

51. Circular letter, Dec. 12, 1919, in Railroad Administration Records, entry 1, File E38-18/4-6. The Progressive editors of the Plumb League's newspaper also endorsed the plan (*Railroad Democracy* [later renamed *Labor*], Sept. 4, 1919).

52. Field's account of the B. and O. experiment ("Designing the Capital-Labor Accord"), by relying on AFL Railway Employees Department records, underestimates the Railway Administration's contributions to the plan.

53. Correspondence from Companies re: Interpretation of National Agreement, Railroad Administration Records, entry 118, in boxes 11–13. Hotly contested issues included the reintroduction of piecework and payment for overtime. Prewar contracts with the same provisions (and even the same language) as Rule 35 are reproduced in United States Railroad Labor Board, *Industrial Relations on Railroads*.

54. Hines, *War History of American Railroads*, 182–84; United States Railroad Administration, "Report of the Division of Labor," *Reports for Fourteen Months* (1920), 82–83.

55. Calculated from Douglas and Wolfe, "Labor Administration in Shipbuilding I," 145–47; and "Data Relative to Shop Employees," Recommendations of the Board of Railroad Wages and Working Conditions 1918–20 (entry 39), Recommendation 99A, U.S. Railroad Administration Records. Hines reported an even smaller increase (8.2 percent) in railroad employment, but he did so to fend off owners' charges that under federal control the labor force had become bloated by political patronage and inefficient management (*Railway Age*, Mar. 14, 1919, p. 600).

56. Official Circular No. 66 (Mar. 15, 1918), in RED Records, ser. 3.

57. On these organizing drives, see Davis, "Bitter Storm," 91–93.

58. Statements by Boilermakers' president Weyand and RED president Jewell, Aug. 18, 1918, in Transcripts of Hearings (entry 291), vol. 1, Hearings of Presidents of National Labor Unions: Boilermakers, USSB Records, p. 672. See also letter, D. R. McBain (chairman of the committee representing regional directors) to F. F. Gaines (chairman of the Board of Wages and Working Conditions), May 6, 1919, RED Records, ser. 4 (misc. folders on National Agreement), protesting job classifications and limits on the work that could be done by helpers; and Wolf, *The Railroad Labor Board*, 40–46.

59. Sirianni, "Workers' Control in Europe," 264–65.

60. Letter, Wade Graham (system federation chairman for the International

and Great Northern Railway) to Jewell, Dec. 17, 1919, RED Records, ser. 1 ("Co-Operation"), folder 1, code no. 36-1 (general cooperation file).

61. Telegram, Hines to Representative J. Hamilton Lewis, undated but probably Aug. 10, 1919, in U.S. Railroad Administration Records, entry 83, folder A-14-30-A.

62. Davis, "Bitter Storm," is the most recent study and adds a great deal of useful detail on developments leading up to the 1922 shop crafts strike. Davis's basic view of the government's role in bringing the strike about matches traditional treatments such as Perlman and Taft, *Labor in the United States,* 516–23.

63. Under the Transportation Act unions nominated labor representatives, but the president appointed them. Harding chose W. C. McMenimen of the Brotherhood of Trainmen over the objections of other railroad unions, and he picked procarrier Ben Hooper as a "public" member. Robert Zieger summarizes the Republican offensive against railroad labor unions in the early 1920s in "From Hostility to Moderation." Even among Democrats and Progressives, however, wartime enthusiasm for federal control and union rights dissipated after the armistice. Only a minority of the Wilsonian liberals, social democrats, and Progressive trust-busters allied in the "Committee of 48" endorsed the Plumb Plan, for example (Shapiro, "The Twilight of Reform," 361–62). See also Kerr, *American Railroad Politics,* 75, 142, on William McAdoo's retreat from wartime Progressive views.

64. Even among activists and officials contributing to the Plumb League's weekly paper, *Labor,* the virtues of government ownership had more to do with preserving wartime gains and improving service than with advancing socialism. Amid the general conservative backlash of 1919–20, however, continued government control of any kind was beyond the pale. On the fate of the Plumb Plan, see Kerr, *American Railroad Politics,* 132–42; Wolf, *The Railroad Labor Board,* 88–94.

65. Most of the Transportation Act dealt with matters other than labor. For example, it continued Interstate Commerce Commission control over rates (something that had been suspended under federal control, benefiting carriers and hurting shippers), and it guaranteed carriers a 5.5 percent rate of return over the next five years.

66. The complex legislative background to these provisions is reviewed in United States Railroad Labor Board, *Railroad Boards of Labor Adjustment;* and Wolf, *The Railroad Labor Board,* 88–94.

67. Letter, Hines to Cummins and Esch, Febr. 14, 1920, in United States Railroad Labor Board, *Railroad Boards of Labor Adjustment,* 12.

68. Proceedings of the United States Railroad Labor Board, Nov. 29, 1920, copy in RED Records, ser. 2, code no. MC-0-14-19 ("Regional Boards of Adjustment"); Wolf, *The Railroad Labor Board,* 266–74.

69. Wolf, *The Railroad Labor Board,* 166–82.

70. United States Railroad Labor Board, *Decisions, 1921,* Decision 119.

71. Quoted in Wolf, *The Railroad Labor Board,* 187. The relevant decisions are 119 and 222. See also *Labor,* Apr. 23, 1921.

72. United States Railroad Labor Board, *Decisions, 1921,* Decision 119, Exhibit B.

73. Ibid., Decision 982 (Indiana Harbor Belt Company), May 9, 1922. Because these rulings came only shortly before the 1922 shopmen's strike, it is impossi-

ble to determine how widely they would have been followed. After the strike anti-union carriers no longer felt obliged to bother disguising their open shop policies. At hearings the day before the shop crafts strike, a number of carriers assured the board that they would discontinue subcontracting, but these pledges were probably designed to persuade President Grable of the Brotherhood of Maintenance-of-Way Employees not to join the strike; see Wolf, *The Railroad Labor Board*, 235–37.

74. National Mediation Board Records, entry 56, Docket 380. Similar cases and decisions include the Chicago, Burlington, and Quincy Railroad (Docket 381) and the Missouri, Kansas, and Texas Railroad (Docket 398).

75. United States Railroad Labor Board, *Decisions, 1921*, Decision No. 119, Exhibit B, Principle 5; Decision 222, Addendum 6, Rules 35 and 36.

76. In these cases the Railroad Labor Board ruled that the fact that a system federation had spoken for employees or signed contracts with management in the past was insufficient evidence of employees' intentions. Accordingly the board ordered elections.

77. Cases include the Virginia Railway Co. (Docket 399), the Long Island Railroad (Docket 403), and the Illinois Terminal Railroad (Docket 449), National Mediation Board Records, S-56. The board further reinforced union control over workplace unionism by assigning responsibility for bringing cases before it to "the chief executive of [the] organization" representing employees (Order No. 1, Apr. 19, 1920, Form B, in United States Railroad Labor Board, *Decisions, 1920*).

78. Plan of Employee Representation, effective June 1, 1920, copy in National Mediation Board Records, S-56, Docket 25; *Railway Age*, Dec. 24, 1920, p. 1114.

79. Letter, F. L. Simmons, supervisor of industrial relations, to C. P. Carrithers, secretary of the Railroad Labor Board, Jan. 24, 1921, with copy of Bennet's notice attached, National Mediation Board Records, S-56, Docket 25-2.

80. Letter to Railroad Labor Board chairman Barton, ibid., Docket 25.

81. Simmons to Carrithers, Jan. 28, 1921, ibid., Docket 25-4 (quotation); Simmons to Carrithers, Jan. 24, 1921, ibid., Docket 25-2.

82. Proceedings of the Labor Board, Docket 353, June 10, 1921, pp. 86–90. Copy in RED Records, ser. 2, code no. MC-144-14A-18.

83. Letter from Charles McKabney, June 6, 1921, in RED Records, ser. 2, code no. MC-144-14A-18.

84. Smith's circular and Jewell's June 4 letter countermanding the vote are in RED Records, ser. 2, code no. MC-144-14A-18.

85. Unsigned letter to Hungerford, Nov. 5, 1921, RED Records, ser. 2, code no. MC-144-14A-18. The letter is probably from Fred Aten and Daniel Goble, officials of the Carmen and the IBEW who represented the RED in its dealings with Pullman.

86. *Labor*, Oct. 1, 1921.

87. Wolf, *The Railroad Labor Board*, 272–75.

88. National Mediation Board Records, S-56, Docket 404. United States Railroad Labor Board, *Decisions, 1921*, Decision 218 and Order in Re: Docket 404, concern the Pennsylvania Railroad case and review its history. See also Wolf, *The Railroad Labor Board*, ch. 13.

89. Wolf, *The Railroad Labor Board*, pp. 130, 137–39, and ch. 8; Armitage, *Poli-*

tics of Decontrol of Industry, 59, 93–97; United States Railroad Labor Board, *Decisions, 1921,* Decision No. 222; Minutes of the National Agreement Committee, Jan. 14, pp. 2–3, in RED Records, series 2, code no. 14A-1.

90. Statement by T. P. Hyland (vice president of the executive board for Division No. 1), Minutes of the National Agreement Committee, Aug. 22–24, 1921, p. 9, RED Records, ser. 2.

91. Davis, "Bitter Storm," 192–93. RED leaders' complaints about unruly and impatient members from late 1921 suggest that officials had less enthusiasm for the strike than did their constituents. See Minutes of the National Agreement Committee, Aug. 22–24, 1921, pp. 13, 15, 18, RED Records, ser. 2; RED Records, ser. 1 (System Federations and Matters Pertaining to Individual System Federations, 1917–61), code no. 22–91, pt. 1; Richberg, *My Hero,* 116.

92. Hooper's denunciation of the strikers and his offer to protect their replacements were part of the official Railroad Labor Board resolution of July 3, 1922 (reprinted in United States Railroad Labor Board, *Decisions, 1922*). Daugherty is quoted by Davis in "Bitter Storm," 216. Davis also provides the best survey of government measures to defeat the strike. The formal request for a federal injunction signaled the temporary victory of anti-union cabinet members over the more conciliatory Herbert Hoover (Commerce) and James Davis (Labor). The balance within the Harding administration (and the GOP) would soon swing the other way (Zieger, "From Hostility to Moderation," 28–29).

93. Resolution, July 3, 1922, in United States Railroad Labor Board, *Decisions, 1922.*

94. Davis, "Bitter Storm," p. 10 and ch. 9.

95. Davis finds that 37.5 percent of shop craft employees were covered by agreements by the end of October ("Bitter Storm," 304–5), and Perlman and Taft report that about 56 percent eventually returned to work with seniority—something unlikely in the absence of agreement (*History of Labor,* 522). At least 36 percent of carriers settled on the basis of the Baltimore Agreement (Wolf, *The Railroad Labor Board,* 259). The contrast to other metalworking industries also shows up in union membership. The International Association of Machinists, which organized throughout the metal trades, lost 63 percent of its members between 1920 and 1923 (Perlman, *The Machinists,* 206); union membership among railroad shop craft workers dropped only 24 percent over the same period (Perlman and Taft, *History of Labor,* 522).

96. Davis, "Bitter Storm," 240–44, 291–96.

97. The basic source on the B. and O. plan is Wood, *Union-Management Cooperation.* See also Jacoby, "Union-Management Cooperation."

98. Wood, *Union-Management Cooperation,* 5–6, 85; Perlman and Taft, *History of American Labor,* 582–84; RED Records, ser. 1 ("Co-Operation") for files on smaller carriers.

99. Jewell to G. H. Stewart (president, System Federation No. 41, Chesapeake and Ohio Railroad), RED Records, ser. 1, code no. 36-8; Wood, *Union-Management Cooperation,* 106, 111.

100. As Jacoby points out ("Union-Management Cooperation"), the industry's financial weakness and the high proportion of costs accounted for by labor also recommended cooperative plans.

101. Stewart to Beyer, Aug. 29, 1924, in RED Records, ser. 1, code no. 36-5; Wood, *Union-Management Cooperation*, 128–29.

102. Letters to Edward Keating (editor of *Labor*) from Beyer and from Jewell, Mar. 31, 1925, RED Records, ser. 1, code no. 36-1. Wood notes that syndicalists did obstruct the plan in a number of locations, but socialists (including IAM president Johnston, a major proponent of the scheme) viewed cooperation as progressive and accepted the plan (*Union-Management Cooperation*, 136).

103. Quotations are from a letter from the officers of the system federation to the management of the Chicago, Milwaukee, St. Paul and Pacific Railroad, Aug. 2; see also letter, Aug. 19, 1926, and copy of Sept. 1926 agreement, all in RED Records, ser. 1, code no. 36-4. For the St. Louis federation, see Davis, "Bitter Storm," 132–33.

CHAPTER 4: STATE POLICY AND UNION AUTHORITY
IN BAY AREA SHIPBUILDING

1. The industry's general trajectory is reviewed by Hutchins, "History and Development of Shipbuilding," 47; Kelly and Allen, *The Shipbuilding Industry;* and Morrison, *New York Ship Yards*, 160–64.

2. Douglas and Wolfe, "Labor Administration in Shipbuilding," 145–47.

3. *Iron Age*, Jan. 4, 1917, p. 35. Everit Macy, chairman of the Shipbuilding Labor Adjustment Board, estimated that skilled mechanics accounted for half of all shipyard employees; see his letter to Felix Frankfurter, Oct. 17, 1917, in USSB Records, General Records (ser. 290), Home Office Records, "Individuals" file.

4. Kelly and Allen, *The Shipbuilding Industry*, 94, 103, 170, 206; Bustard, "The Human Factor," 212.

5. United States Shipping Board, Emergency Fleet Corporation, *Report of Director General*, 87, 147–148; Kelly and Allen, *The Shipbuilding Industry*, 94–97; Douglas and Wolfe, "Labor Administration in Shipbuilding," 171–77, 376–79; Bernard Mergen, "The Government as Manager"; United States Shipping Board, Emergency Fleet Corporation, *Report of Employment Managers' Conference.*

6. On the background and organization of the SLAB, see Douglas and Wolfe, "Labor Administration in Shipbuilding," 150–55; Hotchkiss and Seager, "Shipbuilding Labor Adjustment Board"; and Wehle, *Hidden Threads of History.*

7. Wehle, *Hidden Threads of History*, 39. Those supporting cooperation with labor unions included Wehle, the corporation's legal representative, as well as Henry Seager, an economist and Progressive on loan from Columbia. The SLAB chairman, Everit Macy, came to government service from the National Civic Federation (NCF), one of the few American employers' organizations that endorsed the principles of collective bargaining and trade agreements, even if few NCF members applied those principles in their own businesses.

8. *Boilermakers' Journal*, Sept. 1917, pp. 661–62; Bustard, "The Human Factor," 73–74.

9. Letter, Macy to Frankfurter, Oct. 17, 1917, USSB Records, S-290, Home Office Records, "Individuals" file.

10. Hotchkiss and Seager, "Shipbuilding Labor Adjustment Board," 52.

11. Carpenters' president William Hutcheson alone refused to sign the SLAB

agreement, arguing that it did not ratify closed shops. See Wehle, *Hidden Threads of History*, 41; Douglas and Wolfe, "Labor Administration in Shipbuilding," 150–51.

12. "Memorandum for the Adjustment of Wages, Hours, and Conditions of Labor in Shipbuilding Plants," Dec. 8, 1917. Copy in USSB Records, Decisions and Agreements (S-294).

13. Hotchkiss and Seager, "Shipbuilding Labor Adjustment Board," 14.

14. Letters, O'Connell to Macy, Apr. 19, 1918, and Macy to O'Connell, Apr. 23, May 2, and May 13, 1918, USSB Records, S-290, Home Office Records, "Appeals Board and Unions," box 1; letter, IAM acting president Anderson to Macy, Apr. 24, 1918, USSB Records, S-290, Home Office Records, "Appeals Board and Unions," IAM folder. L. C. Marshall, head of the EFC's Industrial Relations Division, urged national officers to appoint all business agents, thus giving unions "an appropriate form of control over local activities" (letter, Marshall to Boilermakers' union president Franklin, July 3, 1918, USSB Records, EFC Industrial Relations Division, General Records [E-350], File 53857-1, pt. 2). Macy continued to recommend industrywide collective bargaining as the solution for labor unrest after the armistice: "Many causes of irritation could be handled by well paid representatives of the employer and by responsible representatives of the national unions. Petty foremen and small minded local representatives of unions are the greatest source of discord" (speech to the NCF, Dec. 2, 1918, quoted in *Monthly Labor Review*, Feb. 1919, p. 63).

15. Speech by IAM organizer H. F. Nickerson to Duluth shipbuilding workers, quoted in the *Duluth Herald*, Feb. 20, 1918; testimony of Boilermakers' union vice president Weyand, Aug. 18, 1918, in USSB Records, Transcripts of Hearings (S-291), SLAB Hearings of Presidents of International Labor Unions, vol. 1, p. 693; telegram, O'Connell to Bert Swann (Seattle Metal Trades Council secretary), Oct. 4, 1918, in USSB Records, S-290, Home Office Records, "Appeals Board and Unions," AFL folder.

16. *Boilermakers' Journal*, Mar. 1917, p. 200.

17. Complaints about the government's training programs focused on the threat posed to union standards. See, for example, *Tri-City Labor Review* (Oakland), Nov. 16, 1917, for a report on Seattle criticisms; letter, Bert Jewell (Boilermakers' union vice president) to Macy, June 5, 1918, re: Delaware District, USSB Records, S-290, Home Office Records, "Appeals Board and Unions," Boilermakers' folder; Wolfe, *Works Committees and Industrial Councils*, 77–78.

18. Letter from C. D. Bradley, Mar. 25, 1918, USSB Records, S-290, Correspondence from the Field, Middle Atlantic District, James Martin (EFC district manager) file. Similar complaints are scattered through SLAB hearings and correspondence, e.g., from the Great Lakes (S-291: Apr. 8, 1918, hearings, pp. 18–19; and Aug. 10, 1918, hearings, pp. 511–12); the Pacific Coast (S-291: Dec. 6, 1918, hearings); and from New York (S-290: Correspondence from the Field, New York District). See also Hotchkiss and Seager, "Shipbuilding Labor Adjustment Board," 24–25.

19. Union officials regularly lectured members on the importance of discipline and of using the "proper channels" (see, for example, *Boilermakers' Journal*, Apr. 1917, pp. 280, 481), while EFC officials complained of the "disposition which seems to exist . . . to ignore conditions of agreements and authority of the wage

adjustment board" (telegram, San Francisco SLAB examiner Brotherton to H. Blackman [EFC Industrial Relations Division secretary], May 1, 1918, USSB Records, Industrial Relations Division, General Correspondence of the Labor Section [entry 361], daily telegram file). On local hostility to SLAB centralization, see Friedheim, *The Seattle General Strike*; and, for San Francisco, telegram, J. H. Powers to Macy, July 27, 1918, USSB Records, S-290, Correspondence from the Field, South Pacific Coast District.

20. Examiner Brotherton's Weekly Report No. 9, Nov. 15, 1918, USSB Records, S-290, Correspondence from the Field, South Pacific Coast District.

21. Pacific Metal Trades Council report (undated), USSB Records, S-290, Home Office Records, "Appeals Board and Unions," General File folder.

22. Foner, *History of the Labor Movement*, 338; Bing, *War-Time Strikes*, 20–24.

23. Examiners remained in close touch with Hotchkiss and Seager in Washington, and their decisions could be appealed. Nevertheless, the reliance on regional awards and district administration in shipbuilding allowed much more room for local autonomy than did the Railroad Administration or the NWLB. The former exercised control over a unified railroad system and enacted uniform policies for the entire nation; NWLB decisions applied the board's authority directly to specific companies and single occupations rather than to entire cities or local industries.

24. On the unsuccessful prewar open shop drives, see Knight, *Industrial Relations in San Francisco*, 143–50 (1904), 201–3 (1907), and 302–30 (1916).

25. Ibid., 39–44, 375; Boyden, "Craft Consciousness and Labor Revolt," 7–8; Kazin, *Barons of Labor*, ch. 1.

26. Kazin, *Barons of Labor*.

27. *Boilermakers' Journal*, Nov. 1907, pp. 1022–23, 1029, 1050; ibid., Apr. 1908, pp. 241–46; *Labor Clarion*, Oct. 23, 1908, Mar. 1, 1912, and Aug. 30, 1912.

28. *Boilermakers' Journal*, Apr., 1904, p. 216.

29. Boyden, "Craft Consciousness and Labor Revolt," 7.

30. United States Senate, Commission on Industrial Relations, *Final Report*, 6:5236–37; Knight, *Industrial Relations in San Francisco*, 112, 185–90, 214–16, 376–78. The argument that craft production, local product markets, and competitive capital favored strong unions and collective bargaining is consistent with studies of the building and printing trades. See, for example, Jackson, *Formation of Craft Labor Markets*.

31. *Labor Clarion*, Nov. 29, 1912.

32. Kazin, *Barons of Labor*, ch. 8.

33. Saxton, "San Francisco Labor," 422.

34. Ibid., 429–35; Knight, *Industrial Relations in San Francisco*, 244–45; Kazin, *Barons of Labor*, ch. 8.

35. Knight, *Industrial Relations in San Francisco*, 128–29, 177.

36. Boyden, "Craft Consciousness and Labor Revolt," 18; Knight, *Industrial Relations in San Francisco*, 295–338; *California Shipbuilder and Metal Worker*, Sept. 1919, p. 28.

37. *Labor Clarion*, May 19, 1916, and Mar. 23, 1917; *San Francisco Call*, Feb. 20 and Mar. 19, 1917; Knight, *Industrial Relations in San Francisco*, 339–40; *Tri-City Labor Review*, Mar. 9 and 16, 1917, Jan. 4 and 25 and May 24, 1918; Boyden, "Craft

Consciousness and Labor Revolt," 14. The major Bay Area yards were the Union Iron Works and Pacific Coast Steel Company in San Francisco, Moore Shipbuilding in Oakland, and Bethlehem Shipbuilding in Alameda.

38. *Tri-City Labor Review,* Jan. 4, 1918, May 24, 1918, and Sept. 13, 1918; Knight, *Industrial Relations in San Francisco,* 360.

39. See, for example, SLAB examiner Brotherton's Weekly Report No. 11, Nov. 30, 1918, USSB Records, S-290, Correspondence from the Field, South Pacific District; *Tri-City Labor Review,* July 19 and Dec. 13, 1918.

40. Hotchkiss and Seager, "Shipbuilding Labor Adjustment Board," 24–25; *Tri-City Labor Review,* June 7, June 28, and Aug. 9, 1918.

41. Telegrams, Capps to EFC district officer A. F. Pillsbury, Sept. 13 and 14, 1917; telegram, Capps to Special District Officer J. L. Ackerson, Sept. 18, 1917; telegram, Ackerson and Pillsbury to EFC, Sept. 26, 1917; letter, Pillsbury to Capps, Sept. 29, 1917; telegram, Ackerson and Pillsbury to EFC, Oct. 5, 1917 (all in USSB Records, S-290, Correspondence from the Field, South Pacific Coast District); letter, Macy to Felix Frankfurter (at this time, secretary of the President's Mediation Commission), Oct. 17, 1917, USSB Records, S-290, Home Office Records, "Individuals" file; letter, William Blackman (assistant to EFC vice president Piez) to San Francisco ITC, Dec. 1, 1917, USSB Records, Records of Charles Piez (entry 165); Hotchkiss and Seager, "Shipbuilding Labor Adjustment Board," 15–16; *Labor Clarion,* Oct. 5, 1917; *Labor World,* Sept. 21, 1917.

42. *Labor Clarion,* Sept. 28, 1917; *Labor World,* Sept. 21, 1917.

43. The complaint came from W. H. Van Dervoort of the National Metal Trades Association in his letter to Charles Piez, Dec. 31, 1917, USSB Records, S-290, Home Office Records, "Appeals Board and Unions," AFL folder. See also *Labor Clarion,* Oct. 5, 1917; *San Francisco Call,* Dec. 26, 27, and 28, 1917.

44. USSB Records, S-290, Correspondence from the Field, South Pacific District.

45. *Tri-City Labor Review,* Jan. 18, 1918.

46. Copy of Feb. 26, 1918, agreement and Brotherton report to Herbert Fleishhacker (an EFC representative in San Francisco), July 23, 1918, in USSB Records, E-350, File 53957-4; letter, George Armes (Moore Shipbuilding president) to Piez, July 20, 1918, USSB Records, E-165, File 128, pt. 2.

47. *Tri-City Labor Review,* Aug. 9, 1918.

48. Telegram, Wolfe to Macy, June 16, 1918, USSB Records, S-290, Correspondence from the Field, South Pacific District, "Boilermakers and Iron Ship Builders S.F. District" file; *Tri-City Labor Review,* June 14 and July 19, 1918; *Labor Clarion,* July 19, 1918; Brotherton report to Fleishhacker, July 23, 1918, USSB Records, E-350, File 53957-4.

49. *Tri-City Labor Review,* June 7 and 28, 1918.

50. Telegram, Weyand to Wolfe, Sept. 10, 1918, USSB Records, S-290, Home Office Records, "Appeals Board and Unions," Boilermakers' folder; telegram, Brotherton to Macy, Sept. 7, 1918, USSB Records, S-290, Correspondence from the Field, South Pacific District.

51. Telegrams, Brotherton to Macy (Oct. 4 and 7 and Nov. 25, 1918) and Seager (Nov. 23, 1918), and Brotherton's Weekly Report No. 11, Nov. 30, all in USSB Records, S-290, Correspondence from the Field, South Pacific District; telegram, Brotherton to R. W. Leatherbee (of the EFC Industrial Relations Division), Dec.

11, 1918, USSB Records, E-350, File 53831-1; *Tri-City Labor Review*, Oct. 11 and Dec. 13, 1918.

52. *Labor Clarion*, Feb. 7, 1919, 7.

53. Ibid., Jan. 10–Apr. 18, 1919; *Tri-City Labor Review*, Jan. 31–Apr. 4, 1919; Brotherton Weekly Reports, Feb.–Mar., 1919, USSB Records, S-290, Correspondence from the Field, South Pacific District.

54. McGuire and Bethlehem Shipbuilding negotiated the agreement on improvers' rates before Lodge 233 joined the ITC (Brotherton report to Fleishhacker, July 23, 1918, USSB Records, E-350, File 53957–4).

55. *Labor Clarion*, July 26 and Aug. 2, 1918; *Tri-City Labor Review*, Aug. 9, 1918.

56. *Boilermakers' Journal*, July, 1919, p. 422; *Labor Clarion*, Dec. 13, 1918, Feb. 14 and 21 and Mar. 14, 1919; *Tri-City Labor Review*, Feb. 14, Mar. 14, Apr. 18, and May 16, 1919.

57. Undated report of the Pacific Coast Metal Trades Council, USSB Records, S-290, Home Office Records, "Appeals Board and Unions," General File folder; Appeal Board Hearings, Dec. 6, 1918, USSB Records, S-291.

58. *Labor Clarion*, Mar. 22 and May 3, 24, 1918, Jan. 17 and Feb. 28, 1919; *Tri-City Labor Review*, Apr. 19, June 7, and Oct. 4, 1918, Mar. 7 and Apr. 18, 1919.

59. Telegram, Brotherton to Macy, Oct. 9, 1918, USSB Records, S-290, Correspondence from the Field, South Pacific District; *Labor Clarion*, Apr. 5, 1918; *Tri-City Labor Review*, Sept. 27 and Oct. 11, 1918; Knight, *Industrial Relations in San Francisco*, 362 64.

60. *Labor Clarion*, Feb. 28 and June 13, 1919; *Tri-City Labor Review*, Feb. 14 and Mar. 21, 1919.

61. The fact that the two factions of the Bay Area labor movement also clashed on the heated question of Tom Mooney (the unionist sentenced to death for the 1916 Preparedness Day parade bombing in San Francisco) reinforced the insurgents' radical aura. Members of the Oakland unions charged ITC president Burton with failure to support Mooney (*Tri-City Labor Review*, Oct. 11, 1918), and both the Pacific Coast Metal Trades Council and the Pacific Coast Council of Boilermakers voted in favor of a general strike if Mooney's death sentence was not overturned (*Labor World*, May 16, 1918). The one San Francisco craft union lodge to side with the insurgents—IAM Local 68—elected one of the defendants in the bombing case, Ed Nolan, as lodge president in December 1918.

62. Brotherton Weekly Report No. 19, Jan. 25, 1919, USSB Records, S-290, Correspondence from the Field, South Pacific Coast District.

63. Letter, Piez to Warren Hauling, Feb. 11, 1918, USSB Records, E-165, File 126-1.

64. Memo, John Barker (assistant to Hurley) to Piez, July 30, 1918, quoting telegram from Pillsbury, USSB Records, E-165, File 128, pt. 2.

65. Brotherton Weekly Report No. 2, Sept. 14, 1918, USSB Records, S-290, Correspondence from the Field, South Pacific District

66. Brotherton Weekly Report No. 11, Nov. 30, 1918, USSB Records, S-290, Correspondence from the Field, South Pacific District; telegrams, Wolfe to Hurley, Feb. 9, 1918, Blackman to Fisher, Feb. 11, 1918, Moore Shipbuilding to Hurley, Feb. 11, 1918, Fisher to Blackman, Feb. 13, 1918, and Blackman to Fisher, Feb. 14, 1918, all in USSB Records, E-361, Daily Telegram File.

67. Brotherton Weekly Report No. 20, Feb. 1, 1919, and telegram, Brotherton to Macy, Nov. 6, 1918, USSB Records, S-290, Correspondence from the Field, South Pacific District.

68. Telegram, Fleishhacker to Blackman (at this time, secretary of the EFC's Industrial Relations Division), Apr. 10, 1918, USSB Records, entry 361, Daily Telegram file.

69. Telegram, Brotherton to Macy, Oct. 9, 1918, USSB Records, S-290, Correspondence from the Field, South Pacific District.

70. Telegram, Marshall to Berres, Feb. 11, 1919, USSB Records, S-290, Home Office Records, "Individuals" file.

71. *San Francisco Examiner*, Mar. 12, 1919; *Labor Clarion*, May 16 and June 13, 1919. The Shipyard Laborers—born as an AFL Federal union—split between an industrial union faction and AFL loyalists in the spring. The former, frustrated by AFL obstacles to organizing semiskilled workers in the machine trades, joined the International Longshoremen's Association. *Tri-City Labor Review*, May 16, 1919, Jan. 23 and Mar. 26, 1920.

72. *Tri-City Labor Review*, Dec. 5, 1919. See also *Labor Clarion*, May 9 and Aug. 8, 1919; *Tri-City Labor Review*, Oct. 10, 1919.

73. Telegrams, Brotherton to Macy, Mar. 7, 1919, and Hotchkiss to Brotherton, Mar. 8, 1919, both in USSB Records, S-290, Correspondence from the Field, South Pacific District.

74. Report, Special Agent Kerrigan, July 10, 1919, USSB Records, Investigated Files of the Home Office (E-145), case 1316-1.

75. United States Shipping Board, Emergency Fleet Corporation, *Report of Director General*, 154; *Labor Clarion*, Apr.–Sept. 1919.

76. *Labor Clarion*, Sept.–Nov. 1919; telegrams, John O'Connell (secretary of the San Francisco Labor Council) to AFL secretary Frank Morrison, Oct. 23 and Nov. 3, 1919, in San Francisco Labor Council Records, carton 2, "AFL MTD" folder.

77. Quoted by *Labor Clarion*, Jan. 30, 1920, p. 3.

78. *California Shipbuilder and Metal Worker*, May 1920, p. 12.

79. Memo from union presidents and the Pacific Coast Metal Trades Council, filed Sept. 19, 1919; telegram, Brotherton to J. C. Jenkins (EFC staff assistant in charge of industrial relations), Sept. 22, 1919; memo, Jenkins to Ackerson, Sept. 22, 1919; telegram, Brotherton to Jenkins, Sept. 24, 1919; all in USSB Records, E-350, File 53718-6, pt. 1.

80. In South Pacific Coast shipbuilding, 81 percent of EFC work was paid for through lump sum contracts; for Middle Atlantic yards the figure was 56 percent and for Delaware yards only 11 percent (Jenkins report to Ackerson, Aug. 27, USSB Records, E-350, File 580-1222, pt. 2).

81. *Labor Clarion*, Oct. 10, 1919. The president of Moore Shipbuilding asked the EFC's Ackerson to give unions as little information as possible about implementing a wage increase. "We naturally take the position that we are endeavoring to abide by the wishes of the Government . . . to reduce the high cost of living. . . . A positive statement that it is strictly up to the individual builders . . . would make our attempt that much harder" (telegram, Armes to Ackerson, Oct. 22, 1919, USSB Records, E-350, File 54218-1).

82. *Labor Clarion*, Feb. 14, 1919.

83. Ibid., Mar. 19, 1919.

84. *California Shipbuilder and Metal Worker,* Sept. 1919, p. 4.

85. Memo, Jenkins to Ackerson, Sept. 22, 1919, USSB Records, E-350, File 53718-6.

86. Kazin, *Barons of Labor,* ch. 8. Schneirov ("Political Economy and Class Relations") adds that labor's political clout need not be based on a separate political party. It can also be wielded within the two-party system, as in Chicago.

CHAPTER 5: FREEING SHOP COMMITTEES FROM
"PARTISAN PREJUDICES" IN GREAT LAKES SHIPYARDS

1. True, "Sixty Years of Shipbuilding."

2. The company also operated yards in Wyandotte, West Bay City, Chicago, Detroit, and Superior, making it the biggest shipbuilder in the Great Lakes. See Hutchins, "History and Development of Shipbuilding," 47; *Boilermakers' Journal,* Nov. 1904, p. 717, Feb. 1906, p. 68.

3. Miller and Wheeler, *Cleveland,* 64–65, 70–72, 82, 100–102; Lutz, *The Metal Trades,* 13.

4. Lutz, *The Metal Trades,* 21, 24, 97.

5. *Cleveland Press,* Jan. 5, 1917; Kelly and Allen, *The Shipbuilding Industry,* 71, 94–97.

6. The major exceptions were the usual ones, building and printing. Local product markets and entrenched craft control helped skilled men in these industries win collective bargaining rights. In the garment trades, however, where strikes led to trade agreements in New York, Chicago, and elsewhere, Cleveland employers fought off union drives and maintained open shops. See Scharf, "A Woman's View," 185.

7. *Boilermakers' Journal,* May 1907, p. 441, June 1907, pp. 538–39, July 1907, pp. 631, 640, Aug. 1907, pp. 726–27, Oct. 1907, p. 919, Apr. 1908, p. 240.

8. Miggins, "A City of 'Uplifting Influences,'" 143, 154–55; Boryczka and Cary, *No Strength without Union,* 155.

9. *Boilermakers' Journal,* Mar. 1907, p. 267, Mar. 1917, pp. 195–96; *Cleveland Citizen,* Apr. 15, 1916; Judd, *Socialist Cities,* 126.

10. *Boilermakers' Journal,* Apr. 1916, p. 192. In Lorain, National Tube (later U.S. Steel) reinforced residential segregation by dividing the area around its mills into ethnic subdivisions (Judd, *Socialist Cities,* 122).

11. *Cleveland Citizen,* Mar. 7, 1914.

12. Between 1899 and 1908 a majority of the local labor council's officers belonged to the Socialist party. See Sidlo, "Socialism and Trade-Unionism," 135–36, 145–47.

13. See the case studies in Judd, *Socialist Cities.*

14. Campbell, "Mounting Crisis and Reform," 305, 308; *Cleveland Federationist,* Sept. 25, 1913; Sidlo, "Socialism and Trade-Unionism," 150–51.

15. The Great Lakes Engineering Company belonged to the Employers' Association of Detroit (EAD) and followed that organizations' militantly anti-union policies. On the EAD see Klug, "Roots of the Open Shop."

16. American Shipbuilding Company, Annual Reports, 1913–1916, in American Shipbuilding Collection; *Cleveland Press,* Jan. 5, 1917.

17. Letters, Wesley Engelhorn and W. H. Winans to Fred Croxton (head of the Labor Division, Ohio Council of National Defense), undated (Aug. 1917), in Records of the Ohio Branch, Council of National Defense, Ohio Branch Records, Committee on Labor and Industrial Relations, General Correspondence, box 36, File 9; Testimony of American Shipbuilding Company president M. E. Farr, United States Shipping Board, USSB Records, S-291, hearings before the SLAB, "Great Lakes and Vicinity," pp. 413–14.

18. *Cleveland Citizen*, Sept. 4, 1915, p. 14.

19. *Cleveland Press*, Oct. 1–29, 1915; *Cleveland Citizen*, Oct. 9–30, 1915, Mar. 18 and Apr. 15, 1916.

20. *Cleveland Citizen*, Apr. 1 and May 6, 1916. No reliable figures for wartime IAM membership exist, but as late as Sept. 17, 1917, IAM Local 83 (one of four IAM lodges in the city) had fewer than 500 members (IAM Local 83 Minutes, Sept. 17, 1917, International Association of Machinists District 54, IAM District 54 Records, ser. 4 [local lodge files], folder 1974).

21. *Boilermakers' Journal*, Mar. 1917, p. 195, gives Lodge 5 membership as thirty-nine in early 1916; *Cleveland Federationist*, May 18, 1916, Mar. 8, 1917; *Cleveland Citizen*, June 24, 1916, Aug. 17, 1918.

22. *Boilermakers' Journal*, Dec. 1917, p. 942, Feb. 1918, p. 118, Apr. 1918, p. 273.

23. Report, R. W. England (assistant district officer, EFC) to EFC, Oct. 24, 1917; letter, England to Louis Wehle, Oct. 30, 1917; both in USSB Records, EFC Industrial Relations Division, General Records (E-350), File 53917-4.

24. *Cleveland Citizen*, July 13 and Oct. 19, 1918; IAM Local 83 Minutes, June 21, 1918, IAM District 54 Records, ser. 4.

25. *Boilermakers' Journal*, Feb. 1918, p. 110.

26. Transcript of conference, May 31 and June 1, 1918, USSB Records, General Records (S-290), Home Office Records, Great Lakes District; *Boilermakers' Journal*, Aug. 1918, pp. 589, 594.

27. *Cleveland Federationist*, Mar. 21, 28 and June 6, 1918; *Cleveland Citizen*, Mar. 23, 1918.

28. *Boilermakers' Journal*, Aug. 1918, p. 594; *Labor World* (Duluth), June 28 and Sept. 20, 1919; *Toledo Blade*, Aug. 18 and Sept. 17, 1919, Jan. 20, 30 and Mar. 12, 30, 1920.

29. *Cleveland Citizen*, Apr. 6, 13, 1918; *Cleveland Federationist*, June 6, 1918.

30. *Cleveland Federationist*, May 15, 1919; IAM Local 439 Minutes, June 13, June 20, July 11, 1919, IAM District 54 Records, ser. 4.

31. *Cleveland Citizen*, Feb. 3, 1917; informer's report, July 26–27, 1917, Chicago Shipbuilding Company records, American Shipbuilding Collection, box 8, folder 7; *Boilermakers' Journal*, Feb. 1918, p. 118; *Cleveland Federationist*, June 6, 1918; *Toledo Blade*, Apr. 26, 1919. Boilermakers' officials served as stewards or shop committee representatives in the Chicago American Shipbuilding yard and at the Toledo Shipbuilding company (letter, Kellogg Fairbank [president, Chicago Shipbuilding Company] to American Shipbuilding president Farr, May 4, 1918, Chicago Shipbuilding Company records, box 8, folder 1; letter, Boilermakers' organizer A. H. Bathurst to Macy, September 10, 1918, USSB Records, S-290, Home Office Records, Great Lakes District). On the IAM meetings and machinists' stewards generally, see IAM Local 83 Minutes, Feb. 22 and Apr. 19, 1918, and IAM

Local 368 Minutes, Jan. 22, 26, Feb. 12, 19, Mar. 12, Sept. 3, and Nov. 26, 1918, all in IAM District 54 Records, ser. 4.

32. Telegram, Farr to Hurley, May 2, 1918, USSB Records, EFC Industrial Relations Division, General Correspondence of the Labor Section (entry 361), Daily Telegram File; letter, Berres to Seager, undated, USSB Records, S-290, Home Office Records, "Individuals" file.

33. Letter, Bert Jewell (at this time, general organizer for the Boilermakers) to Macy, July 8, 1918, USSB Records, S-290, Home Office Records, "Appeals Board and Unions," Boilermakers folder; testimony of American Shipbuilding president Farr and Great Lakes Engineering president Russel, USSB Records, S-291, Hearings for "Great Lakes and Vicinity," pp. 413–14, 451–53, 463–67.

34. Telegram, Farr to Hurley, May 2, 1918, USSB Records, EFC Industrial Relations Division, General Correspondence of the Labor Section (entry 361), Daily Telegram File.

35. Report by EFC inspectors, Sept. 1918, in American Shipbuilding Company General File, American Shipbuilding Collection.

36. In at least two Cleveland cases, EFC officials went further, suggesting to American Shipbuilding's local manager that police should be called in to break up strikes over union recognition. See telegram, England to EFC, Oct. 24, 1917; A. G. Smith (operating manager, American Shipbuilding Company) to England, Oct. 27, 1917; England to Wehle, Oct. 30, 1917; Smith to Capps, Nov. 6, 1917; Macy to Stevens (USSB vice president), Nov. 20, 1917, all in USSB Records, E-350, File 53917-4.

37. Gitelman, *Legacy of the Ludlow Massacre*, 206. See also Boryczka and Cary, *No Strength without Union*, 155.

38. *Iron Age*, Aug. 17, 1916, pp. 344–49; *Cleveland Citizen*, Mar. 18, 1916.

39. On the relative success of SLAB committees in the Great Lakes, see Wolfe, *Works Committees and Industrial Councils*, 119–21; Douglas and Wolfe, "Labor Administration in Shipbuilding," *Journal of Political Economy*, 370–71.

40. Letter, Bathurst to Fisher, Sept. 13, 1918, USSB Records, S-290, Correspondence from the Field, Great Lakes District, "Boilermakers" file.

41. Letter, Fisher to Bathurst, Sept. 14, 1918, USSB Records, S-290, Correspondence from the Field, Great Lakes District, "Fisher and Pitt, Examiners" file.

42. Report, F. S. Diebler (assistant examiner), July 26–30, 1918, in "Walter Fisher, letters sent by" file; telegram and letter, Fisher to Macy, Sept. 3, 1918, in "Fisher and Pitt, Examiners" file; letter, Hotchkiss to Fisher, Sept. 25, 1918, in "Fisher and Pitt, Examiners" file; telegrams and letters, Seager to Pitt, Oct. 24, Dec. 4, 10, in "Fisher and Pitt, Examiners" file. All in USSB Records, S-290, Correspondence from the Field, Great Lakes District.

43. Letter, Fisher to Macy, July 16, 1918, USSB Records, S-290, Correspondence from the Field, Great Lakes District.

44. Letter, Fisher to Macy, Aug. 19, 1918, USSB Records, S-290, Correspondence from the Field, Great Lakes District, "Fisher and Pitt, Examiners" file.

45. Letter, Pond to James McWeeney, Oct. 8, 1918, USSB Records, S-290, Correspondence from the Field, Great Lakes District.

46. Letter, Pond to John Strong (secretary, Joint Shop Committee, Great Lakes Engineering Works, Ecorse), Sept. 11, 1918, USSB Records, S-290, Correspondence from the Field, Great Lakes District, "W. Fisher, Letters sent by" file.

47. Letter, Seager to Fisher, Sept. 9, 1918, USSB Records, S-290, Correspondence from the Field, Great Lakes District, "Fisher and Pitt, Examiners" file.

48. Transcript of May 31 and June 1 conference, pp. 474–75, USSB Records, S-290, Correspondence from the Field, Great Lakes District.

49. Memo from Pitt, Oct. 30, 1918, USSB Records, E-350, File 53713-1, pt. 3.

50. Union complaints about SLAB committees were not confined to the Great Lakes (see, for example, USSB Records, S-291, hearings before the SLAB, Dec. 6, 1918, pp. 194–206), and examiners in New England, South Atlantic, and Gulf yards seem to have followed Fisher's and Pitt's approach, albeit without their missionary zeal. In better organized districts, by contrast, the SLAB plan was a dead letter.

51. Ironically, Pitt credits IAM vice president H. F. Nickerson with this rationale for using written grievance forms (letter, Pitt to Seager, Nov. 8, 1918, USSB Records, S-290, Correspondence from the Field, Great Lakes District, "Fisher and Pitt, Examiners" file).

52. Letter, Gephart to H. W. Leatherbee (manager, EFC Industrial Relations Division), Feb. 21, 1919, USSB Records, E-350, File 53833-1. See also letter, Gephart to Wright (EFC yard representative for Toledo), Mar. 10, 1919, USSB Records, S-290, Correspondence from the Field, Great Lakes District.

53. Letter, Gephart to Pitt, May 2, 1919, USSB Records, Records Relating to History of the Board (S-295).

54. Hearings, Aug. 22, 1918, pp. 1637–38, USSB Records, S-291; Wolfe, *Works Committees and Industrial Councils*, 121; letter, Gephart to Leatherbee, Mar. 5, 1919, USSB Records, E-350, File 53795-3.

55. Memo from Hotchkiss, Sept. 8, 1918, USSB Records, S-290, Home Office Records, "Individuals" file. See also letter, Fisher to Macy, Aug. 9, 1918, USSB Records, S-290, "Walter Fisher" file.

56. Letter, Fisher to Seager, Sept. 11, 1918, USSB Records, S-290, Correspondence from the Field, Great Lakes District, "Fisher and Pitt, Examiners" file.

57. Pitt to Marshall, Nov. 27, 1918, USSB Records, E-350, File 53713-1, pt. 5.

58. It is not clear whether Fisher's or Pitt's resignation was voluntary, but relations between them and SLAB administrators certainly deteriorated prior to their departures.

59. See, for example, Fisher's testy letters to Macy, Aug. 9, 19, 1918, and Macy to Fisher, Aug. 14, 1918, USSB Records, S-290, Correspondence from the Field, Great Lakes District, "Fisher and Pitt, Examiners" file.

60. Letter, Seager to Pitt, Dec. 11, 1918, USSB Records, S-290, Correspondence from the Field, Great Lakes District, "Fisher and Pitt, Examiners" file.

61. Macy specifically urged that where craft committees insisted on calling in a union representative and the employer objected, the dispute should go to the examiner, who could then rule that the case had to be reviewed by the joint shop committee. "After brief initial period this would result in acceptance of your plan of having everything presented [at the] outset through joint shop committee" (telegram, Macy to Pitt, Dec. 16, 1918, USSB Records, S-290, Correspondence from the Field, Great Lakes District, "Fisher and Pitt, Examiners" file). See also letter, Pitt to Marshall, Dec. 12, 1918, USSB Records, E-350, File 53833-1; letter, Pitt to

Seager, Dec. 13, USSB Records, S-290, Correspondence from the Field, Great Lakes District, "Fisher and Pitt, Examiners" file.

62. Because the SLAB was soon to cease operations and the EFC sought to economize, the examiner's responsibilities were merged with those of the EFC's Industrial Relations Division district representative. Gephart served in this capacity from Jan. 1 to Mar. 31, 1919.

63. United States Shipping Board, Emergency Fleet Corporation, *Report of Director General*, 153–54; Commons, *Industrial Government*, 354–55.

64. Letter, Gephart to Leatherbee, Mar. 26, 1919, USSB Records, E-350, File 53795–3; Minutes of Directors' Meetings, Jan. 22, Feb. 26, Mar. 26, and Apr. 17, 1919, American Shipbuilding Collection; *Boilermakers' Journal*, June, 1919, pp. 350–51.

65. *Cleveland Federationist*, July 31, 1919, report on July 21 Metal Trades Council meeting. Investigators for the National Industrial Conference Board found these resentments to be widespread. "The larger questions of wages, hours, and other working conditions, are left to be settled under this agreement by representatives of the company and of the national and international unions. A field investigator found that there was, on this account, considerable dissatisfaction among members and officials of the local unions" (National Industrial Conference Board, *Works Councils in the United States*, 93–94).

66. Notice, Bathurst to employers, Mar. 7, 1919; letter, Gephart to Berres, Mar. 13, 1919. Both in USSB Records, E-350, File 53833-1.

67. *Cleveland Federationist*, July 31, 1919.

68. Montgomery suggests that the American Shipbuilding Company and the Metal Trades Department formed their pact to fend off a threatened strike for recognition by the Great Lakes Metal Trades Council, with the firm and the MTD reorganizing shop committees along craft rather than solidary lines ("New Tendencies," 102). But in early 1919 the Cleveland and Great Lakes Metal Trades Councils were far less worrisome to the company than were EFC pressures for an agreement. The agreement itself, moreover, did not reorganize shop committees. Instead, it reaffirmed the supremacy of the joint shop committee. In other contexts such a committee might have posed the dangers for employers suggested by Montgomery. Under Great Lakes conditions empowering joint rather than craft committees worked well for employers.

69. Minutes of Directors' Meetings, Feb. 26 and Apr. 17, 1919, American Shipbuilding Collection.

70. Memo, Paul Douglas to Leatherbee, Feb. 11, 1919; letter, Lambright (American Shipbuilding Company executive assistant) to Carroll (EFC district representative), Mar 20, 1919, both in USSB Records, E-350, File 53975-3.

71. Minutes of Directors' Meetings, Mar. 24, 1920, American Shipbuilding Collection.

72. Letter, Gephart to Leatherbee, Mar. 5, 1919, USSB Records, E-350, File 53795-3. See also letter, Gephart to Hotchkiss, May 28, 1919, USSB Records, S-295, box 1.

73. When the Cleveland Metal Trades Council secretary went on night shift early in 1919, the entire organization went into hibernation until he returned to

his duties, and even then attendance continued to be spotty (*Cleveland Federationist*, Mar. 13, 1919; IAM Local 368 Minutes, Feb. 21, 1919, IAM District 54 Records, ser. 4.

74. *Cleveland Federationist*, May 15, 1919.

75. For the few union successes, see Irving Pond report, July 26, 1918, "Walter Fisher" file, re: Saginaw Shipbuilding, and letter, Fisher to Macy, Sept. 3, 1918, "Fisher and Pitt, Examiners" file, re: Superior, both in USSB Records, S-290, Home Office Records, Great Lakes District. SLAB representatives' determination to follow approved procedures is illustrated by two letters: Hotchkiss to Pitt, Dec. 23, 1918, "Fisher and Pitt, Examiners" file, and Bathurst to Macy, Sept. 10, 1918, both in USSB Records, S-290, Correspondence from the Field, Great Lakes District.

76. Diebler report, Sept. 16, 1918, USSB Records, S-290, Correspondence from the Field, Great Lakes District.

77. Telegram, Pitt to Seager, Dec. 10, 1918, USSB Records, S-290, Correspondence from the Field, Great Lakes District, "Fisher and Pitt, Examiners" file.

78. Letter, Gephart to Wright, Mar. 10, 1919, USSB Records, S-290, Correspondence from the Field, Great Lakes District.

79. Letter, Gephart to Leatherbee, Feb. 21, 1919, USSB Records, E-350, File 53833-1.

80. The fact that the surviving completed shop committee grievance forms are typed suggests that management actively cooperated in processing employee claims.

81. IAM Lodge 368 Minutes, Jan. 9, 16 and Oct. 29, 1920; IAM Lodge 83 Minutes, Jan. 10, 31, 1919. Both in IAM District 54 Records, ser. 4.

82. Information on strikes is culled from newspapers, union documents, and government reports. Boryczka and Cary note that in Cleveland generally, wartime walkouts "were purely local in scale" (*No Strength without Union*, 161). They do not try to explain this. In late 1919 it appeared that the pattern might be broken. Union officials meeting at an August conference of the Great Lakes District Shipbuilders' Council resolved to seek a wage increase effective Oct. 1, and they initiated a strike vote for shipyards throughout the Great Lakes. A confrontation similar to that in the Bay Area seemed imminent, especially when owners posted notices that the EFC would not allow further wage hikes. In this case, however, local officials deferred demands pending discussions between the American Shipbuilding Company and Metal Trades Department delegates. The Great Lakes District Shipbuilders' Council revived the demands in January, but by then it had neither the economic leverage (wage cuts and layoffs had already begun as the industry contracted) nor a large or active membership. See *Toledo Blade*, Aug. 18, Sept. 17, 26, 29, and Oct. 8, 29, 1919, and Jan. 20, 1920; *Cleveland Press*, Sept. 29, 30 and Oct. 1, 2, 1919.

83. Letters, Gephart to Jenkins, July 7, 14, 1919, USSB Records, E-350, File 54096-4.

84. *The Labor World*, Apr. 10, 1920.

85. *Cleveland Citizen*, Feb. 14, 1920.

86. Political clout and bargaining leverage, of course, also reinforced skilled workers' position in the labor process.

CONCLUSION

1. *Iron Age,* Jan. 10, 1918, p. 142. The warning came from Walter Drew, a lawyer for the National Erectors' Association and a leading spokesman for the open shop. See Fine, *"Without Blare of Trumpets."*

2. *Iron Age,* May 2, 1918, p. 1141. Barr served as president of the National Founders' Association.

3. Memo, Blyth to MacLeod, Dec. 16, 1918, USSB Records, Investigation Department, Investigated Files of the Home Office, entry 145, case 929.

4. Montgomery, "New Tendencies"; Sirianni, "Workers' Control in Europe"; Maier, *Recasting Bourgeois Europe.*

5. This argument is developed in Haydu, "Employers, Unions, and American Exceptionalism."

6. *Iron Age,* Jan. 10, 1918, p. 142. One familiar interpretation of New Deal employer strategies is that many embraced the AFL only to preempt the more radical Congress of Industrial Organizations (CIO). Efforts to apply a similar argument to the World War I (or prewar) era are less convincing because employers lumped the AFL together with more radical labor organizations and opposed them all. Cf. James Weinstein, *The Corporate Ideal,* chs. 1, 5; Fusfeld, "Government and Radical Labor."

7. For another exception to this pattern, clothing, see Fraser, *Labor Will Rule,* 135–39, 170–75. These internal comparisons also temper Montgomery's claim that U.S. officials, with an eye on Britain, declined to abrogate union standards for fear of inciting an American shop stewards' movement (*House of Labor,* 374). In the munitions industry, federal agencies did not need to suspend craft customs because employers had already done so. Where unions had been more successful in defending work rules and military needs called for dilution—the case in shipbuilding—the government intervened to remove the bottleneck.

8. Dubofsky, *The State and Labor,* ch. 3.

9. J. Smith, "Organized Labor"; Dubofsky, *The State and Labor,* ch. 3; McCartin, "'An American Feeling.'"

10. Michael Burawoy makes an analagous criticism of Skocpol, noting that the problems confronted by different states surely had some impact on policy (*The Politics of Production,* 147). The same point applies to different industries regulated by a single state.

11. Major examples include Orloff, "Origins of America's Welfare State," and Skocpol, "Political Responses to Capitalist Crisis." Both rely on Skowronek, *Building a New American State.*

12. Block, "The Ruling Class"; Engels, *Family, Private Property and State,* 231.

13. This argument also stands Engels on his head, suggesting that as class relations became more balanced politically, the state became *less* independent of class relations in industry.

14. The distinction is emphasized by partisans on both sides. Championing the state and employers against ordinary workers is Zeitlin, "Rank and Filism"; some of the responses to Kimeldorf, "Bringing Unions Back In," tend toward the opposite extreme.

15. Willits, "Employment Managers' Associations," 85.

16. Surveys include Nelson, *Managers and Workers,* and especially Jacoby, *Employing Bureaucracy.*

17. Leiserson, "Employment Management," 215.

18. National Industrial Conference Board, *Experience with Works Councils;* Lescohier and Brandeis, *Labor in the United States,* 349–50. For a fuller discussion of these points, see chapter 2.

19. Focusing more on welfare capitalism than on workplace authority relations in particular, Brody concludes that improved management as well as welfare benefits did appease many workers; see his "Rise and Decline of Welfare Capitalism." Cohen agrees, but with qualifications (*Making a New Deal,* 161–89). Using a higher standard of "success" (employee loyalty to firm), she emphasizes that the square deal succeeded only when consistently applied and that many firms did not do so. Zahavi reaches a similar conclusion in his study of a single firm, *Workers, Managers, and Welfare Capitalism,* chs. 4–5. Focusing explicitly on company unions, Nelson's conclusion is close to Brody's (Nelson, "The Company Union Movement"). See also Harris, "Industrial Democracy and Liberal Capitalism," 56–66.

20. Clegg, Fox, and Thompson, *History of British Trade Unions,* 550; United States Bureau of Labor Statistics, *Strikes in the United States,* 38.

21. Montgomery, *Workers' Control in America,* 102.

22. One interpretation of American exceptionalism is that class consciousness permeated the shop floor but that democratic citizenship and party affiliation crowded out class loyalties and organization in American politics (Katznelson, *City Trenches;* Shefter, "Trade Unions and Political Machines"). In the 1920s, workplace institutions also promoted employees' roles as corporate citizens rather than as members of a trade or class with identities and ties beyond the factory gates.

23. Brody, "Workplace Contractualism"; Burawoy, *Manufactuing Consent,* ch. 7.

24. See Weisbrod, "Economic Power and Political Stability"; Abraham, "Corporatist Compromise" and *Collapse of the Weimar Republic;* L. Jones, *German Liberalism.*

25. See, for example, Gospel, *Markets, Firms, and Management,* 173–74; Maier, "The Two Postwar Eras," 161–66.

26. Cf. Frederic Deyo's conclusion, based on contemporary East Asian cases, that effective enterprise unionism is a functional substitute for state intervention in labor relations; see Deyo, *Beneath the Miracle,* 109.

27. Tomlins, *The State and the Unions,* 122–23; Lazonick, "Technological Change," 128–29. Charles Maier makes a similar point in contrasting political with economic restabilization after World War I and World War II, respectively; see "The Two Postwar Eras."

28. Dawley's "Workers, Capital, and the State" is helpful here, although Dawley applies the analysis too broadly across industries and neglects the state's contributions to outcomes in the 1920s.

29. In his otherwise judicious survey of New Deal labor policy, Dubofsky minimizes this difference to highlight the continuities between Wilsonian and New Deal intervention (*The State and Labor in Modern America,* 166–67).

30. Fraser and Gerstle assemble an excellent collection of essays on this theme in *The Rise and Fall of the New Deal Order.*

31. Kochan and Piore, "New Industrial Relations"; Kochan, Katz, and Mc-Kersie, *American Industrial Relations*, chs. 3–4.

32. Sanford Jacoby, for example, has emphasized the common roots (particularly employer attitudes) of nonunion industrial relations in different periods ("Norms and Cycles"). He attends more closely to differences in "Prospects for Employee Representation," 17–18.

33. For Seymour Martin Lipset, by contrast, the two epochs express the same American character. Union decline since the 1950s merely returns worker organization to normal patterns after the aberrations of the Great Depression and New Deal; see his "North American Labor Movements."

Works Cited

ARCHIVAL MATERIAL

American Federation of Labor, Railway Employees Department. RED Records. Labor-Management Documentation Center, New York State School of Industrial and Labor Relations, Cornell University. Accession no. 5478.

American Shipbuilding Collection. Institute of Great Lakes Research. Bowling Green State University.

American Shipbuilding Company. Institute of Great Lakes Research. Bowling Green State University.

"A.W. Reports." Typescript of reports from a labor spy, planted in the Bridgeport International Association of Machinists, to the Manufacturers' Association of Bridgeport. Bridgeport Public Library.

Council of National Defense, Ohio Branch. Ohio Branch Records. Ohio Historical Society, Columbus, Ohio. Series 1135.

International Association of Machinists, District 54. IAM District 54 Records. Western Reserve Historical Society, Cleveland, Ohio. Mss. no. 4466. Includes IAM Locals 83 and 368.

Manufacturers' Association of the City of Bridgeport. Bulletin. Bridgeport Public Library. Accession no. 1977.25.

Manufacturers' Association of the City of Bridgeport. Minutes of Executive Board and Committee Meetings. Bridgeport Public Library. Accession no. 1981.06.

National War Labor Board. NWLB Records. National Archives Record Group 2.

San Francisco Labor Council. San Francisco Labor Council Records. Bancroft Library, University of California, Berkeley.

United States Department of Labor, Conciliation Service. Conciliation Service Records. National Archives Record Group 280.

United States Railroad Administration. U.S. Railroad Administration Records. National Archives Record Group 14.

United States Railroad Labor Board. National Mediation Board Records. National Archives Record Group 13.

United States Shipping Board. USSB Records. National Archives Record Group 32.

War Labor Policies Board. War Labor Policies Board Records. National Archives Record Group 1.

PERIODICALS

Amalgamated Engineers' Monthly Journal. Published by the Amalgamated Society of Engineers.

American Machinist.

Boilermakers' Journal. Published by the International Brotherhood of Boilermakers and Iron Ship Builders of America.

Bridgeport Herald.

Bridgeport Post.

California Shipbuilder and Metal Worker. Monthly Publication of the California Metal Trades Association.

The Car Worker. Published by the International Association of Car Workers.

The Cleveland Citizen. Published by the Cleveland Socialist party.

The Cleveland Federationist. Published by the Cleveland Federation of Labor.

The Cleveland Press.

Iron Age.

Labor. Begun as *Railroad Democracy,* The Plumb Plan Weekly.

Labor Clarion. Published by the San Francisco Labor Council and the California State Federation of Labor.

Labor Leader. Published by the International Association of Machinists' Lodge 30, Bridgeport.

Labor World. Published by the Oakland Socialist party.

Machinists' Monthly Journal. Published by the International Association of Machinists.

Monthly Labor Review. United States Bureau of Labor Statistics.

Proceedings of the Annual Convention. National Metal Trades Association.

Railway Age.

San Francisco Call.

San Francisco Examiner.

Survey.

Tri-City Labor Review. Published by the Central Labor Council of Alameda, Calif.

GOVERNMENT PUBLICATIONS

Great Britain, Commission of Enquiry into Industrial Unrest. *Summary of the Reports of the Commission.* London: HMSO, 1917.

Great Britain, Ministry of Munitions. *History of the Ministry of Munitions.* 8 vols. London: HMSO, 1922.

Great Britain, Parliament. *Report by a Court of Inquiry concerning the Engineering Trades Dispute, 1922.* London: HMSO, 1922 [Cmd. 1653].

United States Bureau of Labor. *Regulation and Restriction of Output.* 11th Special Report. Washington, D.C.: GPO, 1904.

United States Bureau of Labor Statistics. *Characteristics of Company Unions 1935.* Bulletin no. 634. Washington, D.C.: GPO, 1938.

———. *National War Labor Board.* Bulletin no. 287. Washington, D.C.: GPO, 1922.

———. *Strikes in the United States, 1880–1936.* Bulletin no. 651. Washington, D.C.: GPO, 1938.

United States Congress. House. Committee on Labor. *Hearings before a Special Committee of the House of Representatives to Investigate the Taylor and Other Systems of Shop Management.* 3 vols. Washington, D.C.: GPO, 1912.

———. Senate. Commission on Industrial Relations. *Final Report and Testimony.* 11 vols. Washington, D.C.: GPO, 1916.

United States Department of Labor. Information and Education Service. *Report of the Employers' Industrial Commission.* Washington, D.C.: GPO, 1919.

United States National War Labor Board. *NWLB Docket.* Washington: Bureau of Applied Economics, 1919.

———. *Report of the National War Labor Board for the Twelve Months Ending May 31, 1919.* Washington, D.C.: GPO, 1920.

United States Railroad Administration. *Annual Reports.* Washington, D.C.: GPO, 1918–19.

United States Railroad Administration. *Reports for Fourteen Months Ending March 1, 1920.* Washington, D.C.: GPO, 1920.

United States Railroad Labor Board. *Decisions, 1921.* Washington, D.C.: GPO, 1922.

———. *Decisions, 1922.* Washington, D.C.: GPO, 1923.

———. *Industrial Relations on Railroads prior to 1917.* Chicago: American Federation of Labor, Railway Employees' Department, 1921.

———. *Presentation Made by the Railway Employes' [sic] Department of the American Federation of Labor re: National Agreement.* Chicago: U.S. Railroad Labor Board, 1921.

———. *Railroad Boards of Adjustment.* Chicago: American Federation of Labor, Railway Employees' Department, 1921.

———. *Rules prior to National Agreement.* Chicago: American Federation of Labor, Railway Employees' Department, 1921.

United States Shipping Board, Emergency Fleet Corporation. *Report of Director General Charles Piez.* Washington, D.C.: GPO, 1919.

———. *Report of the Shipyard Employment Managers' Conference, November 9–10, 1917.* Washington, D.C.: GPO, 1918.

United States War Department. *A Report on the Activities of the War Department in the Field of Industrial Relations during the War.* Washington: GPO, 1919.

UNPUBLISHED STUDIES

Boyden, Richard. "Craft Consciousness and Labor Revolt: The Case of San Francisco Metal Workers, 1900–1941." Unpublished paper, 1988.

Bustard, Bruce Irving. "The Human Factor: Labor Administration and Industrial Manpower Mobilization during the First World War." Ph.D. diss., University of Iowa, 1984.

Croucher, Richard. "The Amalgamated Society of Engineers and Local Autonomy, 1898–1914." Master's thesis, University of Warwick, 1971.

Davis, Colin John. "Bitter Storm: The 1922 National Railroad Shopmen's Strike." Ph.D. diss., State University of New York, Binghamton, 1988.

Klug, Thomas A. "The Roots of the Open Shop: Employers, Trade Unions, and Craft Labor Markets in Detroit, 1859–1907." Ph.D. diss., Wayne State University, 1993.

McCartin, Joseph A. "Labor's 'Great War': American Workers, Unions, and the State, 1916–1920." Ph.D. diss., State University of New York–Binghamton, 1990.

Shapiro, Stanley. "Hand and Brain: The Farmer-Labor Party of 1920." Ph.D. diss., University of California, Berkeley, 1967.

True, Dwight. "Sixty Years of Shipbuilding." Paper Presented at Oct. 5, 1956, Meeting of Great Lakes Section, Society of Naval Architects and Marine Engineers. Copy in Institute of Great Lakes Research.

BOOKS AND ARTICLES

Abbott, Andrew. "Sequences of Social Events: Concepts and Methods for the Analysis of Order in Social Processes." *Historical Methods* 16 (1983): 129–47.

Aborn, Willard, and William Shafer. "Representative Shop Committees: America's Industrial Roundtable." *Industrial Management* 58 (July 1919): 29–32.

Abraham, David. *The Collapse of the Weimar Republic: Political Economy and Crisis.* Princeton, N.J.: Princeton University Press, 1981.

———. "Corporatist Compromise and the Re-emergence of the Labor/Capital Conflict in Weimar Germany." *Political Power and Social Theory* 2 (1981): 59–109.

Abrams, Philip. *Historical Sociology.* Ithaca, N.Y.: Cornell University Press, 1982.

Adams, Roy. *Industrial Relations under Liberal Democracy.* Columbia: University of South Carolina Press, 1995.

Aitken, Hugh G. J. *Taylorism at Watertown Arsenal: Scientific Management in Action, 1908–1915.* Cambridge, Mass.: Harvard University Press, 1960.

Aminzade, Ronald. *Ballots and Barricades: Class Formation and Republican Politics in France, 1830–1871.* Princeton, N.J.: Princeton University Press, 1993.

———. "Historical Sociology and Time." *Sociological Methods and Research* 20 (May 1992): 456–80.

Armeson, Robert B. *Total Warfare and Compulsory Labor: A Study of the Military-Industrial Complex in Germany during World War I.* The Hague: Martinus Nijhoff, 1964.

Armitage, Susan. *The Politics of Decontrol of Industry: Britain and the United States.* London School of Economics Research Monograph no. 4. London: Weidenfeld and Nicolson, 1969.

Ashworth, John H. *The Helper and American Trade Unions.* Baltimore: Johns Hopkins University Press, 1915.

Bain, George Sayers, and Robert Price. *Profiles of Union Growth: A Comparative Statistical Portrait of Eight Countries.* Oxford: Blackwell, 1980.

Beaver, Daniel R. *Newton D. Baker and the American War Effort 1917–1919*. Lincoln: University of Nebraska Press, 1966.

Berlanstein, Lenard R., ed. *Rethinking Labor History*. Urbana: University of Illinois Press, 1993.

Bernstein, Irving. *The Lean Years: A History of the American Worker 1920–1933*. Baltimore: Penguin, 1966.

Berthelot, Marcel. *Works Councils in Germany*. International Labour Office Studies and Reports, ser. B, no. 13. Geneva: International Labour Office, 1924.

Bessel, Richard. *Germany after the First World War*. Oxford: Clarendon, 1993.

————. "State and Society in Germany in the Aftermath of the First World War." In *The State and Social Change in Germany, 1880–1980*, ed. W. R. Lee and Eve Rosenhaft, 200–227. New York: Berg, 1990.

Best, Gary Dean. *The Politics of American Individualism: Herbert Hoover in Transition, 1918–1921*. Westport, Conn.: Greenwood, 1975.

Bing, Alexander. *War-Time Strikes and Their Adjustment*. New York: E. P. Dutton, 1921.

Block, Fred. *Revising State Theory: Essays on Politics and Postindustrialism*. Philadelphia: Temple University Press, 1987.

————. "The Ruling Class Does Not Rule: Notes on the Marxist Theory of the State." *Socialist Revolution*, no. 33 (May-June 1977): 6–28.

Bonnett, Clarence E. *Employers' Associations in the United States: A Study of Typical Associations*. New York: Macmillan, 1922.

Boryczka, Raymond, and Lorin Lee Cary. *No Strength without Union: An Illustrated History of Ohio Workers, 1803–1980*. Columbus: Ohio Historical Society, 1982.

Brandes, Stuart. *American Welfare Capitalism 1880–1940*. Chicago: University of Chicago Press, 1976.

Brody, David. *Labor in Crisis: The Steel Strike of 1919*. Urbana: University of Illinois Press, 1987 [1965].

————. "The Rise and Decline of Welfare Capitalism." In *Workers in Industrial America: Essays on the Twentieth Century Struggle*, ed. David Brody, 48–81. New York: Oxford University Press, 1980.

————. *Steelworkers in America: The Nonunion Era*. New York: Harper and Row, 1960.

————. "Workplace Contractualism in Comparative Perspective." In *Industrial Democracy in America: The Ambiguous Promise*, ed. Nelson Lichtenstein and Howell John Harris, 176–205. Washington, D.C. and New York: Woodrow Wilson Center Press and Cambridge University Press, 1993.

Brown, Henry Phelps. *The Origins of Trade Union Power*. Oxford: Oxford University Press, 1983.

Bucki, Cecelia. "Dilution and Craft Traditions: Bridgeport, Connecticut, Munitions Workers, 1915–1919." *Social Science History* 4, no. 1 (Feb. 1980): 105–24.

Burawoy, Michael. *Manufacturing Consent: Changes in the Labor Process under Monopoly Capitalism*. Chicago: University of Chicago Press, 1979.

————. *The Politics of Production*. London: Verso, 1985.

Burdick, Charles B., and Ralph H. Lutz. *The Political Institutions of the German Revolution 1918–1919*. New York: Praeger, 1966.

Bureau of Industrial Research. *American Company Shop Committee Plans*. New York: Bureau of Industrial Research, 1919.

————. *The Industrial Council Plan in Great Britain*. Reprints of the Report on the Whitley Committee on Relations between Employers and Employed of the Ministry of Reconstruction and of Related Documents. New York: Bureau of Industrial Research, 1919.

Burgess, Keith. "The Political Economy of British Engineering Workers during the First World War." In *Strikes, Wars, and Revolutions in an International Perspective: Strike Waves in the Late Nineteenth and Early Twentieth Centuries*, ed. Leopold Haimson and Charles Tilly, 289–320. Cambridge: Cambridge University Press, 1989.

Calvert, Monte A. *The Mechanical Engineer in America, 1830–1910: Professional Cultures in Conflict*. Baltimore: Johns Hopkins Press, 1967.

Campbell, Thomas F. "Mounting Crisis and Reform: Cleveland's Political Development." In *The Birth of Modern Cleveland, 1865–1930*, ed. Thomas F. Campbell and Edward M. Miggins, 298–324. Cleveland: Western Reserve Historical Society, 1988.

Carsten, F. L. *Revolution in Central Europe, 1918–1919*. Berkeley: University of California Press, 1972.

Chandler, Alfred D., Jr. *Scale and Scope: The Dynamics of Industrial Capitalism*. Cambridge, Mass.: Harvard University Press, 1990.

Charles, Rodger. *The Development of Industrial Relations in Britain, 1911–1939: Studies in the Evolution of Collective Bargaining at National and Industry Level*. London: Hutchinson, 1973.

Church, Roy. "Employers, Trade Unions and the State, 1889–1987: The Origins and Decline of Tripartism in the British Coal Industry." In *Workers, Owners and Politics in Coal Mining: An International Comparison of Industrial Relations*, ed. Gerald D. Feldman and Klaus Tenfelde, 12–73. New York: Berg, 1990.

Clark, Victor S. *History of Manufactures in the United States*. 3 vols. New York: Peter Smith, 1949.

Clarkson, Grosvenor B. *Industrial America in the World War: The Strategy behind the Line, 1917–1918*. Boston: Houghton Mifflin, 1923.

Clawson, Dan. *Bureaucracy and the Labor Process: The Transformation of U.S. Industry, 1860–1920*. New York: Monthly Review, 1980.

Clegg, Hugh A. *The System of Industrial Relations in Britain*. 3d ed. Oxford: Blackwell, 1976.

Clegg, Hugh A., Alan Fox, and A. F. Thompson. *A History of British Trade Unions since 1889*. Vol. 2, *1911–1933*. Oxford: Clarendon, 1985.

Cline, Peter. "Winding Down the War Economy: British Plans for Peacetime Recovery, 1916–1919." In *War and the State: The Transformation of British Government, 1914–1919*, ed. Kathleen Burk, 157–81. London: Allen and Unwin, 1982.

Cohen, Lizabeth. *Making a New Deal: Industrial Workers in Chicago, 1919–1939*. Cambridge: Cambridge University Press, 1990.

Cole, G. D. H. *Trade Unionism and Munitions*. Oxford: Clarendon, 1923.

————. *Workshop Organization*. Oxford: Clarendon, 1923.

Colvin, Fred H. *60 Years with Men and Machines: An Autobiography*. New York: McGraw-Hill, 1947.

Commons, John. *Industrial Government*. New York: Macmillan, 1923.

————, ed. *Trade Unionism and Labor Problems*. 2d ser. Boston: Ginn, 1921.

Conner, Valerie Jean. *The National War Labor Board: Stability, Social Justice, and the Voluntary State in World War I*. Chapel Hill: University of North Carolina Press, 1983.

Cornfield, Daniel B. "The U.S. Labor Movement: Its Development and Impact on Social Inequality and Politics." *Annual Review of Sociology* 17 (1991): 27–49.

Cronin, James E. "Coping with Labour, 1918–1926." In *Social Conflict and the Political Order in Modern Britain*, ed. James E. Cronin and Jonathan Schneer, 113–45. New Brunswick, N.J.: Rutgers University Press, 1982.

————. *Labour and Society in Britain 1918–1979*. London: Batsford Academic and Educational, 1984.

Cronin, James E., and Carmen Sirianni, eds. *Work, Community, and Power: The Experience of Labor in Europe and America, 1900–1925*. Philadelphia: Temple University Press, 1983.

Crowell, Benedict. *America's Munitions 1917–1918*. Washington, D.C.: GPO, 1919.

Cuff, Robert D. "The Politics of Labor Administration during World War I." *Labor History* 21, no. 4 (Fall 1980): 546–69.

————. *The War Industries Board: Business-Government Relations during World War I*. Baltimore: Johns Hopkins University Press, 1973.

Currie, Robert. *Industrial Politics*. Oxford: Clarendon, 1979.

Dawley, Alan. *Struggles for Justice: Social Responsibility and the Liberal State*. Cambridge, Mass.: Harvard University Press, 1991.

————. "Workers, Capital, and the State in the Twentieth Century." In *Perspectives on American Labor History: The Problem of Synthesis*, ed. J. Carroll Moody and Alice Kessler-Harris, 152–200. DeKalb: Northern Illinois University Press, 1989.

Derber, Milton. "The Idea of Industrial Democracy in America: 1915–1935." *Labor History* 8, no. 1 (Winter 1967): 3–29.

Deyo, Frederic O. *Beneath the Miracle: Labor Subordination in the New Asian Industrialism*. Berkeley: University of California Press, 1989.

Dixon, Frank Haigh, and Julius H. Parmelee. *War Administration of the Railways in the United States and Great Britain*. New York: Oxford University Press, 1919.

Dore, Ronald. *British Factory—Japanese Factory: The Origins of National Diversity in Industrial Relations*. Berkeley: University of California Press, 1973.

Douglas, Paul, and F. E. Wolfe. "Labor Administration in the Shipbuilding Industry during War Time." *Journal of Political Economy* 27, no. 3 (1919): 145–87 (part 1); 27, no. 5 (1919): 363–96 (part 2).

Dubofsky, Melvyn. "Abortive Reform: The Wilson Administration and Organized Labor, 1913–1920." In *Work, Community, and Power: The Experience of Labor in Europe and America, 1900–1925*, ed. James Cronin and Carmen Sirianni, 197–220. Philadelphia: Temple University Press, 1983.

————. *The State and Labor in Modern America*. Chapel Hill: University of North Carolina Press, 1994.

Dunn, Robert. "The Industrial Welfare Offensive." In *American Labor Dynamics in the Light of Post-War Developments*, ed. J. B. S. Hardman, 213–25. New York: Harcourt, Brace, 1928.

Edwards, P. K. *Strikes in the United States 1881–1974*. New York: St. Martin's, 1981.

Engels, Frederick. *The Origin of the Family, Private Property and the State.* New York: International, 1975.

Ernst, Daniel R. *Lawyers against Labor: From Individual Rights to Corporate Liberalism.* Urbana: University of Illinois Press, 1995.

Evans, Peter, Dietrich Rueschemeyer, and Theda Skocpol, eds. *Bringing the State Back In.* Cambridge: Cambridge University Press, 1985.

Fantasia, Rick. *Cultures of Solidarity: Consciousness, Action, and Contemporary American Workers.* Berkeley: University of California Press, 1988.

Feldman, Gerald D. *Army, Industry, and Labor in Germany, 1914–1918.* Princeton, N.J.: Princeton University Press, 1966.

———. "German Business between War and Revolution: The Origins of the Stinnes-Legien Agreement." In *Entstehung und Wander der Modernen Gesellschaft,* ed. Gerhard A. Ritter, 312–41. Berlin: Walter de Gruyer, 1970.

Field, Gregory. "Designing the Capital-Labour Accord: Railway Labour, The State and the Beyer Plan for Union-Management Co-Operation." *Journal of Management History* 1, no. 2 (1995): 26–37.

Fine, Sidney. *"Without Blare of Trumpets": Walter Drew, the National Erectors' Association, and the Open Shop Movement, 1903–1957.* Ann Arbor: University of Michigan Press, 1995.

Foner, Philip S. *History of the Labor Movement in the United States.* Vol. 7, *Labor and World War I, 1914–1918.* New York: International, 1987.

Foster, John. "Strike Action and Working-Class Politics in Clydeside 1914–1919." *International Review of Social History* 35, no. 1 (1990): 33–70.

———. "Working-Class Mobilisation on the Clyde 1917–1920." In *Challenges of Labour: Central and Western Europe, 1917–1920,* ed. Chris Wrigley, 149–75. London: Routledge, 1993.

Fox, Alan. *History and Heritage: The Social Origins of the British Industrial Relations System.* London: Allen and Unwin, 1985.

Fraser, Steve. "Dress Rehearsal for the New Deal: Shop-Floor Insurgents, Political Elites, and Industrial Democracy in the Amalgamated Clothing Workers." In *Working-Class America: Essays on Labor, Community, and American Society,* ed. Michael H. Frisch and Daniel J. Walkowitz, 212–55. Urbana: University of Illinois Press, 1983.

———. *Labor Will Rule: Sidney Hillman and the Rise of American Labor.* New York: Free Press, 1991.

Fraser, Steve, and Gary Gerstle, eds. *The Rise and Fall of the New Deal Order, 1930–1980.* Princeton, N.J.: Princeton University Press, 1989.

French, Carroll E. *The Shop Committee in the United States.* Baltimore: Johns Hopkins Press, 1923.

Friedheim, Robert L. *The Seattle General Strike.* Seattle: University of Washington Press, 1964.

Friedlander, Henry Egon. "Conflict of Revolutionary Authority: Provisional Government versus Berlin Soviet, November–December 1918." *International Review of Social History* 7, no. 1 (1962): 163–76.

Friedman, Gerald. "The Decline of Paternalism and the Making of the Employer Class: France, 1870–1914." In *Masters to Managers: Historical and Compara-*

tive Perspectives on American Employers, ed. Sanford M. Jacoby, 153–72. New York: Columbia University Press, 1991.

———. "The State and the Making of the Working Class: France and the United States, 1880–1914." *Theory and Society* 17, no. 3 (May 1988): 403–30.

———. "Worker Militancy and Its Consequences: Political Responses to Labor Unrest in the United States, 1877–1914." *International Labor and Working Class History,* no. 40 (Fall 1991): 5–17.

Frisch, Michael H., and Daniel J. Walkowitz, eds. *Working-Class America: Essays in Labor, Community, and American Society.* Urbana: University of Illinois Press, 1983.

Fulcher, James. *Labour Movements, Employers, and the State: Conflict and Co-operation in Britain and Sweden.* Oxford: Clarendon, 1991.

Fusfeld, Daniel R. "Government and the Suppression of Radical Labor, 1877–1918." In *Statemaking and Social Movements: Essays in History and Theory,* ed. Charles Bright and Susan Harding, 344–77. Ann Arbor: University of Michigan Press, 1984.

Gartman, David. *Auto Slavery: The Labor Process in the American Automobile Industry, 1897–1950.* New Brunswick, N.J.: Rutgers University Press, 1986.

Geary, Dick. "The Ruhr: From Social Peace to Social Revolution." *European Studies Review* 10, no. 5 (Oct. 1980): 497–511.

Gerber, Larry. "Corporatism in Comparative Perspective: The Impact of the First World War on American and British Labor Relations." *Business History Review* 62, no. 1 (Spring 1988): 93–127.

Gitelman, H. M. "Being of Two Minds: American Employers Confront the Labor Problem, 1915–1919." *Labor History* 25, no. 2 (Spring 1984): 189–216.

———. *Legacy of the Ludlow Massacre: A Chapter in American Industrial Relations.* Philadelphia: University of Pennsylvania Press, 1988.

Gluckstein, Donny. *The Western Soviets: Workers' Councils versus Parliament 1915–1920.* London: Bookmarks, 1985.

Goldfield, Michael. "Worker Insurgency, Radical Organization, and New Deal Labor Legislation." *American Political Science Review* 83, no. 4 (Dec. 1989): 1257–82.

Goldthorpe, John H. "The End of Convergence: Corporatist and Dualist Tendencies in Modern Western Societies." In *Order and Conflict in Contemporary Capitalism,* ed. John H. Goldthorpe, 315–43. Oxford: Clarendon, 1984.

Goodwyn, Lawrence. *Breaking the Barrier: The Rise of Solidarity in Poland.* New York: Oxford University Press, 1991.

Gordon, Colin. *New Deals: Business, Labor and Politics in America, 1920–1935.* Cambridge: Cambridge University Press, 1994.

Gospel, Howard. "Employers and Managers: Organisation and Strategy, 1914–1939." In *A History of British Industrial Relations,* ed. Chris Wrigley, vol. 2, *1914–1939,* 159–84. Brighton, Sussex: Harvester, 1987.

———. *Markets, Firms, and the Management of Labour in Modern Britain.* Cambridge: Cambridge University Press, 1992.

Gould, Roger V. *Insurgent Identities: Class, Community, and Protest in Paris from 1848 to the Commune.* Chicago: University of Chicago Press, 1995.

Greenwald, Maureen. "Women Workers and World War I: The American Railroad Industry, A Case Study." *Journal of Social History* 9, no. 2 (Winter 1975):
154–74.

Griffin, Larry J. "Temporality, Events, and Explanation in Historical Sociology."
Sociological Methods and Research 20, no. 4 (May 1992): 403–27.

Griffin, Larry J., Michael E. Wallace, and Beth A. Rubin. "Capitalist Resistance
to the Organization of Labor before the New Deal: Why? How? Success?"
American Sociological Review 51, no. 2 (Apr. 1986): 146–67.

Guillebaud, C. W. *The Works Council: A German Experiment in Industrial Democracy.* Cambridge: Cambridge University Press, 1928.

Habakkuk, H. J. *American and British Technology in the Nineteenth Century: The
Search for Labor Saving Inventions.* Cambridge: Cambridge University Press,
1967.

Haber, Samuel. *Efficiency and Uplift: Scientific Management in the Progressive Era,
1890–1920.* Chicago: University of Chicago Press, 1964.

Haimson, Leopold, and Charles Tilly, eds. *Strikes, Wars, and Revolutions in an
International Perspective: Strike Waves in the Late Nineteenth and Early Twentieth
Centuries.* Cambridge: Cambridge University Press, 1989.

Halevy, Elie. *The Era of Tyrannies.* New York: New York University Press, 1966.

Halle, David. *America's Working Man: Work, Home, and Politics among Blue-Collar
Property Owners.* Chicago: University of Chicago Press, 1984.

Hardach, Gerd. *The First World War, 1914–1918.* Berkeley: University of California Press, 1977.

Harris, Howell. "Employers' Collective Action in the Open-Shop Era: The Metal Manufacturers' Association of Philadelphia, c. 1903–1933." In *The Power to
Manage? Employers and Industrial Relations in Comparative-Historical Perspective,*
ed. Steven Tolliday and Jonathan Zeitlin, 117–46. London: Routledge, 1991.

———. "Getting It Together: The Metal Manufacturers Association of Philadelphia, c. 1900–1930." In *Masters to Managers: Historical and Comparative Perspectives on American Employers,* ed. Sanford M. Jacoby, 111–31. New York: Columbia University Press, 1991.

———. "Industrial Democracy and Liberal Capitalism, 1890–1925." In *Industrial Democracy in America: The Ambiguous Promise,* ed. Nelson Lichtenstein and
Howell John Harris, 43–66. Washington, D.C., and New York: Woodrow Wilson Center Press and Cambridge University Press, 1993.

———. "The Snares of Liberalism? Politicians, Bureaucrats, and the Shaping of
Federal Labour Relations Policy in the United States, ca. 1915–1947." In *Shop
Floor Bargaining and the State: Historical and Comparative Perspectives,* ed. Steven
Tolliday and Jonathan Zeitlin, 148–91. Cambridge: Cambridge University
Press, 1985.

Harvey, Charles E. "John D. Rockefeller, Jr., Herbert Hoover, and President Wil-
son's Industrial Conferences of 1919–1920." In *Voluntarism, Planning, and the
State: The American Planning Experience, 1914–1946,* ed. Jerold E. Brown and
Patrick D. Reagan, 25–46. New York: Greenwood, 1988.

Hattam, Victoria. "Economic Visions and Political Strategies: American Labor and
the State, 1865–1896." *Studies in American Political Development* 4, no. 1 (Spring
1990): 82–129.

————. *Labor Visions and State Power: The Origins of Business Unionism in the United States*. Princeton, N.J.: Princeton University Press, 1993.

Hawley, Ellis W. *The Great War and the Search for a Modern Order: A History of the American People and Their Institutions, 1917–1933*. New York: St. Martin's, 1979.

Hawley, George. "Bridgeport Employers Report Shop Committees Successful." *New York Evening Post*, Apr. 22, 1920.

Haydu, Jeffrey. *Between Craft and Class: Skilled Workers and Factory Politics in Great Britain and the United States, 1890–1922*. Berkeley: University of California Press, 1988.

————. "Employers, Unions, and American Exceptionalism: A Comparative View." *International Review of Social History* 33, no. 1 (1988): 25–41.

Herwig, Holger H. "The First German Congress of Workers' and Soldiers' Councils and the Problem of Military Reforms." *Central European History* 1, no. 2 (June 1968): 150–65.

Hines, Walker D. *War History of American Railroads*. New Haven, Conn.: Yale University Press, 1928.

Hinton, James. *The First Shop Stewards' Movement*. London: Allen and Unwin, 1973.

————. *Labour and Socialism: A History of the British Labour Movement 1867–1974*. Amherst: University of Massachusetts Press, 1983.

Hogler, Raymond. "Labor History and Critical Labor Law: An Interdisciplinary Approach to Workers' Control." *Labor History* 30, no. 2 (Spring 1989): 165–92.

Holt, James. "Trade Unionism in the British and U.S. Steel Industries, 1880–1914." *Labor History* 18, no. 1 (Winter 1977): 5–35.

Holt, Wythe. "The New American Labor Law History." *Labor History* 30, no. 2 (Spring 1989): 275–93.

Holton, Bob. *British Syndicalism 1900–1914: Myths and Realities*. London: Pluto, 1976.

Horne, John N. *Labour at War: France and Britain 1914–1918*. Oxford: Clarendon, 1991.

Hotchkiss, Willard E., and Henry R. Seager. "History of the Shipbuilding Labor Adjustment Board 1917–1919." *Bulletin of the United States Bureau of Labor Statistics*, no. 283 (May 1921).

Hurwitz, Samuel J. *State Intervention in Great Britain: A Study of Economic Control and Social Response, 1914–1919*. New York: Columbia University Press, 1949.

Hutchins, John G. B. "History and Development of Shipbuilding 1776–1944." In *The Shipbuilding Business in the United States of America*, 2 vols., ed. F. G. Fassett Jr., 1:14–60. New York: Society of Naval Architects and Marine Engineers, 1948.

International Labour Office. *Works Councils in Germany*. Studies and Reports Series B, no. 6. Geneva: International Labour Office, 1921.

Jackson, Robert Max. *The Formation of Craft Labor Markets*. Orlando, Fla.: Academic, 1984.

Jacoby, Sanford M. "American Exceptionalism Revisited: The Importance of Management." In *Masters to Managers: Historical and Comparative Perspectives on American Employers*, ed. Sanford M. Jacoby, 172–200. New York: Columbia University Press, 1991.

———. *Employing Bureaucracy: Managers, Unions, and the Transformation of Work in American Industry, 1900–1945.* New York: Columbia University Press, 1985.

———, ed. *Masters to Managers: Historical and Comparative Perspectives on American Employers.* New York: Columbia University Press, 1991.

———. "Norms and Cycles: The Dynamics of Nonunion Industrial Relations in the United States, 1897–1987." In *New Developments in the Labor Market: Toward a New Institutional Paradigm,* ed. Katharine G. Abraham and Robert B. McKersie, 19–57. Cambridge, Mass.: MIT Press, 1990.

———. "Prospects for Employee Representation in the United States: Old Wine in New Bottles?" Working Paper 278. Institute of Industrial Relations, University of California, Los Angeles, 1994.

———. "Union-Management Cooperation in the United States: Lessons from the 1920s." *Industrial and Labor Relations Review* 37, no. 1 (Oct. 1983): 18–31.

Jefferys, James B. *The Story of the Engineers, 1800–1945.* London: Lawrence and Wishart, 1945.

Jenkins, Craig, and Barbara Brents. "Social Protest, Hegemonic Competition, and Social Reform: A Political Struggle Interpretation of the Origins of the American Welfare State." *American Sociological Review* 54, no. 6 (Dec. 1989): 891–909.

Jessop, Bob. *The Capitalist State: Marxist Theories and Methods.* New York: New York University Press, 1982.

Johnson, James P. *The Politics of Soft Coal: The Bituminous Industry from World War I through the New Deal.* Urbana: University of Illinois Press, 1979.

Jones, Gareth Stedman. "The Language of Chartism." In *The Chartist Experience: Studies in Working-Class Radicalism and Culture, 1830–60,* ed. James Epstein and Dorothy Thompson, 3–58. London: Macmillan, 1982.

Jones, Larry Eugene. *German Liberalism and the Dissolution of the Weimar Party System, 1918–1933.* Chapel Hill: University of North Carolina Press, 1988.

Judd, Richard. *Socialist Cities: Municipal Politics and the Grass Roots of American Socialism.* Albany: State University of New York Press, 1989.

Kahn-Freund, Otto. *Labour Law and Politics in the Weimar Republic.* Oxford: Blackwell, 1981.

Kaplan, Sidney. "Social Engineers as Saviors: Effects of World War I on Some American Liberals." *Journal of the History of Ideas* 17, no. 3 (June 1956): 347–69.

Katznelson, Ira. "The 'Bourgeois' Dimension: A Provocation about Institutions, Politics, and the Future of Labor History." *International Labor and Working-Class History* 46 (Fall 1994): 7–32.

———. *City Trenches: Urban Politics and the Patterning of Class in the United States.* New York: Pantheon, 1981.

———. "Working-Class Formation: Constructing Cases and Comparisons." In *Working-Class Formation: Nineteenth-Century Patterns in Western Europe and the United States,* ed. Ira Katznelson and Aristide R. Zolberg, 3–41. Princeton, N.J.: Princeton University Press, 1986.

———. "Working-Class Formation and the State: Nineteenth-Century England in American Perspective." In *Bringing the State Back In,* ed. Peter Evans, Dietrich Rueschemeyer, and Theda Skocpol, 257–84. Cambridge: Cambridge University Press, 1985.

Kazin, Michael. *Barons of Labor: The San Francisco Building Trades and Union Power in the Progressive Era.* Urbana: University of Illinois Press, 1987.

Kelly, Roy Willmarth, and Frederick J. Allen. *The Shipbuilding Industry.* Boston: Houghton Mifflin, 1918.

Kendall, Walter. *The Revolutionary Movement in Britain 1900–1921: The Origins of British Communism.* London: Weidenfeld and Nicolson, 1969.

Kennedy, David M. *Over Here: The First World War and American Society.* New York: Oxford University Press, 1980.

Kerr, K. Austin. *American Railroad Politics, 1914–1920.* Pittsburgh: University of Pittsburgh Press, 1968.

Kimeldorf, Howard. "Bringing Unions Back In." *Labor History* 32, no. 1 (Winter 1991): 91–103.

———. *Reds or Rackets? The Making of Radical and Conservative Unions on the Waterfront.* Berkeley: University of California Press, 1988.

Kimeldorf, Howard, and Judith Stepan-Norris. "Historical Studies of Labor Movements in the United States." *Annual Review of Sociology* 18 (1992): 495–517.

Kirk, Neville. *Labour and Society in Britain and the USA.* Vol. 2, *Challenge and Accommodation, 1850–1939.* Aldershot, Hampshire: Scolar, 1994.

Knight, Robert Edward Lee. *Industrial Relations in the San Francisco Bay Area, 1900–1918.* Berkeley: University of California Press, 1960.

Kochan, Thomas A., Harry C. Katz, and Robert B. McKersie. *The Transformation of American Industrial Relations.* New York: Basic, 1986.

Kochan, Thomas A., and Michael J. Piore. "Will the New Industrial Relations Last? Implications for the American Labor Movement." *Annals of the American Academy of Political and Social Sciences* 473 (May 1984): 177–89.

Kocka, Jürgen. *Facing Total War: German Society 1914–1918.* Leamington Spa, Warwickshire: Berg, 1984.

Kolko, Gabriel. *The Triumph of Conservatism: A Reinterpretation of American History, 1900–1916.* Chicago: Quadrangle, 1967.

Kopald, Sylvia. *Rebellion in Labor Unions.* New York: Boni and Liveright, 1924.

Labour Research Department. *Labour and Capital in the Engineering Trades.* London: Labour Publishing, 1922.

Laraña, Enrique, Hank Johnston, and Joseph R. Gusfield, eds. *New Social Movements: From Ideology to Identity.* Philadelphia: Temple University Press, 1994.

Laslett, John H. M. "State Policy toward Labour and Labour Organizations, 1830–1939: Anglo-American Union Movement." In *The Cambridge Economic History of Europe,* vol. 8, *The Industrial Economies: The Development of Economic and Social Policies,* ed. Peter Mathias and Sidney Pollard, 495–548. Cambridge: Cambridge University Press, 1989.

Lazonick, William H. "Technological Change and the Control of Work: The Development of Capital-Labour Relations in US Mass Production Industries." In *Managerial Strategies and Industrial Relations: An Historical and Comparative Study,* ed. Howard F. Gospel and Craig Littler, 111–36. London: Heinemann, 1983.

Leahey, Patrick. "Skilled Labor and the Rise of the Modern Corporation: The Case of the Electrical Industry." *Labor History* 27, no. 1 (Winter 1985–86): 31–53.

Lecht, Leonard A. *Experience under Railway Labor Legislation.* New York: Columbia University Press, 1955.

Leiserson, William. "Employment Management." *Monthly Labor Review,* Oct. 1919, pp. 207–16.

Lescohier, Don, and Elizabeth Brandeis. *History of Labor in the United States, 1896–1932: Working Conditions and Labor Legislation.* New York: Macmillan, 1935.

Levine, Rhonda F. *Class Struggle and the New Deal: Industrial Labor, Industrial Capital, and the State.* Lawrence: University of Kansas Press, 1988.

Lewchuk, Wayne. "Fordism and the Moving Assembly Line: The British and American Experience, 1895–1930." In *On the Line: Essays in the History of Auto Work,* ed. Nelson Lichtenstein and Stephen Meyer, 17–41. Urbana: University of Illinois Press, 1989.

Licht, Walter. *Working for the Railroad: The Organization of Work in the Nineteenth Century.* Princeton, N.J.: Princeton University Press, 1983.

Lichtenstein, Nelson, and Howell John Harris, eds. *Industrial Democracy in America: The Ambiguous Promise.* Washington, D.C., and New York: Woodrow Wilson Center Press and Cambridge University Press, 1993.

Lindemann, Albert S. *The "Red Years": European Socialism versus Bolshevism, 1919–1921.* Berkeley: University of California Press, 1974.

Lipset, Seymour Martin. "North American Labor Movements: A Comparative Perspective." In *Unions in Transition: Entering the Second Century,* ed. Seymour Martin Lipset, 421–52. San Francisco: Institute for Contemporary Studies, 1986.

———. "Why No Socialism in the United States?" In *Sources of Contemporary Radicalism,* ed. S. Bialer and S. Sluzar, 31–149. Boulder, Colo.: Westview, 1977.

Lombardi, John. *Labor's Voice in the Cabinet: A History of the Department of Labor from Its Origin to 1921.* New York: AMS, 1968 [1942].

Lowe, Rodney. *Adjusting to Democracy: The Role of the Ministry of Labour in British Politics, 1916–1939.* Oxford: Clarendon, 1986.

———. "The Government and Industrial Relations, 1919–1939." In *A History of British Industrial Relations,* ed. Chris Wrigley, vol. 2, *1914–1939,* 185–210. Brighton, Sussex: Harvester, 1987.

Lutz, R. R. *The Metal Trades.* Cleveland: Survey Committee of the Cleveland Foundation, 1916.

Lyddon, Dave. "Industrial-Relations Theory and Labor History." *International Labor and Working-Class History* 46 (Fall 1994): 122–41.

Maier, Charles S. "The 1920s—Consolation or Warning?: A Response to David Montgomery." *International Labor and Working Class History* 32 (Fall 1987): 25–30.

———. *Recasting Bourgeois Europe: Stabilization in France, Germany, and Italy in the Decade after World War I.* Princeton, N.J.: Princeton University Press, 1975.

———. "The Two Postwar Eras and the Conditions for Stability in Twentieth-Century Western Europe." In *In Search of Stability: Explorations in Historical Political Economy,* ed. Charles Maier, 153–84. Cambridge: Cambridge University Press, 1987.

Marks, Gary. *Unions in Politics: Britain, Germany, and the United States in the Nineteenth and Early Twentieth Centuries.* Princeton, N.J.: Princeton University Press, 1989.

Marwick, Arthur. *The Deluge: British Society and the First World War.* New York: Norton, 1970.

McAdam, Doug. *Political Process and the Development of Black Insurgency, 1930–1970*. Chicago: University of Chicago Press, 1982.

McAdoo, William G. *Crowded Years*. Boston: Houghton Mifflin, 1931.

McCartin, Joseph A. "'An American Feeling': Workers, Managers, and the Struggle over Industrial Democracy in the World War I Era." In *Industrial Democracy in America: The Ambiguous Promise*, ed. Nelson Lichtenstein and Howell John Harris, 67–86. Washington, D.C., and New York: Woodrow Wilson Center Press and Cambridge University Press, 1993.

McClymer, John F. *War and Welfare: Social Engineering in America, 1890–1925*. Westport, Conn.: Greenwood, 1980.

McIvor, Arthur J. *Organised Capital: Employers' Associations and Industrial Relations in Northern England, 1880–1939*. New York: Cambridge University Press, 1996.

McLean, Iain. *The Legend of Red Clydeside*. Edinburgh: John Donald, 1983.

McQuaid, Kim. "Corporate Liberalism in the American Business Community, 1920–1940." *Business History Review* 52, no. 3 (Autumn 1978): 342–68.

Meeker, Royal. "Employees' Representation in Management of Industry." *Monthly Labor Review*, Feb. 1920, pp. 305–18.

Mergen, Bernard. "The Government as Manager: Emergency Fleet Shipbuilding, 1917–1919." In *Business and Its Environment: Essays for Thomas C. Cochran*, ed. Harold Issadore Sharlin, 49–80. Westport, Conn.: Greenwood, 1983.

Meyer, Stephen III. *The Five Dollar Day: Labor Management and Social Control in the Ford Motor Company, 1908–1921*. Albany: State University of New York Press, 1981.

Middlemas, Keith. *Politics in Industrial Society: The Experience of the British System since 1911*. London: Andre Deutsch, 1979.

Miggins, Edward M. "A City of 'Uplifting Influences': From 'Sweet Charity' to Modern Social Welfare and Philanthropy." In *The Birth of Modern Cleveland, 1865–1930*, ed. Thomas F. Campbell and Edward M. Miggins, 141–71. Cleveland: Western Reserve Historical Society, 1988.

Miller, Carol Poh, and Robert Wheeler. *Cleveland: A Concise History, 1796–1990*. Bloomington: Indiana University Press, 1990.

Mommsen, Hans. "The Free Trade Unions and Social Democracy in Imperial Germany." In *The Development of Trade Unionism in Great Britain and Germany, 1880–1914*, ed. Wolfgang J. Mommsen and Hans-Gerhard Husung, 371–89. London: Allen and Unwin, 1985.

Mommsen, Wolfgang J. "The German Revolution 1918–1920: Political Revolution and Social Protest Movement." In *Social Change and Political Development in Weimar Germany*, ed. Richard Bessel and E. J. Feuchtwanger, 21–54. London: Croom Helm, 1981.

Mommsen, Wolfgang J., and Hans-Gerhard Husung, eds. *The Development of Trade Unionism in Great Britain and Germany, 1880–1914*. London: Allen and Unwin, 1985.

Montgomery, David. *The Fall of the House of Labor: The Workplace, the State, and American Labor Activism, 1865–1925*. Cambridge: Cambridge University Press, 1987.

———. "Industrial Democracy or Democracy in Industry?: The Theory and Practice of the Labor Movement, 1870–1925." In *Industrial Democracy in America:*

The Ambiguous Promise, ed. Nelson Lichtenstein and Howell John Harris, 20–42. Washington, D.C., and New York: Woodrow Wilson Center Press and Cambridge University Press, 1993.

———. "New Tendencies in Union Struggles and Strategies in Europe and the United States, 1916–1922." In *Work, Community, and Power: The Experience of Labor in Europe and America, 1900–1925,* ed. James E. Cronin and Carmen Sirianni, 88–116. Philadelphia: Temple University Press, 1983.

———. "Thinking about American Workers in the 1920s." *International Labor and Working Class History* 32 (Fall 1987): 4–24.

———. *Workers' Control in America: Studies in the History of Work, Technology, and Labor Struggles.* Cambridge: Cambridge University Press, 1979.

Moore, Barrington, Jr. *Social Origins of Dictatorship and Democracy: Lord and Peasant in the Making of the Modern World.* Boston: Beacon, 1966.

Morgan, David W. *The Socialist Left and the German Revolution: A History of the German Independent Social Democratic Party, 1917–1922.* Ithaca, N.Y.: Cornell University Press, 1975.

Morgan, Kenneth O. *Consensus and Disunity: The Lloyd George Coalition Government 1918–1922.* Oxford: Clarendon, 1979.

Morrison, John H. *History of the New York Ship Yards.* New York: William F. Sametz, 1909.

Moses, John. "The Concept of Economic Democracy within the German Socialist Trade Unions during the Weimar Republic: The Emergence of an Alternative Route to Socialism." *Labour History,* no. 34 (May 1978): 45–57.

———. *Trade Unionism in Germany from Bismark to Hitler, 1869–1933.* 2 vols. Totowa, N.J.: Barnes and Noble, 1982.

Muller, Dirk H. "Syndicalism and Localism in the German Trade Union Movement." In *The Development of Trade Unionism in Great Britain and Germany, 1880–1914,* ed. Wolfgang J. Mommsen and Hans-Gerhard Husung, 239–49. London: Allen and Unwin, 1985.

Murphy, Donald J. "John Andrews, the American Association for Labor Legislation, and Unemployment Reform, 1914–1929." In *Voluntarism, Planning, and the State: The American Planning Experience, 1914–1946,* ed. Jerold E. Brown and Patrick D. Reagan, 1–23. New York: Greenwood, 1988.

Murray, Robert K. *Red Scare: A Study in National Hysteria, 1919–1920.* Minneapolis: University of Minnesota Press, 1955.

National Industrial Conference Board. *Experience with Works Councils in the United States.* New York: Century, 1922.

———. *Strikes in American Industry in Wartime, April 6 to October 6, 1917.* Research Report no. 3. Boston: NICB, 1918.

———. *Wartime Employment of Women in the Metal Trades.* Research Report no. 8. Boston: NICB, 1918.

———. *Works Councils in the United States.* Research Report no. 21. Boston: NICB, 1919.

National Metal Trades Association. *Report of the Committee on Works Councils in the Metal Trades.* Chicago: National Metal Trades Association, 1919.

Nelson, Daniel. "The Company Union Movement, 1900–1937: A Reexamination." *Business History Review* 56, no. 3 (Autumn 1982): 335–57.

————. *Fredrick Taylor and the Rise of Scientific Management.* Madison: University of Wisconsin Press, 1980.

————. *Managers and Workers: Origins of the New Factory System in the United States, 1880–1920.* Madison: University of Wisconsin Press, 1975.

Nocken, Ulrich. "Corporatism and Pluralism in Modern German History." In *Industrielle Gesellschaft und Politisches System,* ed. Dirk Stegmann, Bernd-Jürgen Wendt, and Peter-Christian Witt, 37–56. Bonn: Verlag Neue Gesellschaft, 1978.

Nolan, Mary. *Social Democracy and Society: Working-Class Radicalism in Düsseldorf, 1890–1920.* Cambridge: Cambridge University Press, 1981.

Nottingham, Christopher J. "Recasting Bourgeois Britain? The British State in the Years Which Followed the First World War." *International Review of Social History* 31, no. 3 (1986): 227–47.

Oestreicher, Richard. "Urban Working-Class Political Behavior and Theories of American Electoral Politics, 1870–1940." *Journal of American History* 74, no. 4 (Mar. 1988): 1257–86.

Orloff, Ann Shola. "The Political Origins of America's Belated Welfare State." In *The Politics of Social Policy in the United States,* ed. Margaret Weir, Ann Shola Orloff, and Theda Skocpol, 37–80. Princeton, N.J.: Princeton University Press, 1988.

Orren, Karen. *Belated Feudalism: Labor, the Law, and Liberal Development in the United States.* Cambridge: Cambridge University Press, 1991.

Ozanne, Robert. *A Century of Labor-Management Relations at McCormick and International Harvester.* Madison: University of Wisconsin Press, 1967.

Perlman, Mark. *The Machinists: A New Study in American Trade Unionism.* Cambridge, Mass.: Harvard University Press, 1961.

Perlman, Selig, and Philip Taft. *History of Labor in the United States, 1896–1932.* Vol. 4, *Labor Movements.* New York: Macmillan, 1935.

Peterson, Joyce Shaw. *American Automobile Workers, 1900–1933.* Albany: State University of New York Press, 1987.

Peukert, Detlev J. K. *The Weimar Republic: The Crisis of Classical Modernity.* London: Penguin, 1991.

Piore, Michael J., and Charles F. Sabel. *The Second Industrial Divide: Possibilities for Prosperity.* New York: Basic, 1984.

Piven, Frances Fox, and Richard A. Cloward. *Poor People's Movements: Why They Succeed, How They Fail.* New York: Vintage, 1979.

Potter, Zenas. "War-Boom Towns I: Bridgeport." *The Survey,* Dec. 4, 1915, pp. 237–41.

Poulantzas, Nicos. *Political Power and Social Classes.* London: New Left, 1973.

Powell, David. *British Politics and the Labour Question, 1868–1990.* New York: St. Martin's, 1992.

Preston, William. *Aliens and Dissenters: Federal Suppression of Radicals, 1903–1933.* Cambridge, Mass.: Harvard University Press, 1963.

Pribicevic, Branko. *The Shop Stewards' Movement and Workers' Control, 1910–1922.* Oxford: Blackwell, 1959.

Price, Richard. *Labour in British Society: An Interpretive History.* London: Croom Helm, 1986.

Prothero, James W. *Dollar Decade: Business Ideas in the 1920s.* Baton Rouge: Louisiana State University Press, 1954.

Quadagno, Jill. "Welfare Capitalism and the Social Security Act of 1935." *American Sociological Review* 49, no. 5 (Oct. 1984): 632–47.

Ramirez, Bruno. *When Workers Fight: The Politics of Industrial Relations in the Progressive Era, 1898–1916.* Westport, Conn.: Greenwood, 1978.

Rancière, Jacques. "The Myth of the Artisan: Critical Reflections on a Category of Social History." In *Work in France: Representations, Meaning, Organization, and Practice,* ed. Steven Lawrence Kaplan and Cynthia J. Koepp, 317–34. Ithaca, N.Y.: Cornell University Press, 1986.

Reddy, William. *The Rise of Market Culture: The Textile Trade and French Society.* Cambridge: Cambridge University Press, 1984.

Reich, Nathan. *Labour Relations in Republican Germany: An Experiment in Industrial Democracy, 1918–1933.* New York: Oxford University Press, 1938.

Reid, Alastair. "Dilution, Trade Unionism and the State in Britain during the First World War." In *Shop Floor Bargaining and the State: Historical and Comparative Perspectives,* ed. Steven Tolliday and Jonathan Zeitlin, 46–74. Cambridge: Cambridge University Press, 1985.

Richberg, Donald R. *My Hero: The Indiscreet Memoirs of an Eventful but Unheroic Life.* New York: Putnam's, 1954.

Robertson, David Brian. "The Bias of American Federalism: The Limits of Welfare-State Development in the Progressive Era." *Journal of Policy History* 1, no. 3 (1989): 261–91.

Rogers, Fred. "Developments in Machine-Shop Practice during the Last Decade." *Transactions* [American Society of Mechanical Engineers], 34 (1912): 847–65.

Rosenberg, Arthur. *A History of the German Republic.* New York: Russell and Russell, 1965 [1936].

———. *Imperial Germany: The Birth of the German Republic 1871–1918.* Boston: Beacon, 1964 [1931].

Rosenzweig, Roy. *Eight Hours for What We Will: Workers and Leisure in an Industrial City, 1870–1920.* Cambridge: Cambridge University Press, 1983.

Rubin, Gerry R. "Law as a Bargaining Weapon: British Labour and the Restoration of Pre-War Practices Act 1919." *Historical Journal* 32, no. 4 (Dec. 1989): 925–45.

———. *War, Law, and Labour: The Munitions Acts, State Regulation, and the Unions, 1915–1921.* Oxford: Clarendon, 1987.

Ryder, A. J. *The German Revolution of 1918: A Study of German Socialism in War and Revolt.* Cambridge: Cambridge University Press, 1967.

Saxton, Alexander. "San Francisco Labor and the Populist and Progressive Insurgencies." *Pacific Historical Review* 34, no. 4 (1965): 421–38.

Schacht, John N. "Toward Industrial Unionism: Bell Telephone Workers and Company Unions, 1919–1937." *Labor History* 16, no. 1 (Winter 1975): 5–36.

Scharf, Lois. "A Woman's View of Cleveland's Labor Force: Two Case Studies." In *The Birth of Modern Cleveland, 1865–1930,* ed. Thomas F. Campbell and Edward M. Miggins, 172–94. Cleveland: Western Reserve Historical Society, 1988.

Schneer, Jonathan. "The War, the State and the Workplace: British Dockers during 1914–1918." In *Social Conflict and the Political Order in Modern Britain,* ed. James E. Cronin and Jonathan Schneer, 96–112. New Brunswick, N.J.: Rutgers University Press, 1982.

Schneider, Michael. *A Brief History of the German Trade Unions.* Bonn: Dietz, 1991.

Schneirov, Richard. "Political Economy and Class Relations: A Path to a Synthesis in Labor History." *Reviews in American History* 16, no. 3 (Sept. 1988): 435–42.

Schonhoven, Klaus. "Localism—Craft Union—Industrial Union: Organizational Patterns in German Trade Unionism." In *The Development of Trade Unionism in Great Britain and Germany, 1880–1914*, ed. Wolfgang J. Mommsen and Hans-Gerhard Husung, 219–35. London: Allen and Unwin, 1985.

Schorske, Carl E. *German Social Democracy 1905–1917: The Development of the Great Schism*. New York: Wiley, 1955.

Sewell, William H., Jr. "Three Temporalities: Toward an Eventful Sociology." In *The Historic Turn in the Human Sciences*, ed. Terrence J. McDonald. Ann Arbor: University of Michigan Press, forthcoming.

———. *Work and Revolution in France: The Language of Labor from the Old Regime to 1848*. Cambridge: Cambridge University Press, 1980.

Seymour, John Barton. *The Whitley Councils Scheme*. London: P. S. King, 1932.

Shafer, Byron E., ed. *Is America Different? A New Look at American Exceptionalism*. Oxford: Clarendon, 1991.

Shalev, Michael, and Walter Korpi. "Working Class Mobilization and American Exceptionalism." *Economic and Industrial Democracy* 1 (1980): 31–61.

Shapiro, Stanley. "The Great War and Reform: Liberals and Labor, 1917–1919." *Labor History* 12, no. 3 (Summer 1971): 323–44.

———. "The Twilight of Reform: Advanced Progressives after the Armistice." *The Historian* 33, no. 3 (May 1971): 349–64.

Shefter, Martin. "Trade Unions and Political Machines: The Organization and Disorganization of the American Working Class in the Late Nineteenth Century." In *Working-Class Formation: Nineteenth-Century Patterns in Western Europe and the United States*, ed. Ira Katznelson and Aristide R. Zolberg, 197–276. Princeton, N.J.: Princeton University Press, 1986.

Sheldrake, John. *Industrial Relations and Politics in Britain, 1880–1989*. London: Pinter, 1991.

Shepard, George H. "Industrial Representation and the Fair Deal—I." *Industrial Management* 63, no. 2 (Feb. 1922): 81–85.

Sidlo, T. L. "Socialism and Trade-Unionism: A Study of Their Relationship in Cleveland." *Western Reserve University Bulletin* 12, no. 6 (Nov. 1909): 126–53.

Sirianni, Carmen. *Workers' Control and Socialist Democracy: The Soviet Experience*. London: Verso, 1982.

———. "Workers' Control in Europe: A Comparative Sociological Analysis." In *Work, Community, and Power: The Experience of Labor in Europe and America, 1900–1925*, ed. James E. Cronin and Carmen Sirianni, 254–310. Philadelphia: Temple University Press, 1983.

Sisson, Keith. "Employers and the Structure of Collective Bargaining: Distinguishing Cause and Effect." In *The Power to Manage? Employers and Industrial Relations in Comparative-Historical Perspective*, ed. Steven Tolliday and Jonathan Zeitlin, 256–71. London: Routledge, 1991.

———. *The Management of Collective Bargaining: An International Comparison*. Oxford: Blackwell, 1987.

Sklar, Martin J. *The Corporate Reconstruction of American Capitalism, 1890–1916: The Market, the Law, and Politics*. Cambridge: Cambridge University Press, 1988.

Skocpol, Theda. "Bringing the State Back In: Strategies of Analysis in Current Research." In *Bringing the State Back In*, ed. Peter B. Evans, Dietrich Rueschmeyer, and Theda Skocpol, 3–37. New York: Cambridge University Press, 1985.

———. "Political Responses to Capitalist Crisis: Neo-Marxist Theories of the State and the Case of the New Deal." *Politics and Society* 10, no. 2 (1980): 155–201.

———. *Protecting Soldiers and Mothers: The Political Origins of Social Policy in the United States*. Cambridge, Mass.: Harvard University Press, 1992.

———. *States and Social Revolutions: A Comparative Analysis of France, Russia, and China*. Cambridge: Cambridge University Press, 1979.

Skowronek, Stephen. *Building a New American State: The Expansion of Administrative Capacities, 1877–1920*. Cambridge: Cambridge University Press, 1982.

Smith, John S. "Organized Labor and Government in the Wilson Era, 1913–1921: Some Conclusions." *Labor History* 3, no. 3 (Fall 1962): 265–86.

Smith, Merritt Roe. *Harpers Ferry Armory and the New Technology: The Challenge of Change*. Ithaca, N.Y.: Cornell University Press, 1977.

Spencer, Elaine Glovka. *Management and Labor in Imperial Germany: Ruhr Industrialists as Employers, 1896–1914*. New Brunswick, N.J.: Rutgers University Press, 1984.

Stephens, John D. *The Transition from Capitalism to Socialism*. London: Macmillan, 1979.

Stern, Boris. *Works Council Movement in Germany*. Bulletin of the United States Bureau of Labor Statistics no. 383. Washington, D.C.: GPO, 1925.

Stromquist, Shelton. *A Generation of Boomers: The Pattern of Railroad Labor Conflict in Nineteenth-Century America*. Urbana: University of Illinois Press, 1987.

Tampke, Jürgen. *The Ruhr and Revolution: The Revolutionary Movement in the Rhenish-Westphalian Industrial Region 1912–1919*. London: Croom Helm, 1979.

Tanner, Duncan. *Political Change and the Labour Party 1900–1918*. Cambridge: Cambridge University Press, 1990.

Tilly, Charles. *As Sociology Meets History*. New York: Academic, 1981.

———. *From Mobilization to Revolution*. New York: Random House, 1978.

Tipper, Harry. "How to Check the Radical in Labor Circles." *Automotive Industries*, Oct. 9, 1919.

Tobin, Elizabeth H. "War and the Working Class: The Case of Dusseldorf 1914–1918." *Central European History* 18, no. 3/4 (Sept./Dec. 1985): 257–98.

Tobin, Eugene M. *Organize or Perish: America's Independent Progressives, 1913–1933*. Westport, Conn.: Greenwood, 1986.

Toller, Ernst. *I Was a German: An Autobiography*. London: John Lane, The Bodley Head, 1934.

Tolliday, Steven, and Jonathan Zeitlin, eds. *The Power to Manage? Employers and Industrial Relations in Comparative-Historical Perspective*. London: Routledge, 1991.

———, eds. *Shop Floor Bargaining and the State: Historical and Comparative Perspectives*. Cambridge: Cambridge University Press, 1985.

Tomlins, Christopher L. *The State and the Unions: Labor Relations, Law, and the Organized Labor Movement in America, 1880–1960*. Cambridge: Cambridge University Press, 1985.

Traugott, Mark. *Armies of the Poor: Determinants of Working-Class Participation in the Parisian Insurrection of June 1848.* Princeton, N.J.: Princeton University Press, 1985.

Troy, Leo. "Labor Representation in American Railways." *Labor History* 2, no. 3 (Fall 1961): 295–322.

Turner, John. *British Politics and the Great War: Coalition and Conflict, 1915–1918.* New Haven, Conn.: Yale University Press, 1992.

Urofsky, Melvin I. *Big Steel and the Wilson Administration: A Study in Business-Government Relations.* Columbus: Ohio State University Press, 1969.

Valocchi, Stephen. "The Class Basis of the State and the Origins of Welfare Policy in Britain, Sweden, and Germany." In *Bringing Class Back In: Contemporary and Historical Perspectives,* ed. Scott G. McNall, Rhonda F. Levine, and Rick Fantasia, 167–83. Boulder, Colo.: Westview, 1991.

Voss, Kim. *The Making of American Exceptionalism: The Knights of Labor and Class Formation in the Nineteenth Century.* Ithaca, N.Y.: Cornell University Press, 1993.

Wagoner, Harless D. *The U.S. Machine Tool Industry from 1900 to 1950.* Cambridge, Mass.: MIT Press, 1968.

Wakstein, Allen. "The Origins of the Open Shop Movement, 1919–20." *Journal of American History* 51, no. 3 (Dec. 1964): 460–75.

Warne, Frank Julian. *The Workers at War.* New York: Century, 1920.

Watson, W. F. *Machines and Men: An Autobiography of an Itinerant Mechanic.* London: Allen and Unwin, 1935.

Wehle, Louis B. "The Adjustment of Labor Disputes Incident to Production for War in the United States." *Quarterly Journal of Economics* 32 (Nov. 1917): 122–41.

———. *Hidden Threads of History: Wilson through Roosevelt.* New York: Macmillan, 1953.

———. "War Labor Policies and Their Outcome in Peace." *Quarterly Journal of Economics* 33 (Feb. 1919): 321–43.

Weinstein, James. *The Corporate Ideal in the Liberal State: 1900–1918.* Boston: Beacon, 1968.

Weir, Margaret, Ann Shola Orloff, and Theda Skocpol, eds. *The Politics of Social Policy in the United States.* Princeton, N.J.: Princeton University Press, 1988.

Weisbrod, Bernd. "Economic Power and Political Stability Reconsidered: Heavy Industry in Weimar Germany." *Social History* 4, no. 2 (May 1979): 241–63.

———. "Entrepreneurial Politics and Industrial Relations in Mining in the Ruhr Region: From Managerial Absolutism to Co-determination." In *Workers, Owners and Politics in Coal Mining: An International Comparison of Industrial Relations,* ed. Gerald D. Feldman and Klaus Tenfelde, 118–202. New York: Berg, 1990.

Wiebe, Robert H. *The Search for Order, 1877–1920.* New York: Hill and Wang, 1967.

Wigham, Eric. *The Power to Manage: A History of the Engineering Employers' Federation.* London: Macmillan, 1973.

Wilentz, Sean. "Against Exceptionalism: Class Consciousness and the American Labor Movement, 1790–1920." *International Labor and Working Class History* 26 (Fall 1984): 1–24.

———. *Chants Democratic: New York City and the Rise of the American Working Class, 1788–1850.* New York: Oxford University Press, 1984.

Williams, Gwyn A. *Proletarian Order: Antonio Gramsci, Factory Councils and the Origins of Italian Communism 1911–1921.* London: Pluto Press, 1975.

Williams, John. *The Home Fronts: Britain, France and Germany 1914–1918*. London: Constable, 1972.

Willits, J. H. "Development of Employment Managers' Associations." *Monthly Labor Review* Sept. 1917, 85–87.

Wilson, Woodrow. *The Papers of Woodrow Wilson*. Vol. 45. Ed. Arthur S. Link. Princeton, N.J.: Princeton University Press, 1984.

Wolf, H. D. *The Railroad Labor Board*. Chicago: University of Chicago Press, 1927.

Wolfe, A. B. *Works Committees and Joint Industrial Councils*. Philadelphia: United States Shipping Board, Emergency Fleet Corporation, Industrial Relations Division, 1919.

Wolman, Leo. *Ebb and Flow in Trade Unionism*. New York: National Bureau of Economic Research, 1936.

———. *The Growth of American Trade Unions, 1880–1923*. New York: National Bureau of Economic Research, 1924.

Wood, Louis Aubrey. *Union-Management Cooperation on the Railroads*. New Haven, Conn.: Yale University Press, 1931.

Wrigley, Chris. *David Lloyd George and the British Labour Movement*. Brighton, Sussex: Harvester, 1976.

———. "The First World War and State Intervention in Industrial Relations, 1914–1918." In *A History of British Industrial Relations*, ed. Chris Wrigley, vol. 2, *1914–1939*, 23–70. Brighton, Sussex: Harvester, 1987.

———. *Lloyd George and the Challenge of Labour: The Post-War Coalition, 1918–1922*. New York: Harvester Wheatsheaf, 1990.

———. "The Ministry of Munitions: An Innovatory Department." In *War and the State: The Transformation of British Government, 1914–1919*, ed. Kathleen Burk, 32–56. London: Allen and Unwin, 1982.

———. "The State and the Challenge of Labour in Britain 1917–1920." In *Challenges of Labour: Central and Western Europe, 1917–1920*, ed. Chris Wrigley, 262–88. London: Routledge, 1993.

Wunderlich, Frieda. *Labor under German Democracy: Arbitration 1918–1933*. New York: New School for Social Research, 1940.

Yellowitz, Irwin. "Skilled Workers and Mechanization: The Lasters in the 1890s." *Labor History* 18, no. 2 (Spring 1977): 197–213.

Zahavi, Gerald. *Workers, Managers, and Welfare Capitalism: The Shoeworkers and Tanners of Endicott Johnson, 1890–1950*. Urbana: University of Illinois Press, 1988.

Zeitlin, Jonathan. "The Internal Politics of Employer Organization: The Engineering Employers' Federation 1896–1939." In *The Power to Manage? Employers and Industrial Relations in Comparative-Historical Perspective*, ed. Steven Tolliday and Jonathan Zeitlin, 52–80. London: Routledge, 1991.

———. "Rank and Filism and Labour History." *International Review of Social History* 34, no. 1 (1989): 42–61, 89–102.

Zieger, Robert. "From Hostility to Moderation: Railroad Labor Policy in the 1920s." *Labor History* 9, no. 1 (Winter 1968): 23–38.

Zolberg, Aristide R. "How Many Exceptionalisms?" In *Working-Class Formation: Nineteenth-Century Patterns in Western Europe and the United States*, ed. Ira Katznelson and Aristide R. Zolberg, 397–455. Princeton, N.J.: Princeton University Press, 1986.

Index